ROUTLEDGE LIBRARY EDITIONS: EVOLUTION

Volume 14

HOMO FABER

HOMO FABER

A Study of Man's Mental Evolution

G. N. M. TYRRELL

Routledge
Taylor & Francis Group

LONDON AND NEW YORK

First published in 1951 by Methuen & Co. Ltd.

This edition first published in 2020
by Routledge
2 Park Square, Milton Park, Abingdon, Oxon OX14 4RN

and by Routledge
52 Vanderbilt Avenue, New York, NY 10017

Routledge is an imprint of the Taylor & Francis Group, an informa business

British Library Cataloguing in Publication Data
A catalogue record for this book is available from the British Library

ISBN: 978-0-367-27938-7 (Set)
ISBN: 978-0-429-31628-9 (Set) (ebk)
ISBN: 978-0-367-27353-8 (Volume 14) (hbk)
ISBN: 978-0-367-27356-9 (Volume 14) (pbk)
ISBN: 978-0-429-29633-8 (Volume 14) (ebk)

Publisher's Note
The publisher has gone to great lengths to ensure the quality of this reprint but points out that some imperfections in the original copies may be apparent.

Disclaimer
The publisher has made every effort to trace copyright holders and would welcome correspondence from those they have been unable to trace.

HOMO FABER

A Study of Man's Mental Evolution

by

G. N. M. TYRRELL

METHUEN & CO. LTD. LONDON
36 Essex Street, Strand, W.C.2

First published in 1951

CATALOGUE NO. 5349/U

PRINTED IN GREAT BRITAIN

PREFACE

THE theme developed in the following chapters is invested with a certain intangibility, and to some it may seem that the quarry pursued is too elusive. But the underlying idea is neither intricate nor complicated. It is extremely simple: its elusiveness is wholly due to the fact that it is not easily reconciled with our customary habits of thought. In order to grasp it, we must step out of the grooves in which we habitually move and go forward, rendering ourselves receptive to the new. To this adventure, the mind is naturally resistant. It has therefore been necessary, in writing this book, deliberately to introduce repetition of the idea, which is repeatedly presented from slightly differing angles. While the intellect does not need constant repetition of a proposition, the entire mind, with its elements of habit, does so. Any conception which is strange can only be grasped by slow infiltration.

The method employed in developing this theme differs entirely from that used in the technical and specialist literature with which we are to-day so familiar. The approach is synthetic and not analytical; and the point of view is non-specialist as opposed to specialist. Where, in dealing with the questions raised, it has been necessary to enter specialist territory, the information is drawn from special sources. In consequence, a large number of quotations are inevitable.

I take this opportunity of acknowledging my indebtedness to the following authors and publishers for permission to quote passages which exceed in length the limits customarily open for free comment: Professor C. D. Broad, *The Mind and Its Place in Nature*; also to Messrs. Routledge and Kegan Paul Ltd.; the Cambridge University Press for permission to quote from Sir Arthur Eddington's book, *The Philosophy of Physical Science*; Dr. V. H. Mottram for permission to quote from his book, *The Physical Basis of Personality*; Dr. Joseph Needham for permission to quote from his book, *Man a Machine*; also to the Orthological Institute: Dr. E. S. Russell for permission to quote from his book, *The Directiveness of Organic Activities*; also to the Cambridge University Press: Professor W. T. Stace for permission to quote from his article, "Man against Darkness," in *The Atlantic Monthly* for September, 1948; Dr. Arnold Toynbee for permission to quote from *Civilization on Trial*; also to the Oxford University Press: Sir Edmund Whittaker for permission to quote from his collected lectures, *The Beginning and End of the World*; *The Times* for permission to quote from issues of September 8th and 12th, 1933, June 12th, 1948, September 9th, 1948, November 12th, 1948, and December 13th, 1948, the authors or titles of these extracts being Dr. H. Gray, Dr. F. E. Lloyd, "Abortive Atomic Talks," Sir Henry Tizard, Sir Henry Dale, and an article on the United Nations; *The Times Literary Supplement* for permission to quote from a review of Professor A. M. Low's book, *Your World To-morrow*, October 11th, 1947; also for permission to quote from a review of Dr. Julian Huxley's book, *Evolutionary Ethics*, March 20th, 1948.

My thanks are also due to those who have assisted in the preparation of this book, especially to Miss G. M. Johnson, through whose intuitive insight the main ideas have been assisted to emerge; and to my wife for much assistance with the typescript. Also to Dr. E. V. Rieu for valuable constructive criticism.

REIGATE

April, 1950

CONTENTS

ABBREVIATIONS

IN order to save space, the following abbreviations have been used in the footnotes to indicate books to which more than one reference has been made:

Bergson, H., *Creative Evolution*	*C.E.*
Bevan, E., *Sybils and Seers*	*S.S.*
Broad, C. D., *The Mind and Its Place in Nature*	*M.P.N.*
Collingwood, R. G., *Speculum Mentis*	*S.M.*
Eddington, A. S., *The Philosophy of Physical Science*	*P.P.S.*
Freud, S., *The Future of an Illusion*	*F.I.*
Haldane, J. S., *The Philosophy of a Biologist*	*P.B.*
Harding, R., *An Anatomy of Inspiration*	*A.I.*
Henderson, L. J., *The Fitness of the Environment*	*F.E.*
Holmes, E., *The Headquarters of Reality*	*H.R.*
Jung, C. G., *Modern Man in Search of a Soul*	*M.M.S.S.*
Lloyd Morgan, C., *Emergent Evolution*	*E.E.*
McDougall, W., *Modern Materialism*	*M.M.*
Needham, J., *Biochemistry and Morphogenesis*	*B.M.*
Needham, J., *Man a Machine*	*M. a M.*
Russell, B., *What I Believe*	*W.I.B.*
Russell, E. S., *The Directiveness of Organic Activities*	*D.O.A.*
Stebbing, L. S., *Philosophy and the Physicists*	*P.P.*
Toynbee, A., *Civilization on Trial*	*C.T.*
Watson, J. B., *Psychology from the Standpoint of the Behaviorists*	*P.S.B.*
Whittaker, E. T., *The Beginning and End of the World*	*B.E.W.*

Now we see through a glass, darkly.

St. Paul

CHAPTER I

INTRODUCTORY

TO-DAY the specialist is king. If a non-specialist ventures to raise his voice on any matter of importance, his views are likely to be dismissed as those of a mere amateur, trespassing on matters he does not understand. Specialist inquiry has been carried into so many departments of knowledge that it appears as if everything has been brought under its sway and that it has given us, not only infallible truth about every detail, but also a valid picture of the whole. Has not the scientific method proved itself to be infallible and omnipotent? Has it not succeeded in carrying everything before it? Has it not launched humanity on the first epoch of genuine progress known to history?

This is the current opinion of our time; and it is held with curious tenacity despite the tremendous problems which science has raised, despite the fact that scientific achievement has left human morality and wisdom so far behind that it has passed beyond human control. It is tenaciously clung to, despite the black and pessimistic picture of the universe which science has drawn. Many believe that no light can shine from any other quarter.

It is not our present aim to deny the validity of the scientific method within its limitations nor to deny the immense successes which this method has achieved. But, in the following chapters, we shall question whether the method is a fool-proof instrument. It will be gradually disclosed to us that there is a subtle factor underlying the scientific method, and also underlying much else; and we shall see that this factor has never been fully and consciously recognized or taken into account. We shall question whether the rational faculty of man is as immaculate and immune from error as it is tacitly assumed to be. We shall maintain that it has not escaped the moulding hand of Nature but has been adapted, along with the physical side of man, to the highly special conditions of the world we live in.

This will not result in the degradation of reason; for the progress of the human mind has always been the result of an uprising from the level on which it was adapted by nature to a condition of freer consciousness, in which reason comes more and more to its own.

It will be shown that the adapted characteristics of the mind act beneficially in the ordinary situations of life, which include the region of applied science; and that it is only when remoter types of problem arise

that they are apt to lead the mind astray. This has happened in the formation of the general conception of the cosmos, which has arisen during the
scientific epoch. This adapting factor is intangible and cannot easily be
defined, for it lies outside the usual province of metaphysics and epistemological theory, which is based on reason. It is difficult to take hold of and
only gradually does it filter into the mind as we come to realize its presence
by looking at it from different angles. Yet it is fundamental and all-
pervasive. The scientific method cannot detect it because it is inserted in
the mind at a lowly level and is already operating before that method
begins. The influence it exerts is invisible. Specialist technique has, indeed,
the effect of rendering it more obscure instead of bringing it to light; for
it introduces into that technique unconsciously accepted premises. If
we liken the scientific method to a biochemist's filter, then this elusive
factor is like a micro-organism which passes through the filter unobserved.
The scientist, because tied to his own method, looks only at what the
filter has arrested. It is outside his province to examine the filtrate. But it
is in the filtrate that this all-important element lies. It *can* be detected, but
not by cut-and-dried specialist technique. It becomes visible only when
seen from the non-specialist's angle of approach, which consists in making
a comprehensive survey and in keeping the mind alive to every situation.
From this point of view, it becomes obvious that the specialist has failed
to see that introspection is a vital factor and that by omitting it he has
started his investigation a step too late.

Part of the subtlety of the undetected factor arises from the fact that it
is inherent in its own character that it should remain invisible. The natural
reaction of the mind is therefore to deny its existence. It may seem at first
sight that the existence of such a tendency, even if admitted, would be no
more than an academic matter, the concern of philosophers, perhaps, but
of no practical importance to mankind. But it turns out, as we look into
it, that the more the existence of this hidden factor is realized the more
practical importance it is seen to possess. So long as the mind of man is
trying to deal with practical matters in the world to which nature has
adapted him, this unperceived factor *assists* him in arriving at the truth.
But the more the mind attempts to leave the familiar world and to
explore into far removed matters the more this factor deflects it away from
truth and fosters illusion. In the end, this deflecting tendency becomes a
matter of central importance in the human situation. The micro-organism
has passed into the human system.

It may be asked, how can one who is no specialist in psychology hope
to detect a psychological factor in the human mind? The answer is that the
specialist's method of analysing data supplied by his senses compels him

to keep his face close to the ground. On the other hand, the non-specialist is able to take a bird's-eye view of the scene as a whole. If a party of archæologists are at work on the site of some ancient building, they trench, they dig, they sift with all the skill of trained specialists and only by means of these methods are their detailed finds secured. But an airman, who may know little or nothing of archæology, flying above the site, can see the outline of all the buried foundations extending to a distance, which the experts on the ground cannot see at all. It is the airman and not the specialist who obtains the correct general view of things. It would be entirely wrong to regard him as a meddling interloper trespassing in matters he does not understand. He assists the experts. He does not interfere with them. His work and theirs are mutually complementary.

So it is with the sciences which are the products of expert technique. They have accumulated mountains of detailed knowledge. This knowledge is true so long as we regard it as a collection of piecemeal facts, like objects unearthed by the archæologists. Yet these objects do not reveal the plan of the original builders in the enlightening and informative manner of a picture taken from the air. Specialist scientific information resembles a collection of photographs of the streets and buildings of a town, placed side by side and seen independently. They may be extremely accurate photographs but they will not give the instantaneous conception of the town as a whole which a single aerial photograph will produce. It is an aerial picture, in general outline, that we shall attempt to construct in the following chapters.

Science has illuminated the world which is given by the senses as if with a searchlight and modern philosophy has, to a great extent, been drawn into the searchlight area and has assumed that a valid perspective of the cosmic whole can be constructed by analysing the sense-world. At the same time the physical universe, sense-revealed, is to-day accepted unquestioningly as embracing the entire cosmos. The underlying cause responsible for everything is taken to be a meaningless flux of physical forces from which mankind has emerged, a product of purposeless, physical change. Religion is looked upon as a delusion, born in the mind of ignorant man before the dawn of scientific illumination and as no more than a product of wishful thinking. It is taken as axiomatic that reality does not extend beyond the realm that the senses reveal. Everything is projected upon the flat screen that the sense-world provides. The universe, as seen to-day, is without perspective; and it is assumed that the entire cosmos can be grasped in principle by the human intellect. Side by side with this assumption, and in grotesque contrast with it, is the belief that this intellect arose from a chance combination of material particles. The whole modern outlook is a combination of childish naïvety with the superb analytical skill of the specialist.

In examining Materialism, our object is not to defend religious orthodoxy against the current philosophy which has been produced by science, but rather to examine from a non-technical and non-specialist standpoint the foundations on which Materialism has been built. And it is not the materialist doctrine alone with which we are concerned but also the far-reaching results, which ramify in many directions, of certain instinctive acceptances which have been fixed by nature in the base of the human mind. It is these which scientists, among others, have unconsciously, but with momentous consequences, incorporated into their system of thought. As we proceed it will become more and more evident that conscious recognition of this instinctive mental structure throws light, not only on the nature of science, but on the whole situation of man. The organism which has passed unnoticed through the scientist's filter is among the most important factors of all.

CHAPTER II

THE NON-SPECIALIST STANDPOINT

A UNIVERSAL difficulty presents itself whenever the human mind tries fully to understand. The question or problem that arises, the fact with which it is faced, may appear simple at first sight; but the more thoroughly it tries to understand it, the more complex and the more elusive it becomes. In dealing with it mentally, we are therefor obliged to shape it to fit *ourselves*, so that when we say that we understand it, we understand something that is partly a creation of our own. We have drawn it into a mould of our own making and have fitted it to the structure of our own mind. We simplify, we abstract, we modify until this is achieved. The idea that is needed in order to grasp the thing as it is, must be modified until it assumes a form which can be expressed by our existing vocabulary. A rough simile of the kind of difficulty we encounter when we try to understand anything exhaustively, is provided by the act of looking at a contour-map. The eye takes it in at a glance, but to give a full description in words of the relation of all the features which the map contains would be an impossible task.

This difficulty permeates human knowledge. The more precisely we attempt to define a thing, the more the indefinable in it escapes us. We realize this very little because a partial understanding of things is all that is needed for practical life, and that partial understanding can be rendered clear and simple and can remain within the competence of words. In fact, it is the adequacy of language, when dealing with practical matters, which has created the belief that language is universally valid. Science has done much to strengthen this belief, for it arose in the practical world by dealing practically with visible and tangible things and has continued to assume that what serves for them will serve for everything. The result is that the scientific picture keeps on growing, but never integrates. No specific answer is forthcoming to the question: What picture of the universe has science produced? The picture is not in the nature of a conclusion methodically arrived at, but has grown up by itself out of masses of detail accumulated by specialists. However inadequate or distorted this picture may be when seen from a distance, it appears to the specialist, from his ground-level standpoint, to be complete. It is quite understandable that this should be so. If we stand on the shore of a lake and look out over the water, it seems to us that we are looking at a complete and perfectly proportioned scene. But when we climb the mountain behind the lake and look down on the same scene from above, we see how distorted the ground-level view really was. Only when we get away from the ground-level and survey the maplike outline of the lake and its islands from the mountain-top do we see it as it really is.

I was once invited to attend a series of lectures on the philosophy of science, and I rejoiced at what I supposed to be an opportunity of learning from experts the significance which each science had for knowledge as a whole. But each lecturer gave a clear epitome of his own science, and then, remembering the title of the course, bowed politely to the philosophers and handed the general significance over to them. Having reached the limits of his special preserve, he tossed the ball to the group of specialists next door. Indeed, philosophy has become far more a technical study within a fence of its own than a general interpretation of knowledge. Surrounded, as we are, by mountains of print and masses of detail, our great need is to find a single thread which will lead us through the maze of specialist learning and show us a true outline of what it means and whither it is leading. But we cannot expect such an outline to be supplied by more and more analysis: it must be reached by synthesis; and synthesis means a departure from the analytical technique of specialists.

It is our object in the present volume to attempt a contribution, however small, towards the creation of an outline-view set in a perspective which only the non-specialist can provide. Technical problems of science and philosophy will be left, as far as possible, to the specialist and the expert while we endeavour to stand back and look at their creations from afar. The risk of being prosecuted for trespass is one which we must unavoidably run. Many questions arise as we stand back and look at science as a whole; and one of these is whether the analytical method on which scientists so largely depend is adequate even for science itself. The following pertinent passage occurred in a paper read by Dr. J. Gray to the Zoological Section of the British Association in 1933: "Each year it becomes more difficult to review the progress which is being made in the diverse fields of modern zoology, for as individuals we are necessarily specialists, and we tend to forget that the greatest contribution which zoology has ever made to human thought was not the result of a specialized inquiry. The concept of organic evolution was, on the contrary, a brilliant process of integration from every branch of the subject, which spread its effect far beyond the confines of zoology itself."[1]

Integration here revealed a vast, general principle. Yet one feels that the routine-minded specialist strongly objects to integrative methods. I

[1] *The Times*, September 8th, 1933.

believe it has been doubted by some whether the work of Darwin should be classed as scientific, because it did not depend on quantitative methods or on analysis. A. N. Whitehead throws out the idea that the concepts to which analysis leads are dangerously narrow: "Is it not possible", he asks, "that the standardized concepts of science are only valid within narrow limitations, perhaps too narrow for science itself?"

How can we obtain a picture which is an integrated whole, and not a collection of detailed pictures placed side by side?

It must be admitted that the non-specialist who, in the present age, attempts to review the work of specialists, suffers from serious disadvantages. His method, for one thing, is altogether out of favour. Instead of minutely examining samples of what lies before him, he closes his eyes to detail and tries to acquire an impression of the whole. In contrast to analysis, his method, if it were to receive a name, would have to be called "convergent synthesis"; for he does not work on the inductive principle of generalization from examples but on the quite different principle of allowing light to converge from many different sources until a picture of the situation grows up in his mind. It is a method which depends more on intuition than on logic and is therefore likely to be opposed by the specialist, although the latter often relies on intuition without being fully aware of it.

The non-specialist suffers also from the lack of a recognized position and the lack of credentials. A forceful argument is likely to be brought against him. It will be said: How can you expect to deal with anything unless you have the exact knowledge and the power of precise expression which come only from special training? Without these, you will wander away into vagueness and, in the end, you will get nowhere. The reader must decide, if he pursues the present volume to the end, whether this indictment is true.

Again, the specialist has the advantage of a recognized position, which the non-specialist (as a non-specialist) necessarily lacks. If argument fails, the former can always point to his position:

> *Whatever you may say, Sir*
> *I am the vicar of Bray, Sir.*

Also a non-specialist is almost sure to be misrepresented as an amateur attempting to compete with experts; whereas he is, in reality, taking, from quite a different standpoint, a view which includes much that specialists are unaware of or ignore.

But the advantages are not all on the specialist's side. The non-specialist is a free lance. In the true sense of the word, he is a "free thinker". He is immersed in no groove: he is attached to no camp: he is not obliged to weigh every word he utters in the light of its probable effect on his reputation. Also, he need not stop short at the artificial boundaries which divide one specialist province from another: he can appeal from any fact to any other fact, however widely separated the two may be. By doing this he has a chance of lighting upon ideas that the specialist would never think of. He can make light from different quarters converge.

It is a prevalent idea to-day that only a specialist can arrive at a goal. But we shall boldly turn the tables. While admitting the specialist's supremacy in his own field, we shall maintain that only the non-specialist can see the whole in proper proportion. It is, of course, possible for the same individual to adopt both the specialist's and the non-specialist's angle of approach; but this is rarely done. People who have looked at things broadly have, however, realized something of the advantage of the non-specialist's position. Sir Auckland Geddes, for example, in a speech on medical education, said: "The root of the present discontent seems to be that all medical students learn some zoology, physics, chemistry, anatomy, physiology, pathology, etc., but they are never given a chance systematically to study Man as a whole. Man is much more than a physical body. The better you know him as he lives his life in the city or faces death in his job or in some wild adventure, the more fully you realize how far removed from a picture of what man really is, the portrait given by each of the sciences is. Even a synthesis of the portraits fails to represent reality."[1] The special sciences, in other words, do not provide the aerial view.

But perhaps the most important advantage that the non-specialist possesses is that he is in a position to notice things that the specialist is liable to miss. His thinking begins a step earlier. For example, there are two ways in which a thing may be hidden. It may be hidden because it is thoroughly concealed: or it may be hidden because it is so obvious that no one notices it. The latter is by far the most effectual mode of conceal- ment; but the specialist in his search for truth plunges into a routine which is admirably devised for bringing to light what is concealed, but he omits the preliminary survey of his data which brings to light the obvious. The non-specialist, on the other hand, looks round in a leisurely way, without a fixed method of procedure, and notices things which the specialist has inadvertently taken for granted. But the things the non-specialist notices lead him into a different manner of thinking from that which the specialist adopts, and it seems probable that that which is revealed by the non-specialist mode of thought is likely to be ignored by

[1] *A Voice from the Grand-stand.*

those wholly immersed in a special routine. His way of thought is not consonant with the ingrained habits of the human mind. Yet it is hoped the reader may see that there is method in this non-specialist's madness nevertheless. In any case I invite the reader to suspend judgment for the moment and to accompany me to a little hill apart—the non-specialist's vantage-point—from which we may survey the scene spread out before us. From it we will try to trace an outline-picture of the human situation as seen from this unusual standpoint.

CHAPTER III

SCIENCE IN ACTION

L OOKING at science, the major factor in the world to-day, not as a scientist or a philosopher or a historian or a sociologist looks at it, but from a non-specialist angle, we see that there is a peculiar rift in it. This is visible only from afar. At first the division is shadowy and its significance far from obvious. But, when we develop our view synthetically, the division begins to clarify. There seems at first sight to be some disjunction between pure and applied science. This the specialist would be likely to deny. Theory and practice, he would say, act and react on one another and form an integral whole. There is no ground for regarding the two as separate. Science is not a dichotomy.

But we have not as yet correctly caught sight of the nature of the distinction. The synthetic mode of detecting what is hidden operates gradually. While it is growing, it can easily be attacked. Ideas which develop in this way are like tender plants, defenceless while they are forming, but immensely valuable when they are formed. At this early stage it may be said that at any rate we can see this difference: the applied scientist is at work in the clearly defined foreground while the pure scientist is trying to peer into the shadowy background, so that their objectives are not on one plane. We must leave the matter there for the present and glance briefly at the two main departments of science—applied and pure—in order to understand what it is that science is achieving and what effects it is producing on mankind.

Applied science is engaged in doing things and making things, while pure science is engaged in discovering things. Instead of speaking of applied and pure science, it will be better to speak of science in action and science in discovery. The two are not at work on the same plane, though specialists would be slow to recognize that this difference has any important significance. It is commonly assumed that scientific methods are equally valid in the background and in the foreground—in problems concerned with practical achievements and in problems concerned with unlimited discovery—in fact, that they are valid universally. A. N. Whitehead, when discussing the nature of science, makes a statement that most men of science would accept as axiomatic: "I do not think, however, that I have even yet brought out the greatest contribution of medievalism to the formation of the scientific movement, I mean the inexpugnable belief that every detailed occurrence can be correlated with its antecedents in a perfectly definite manner, exemplifying general principles. Without this belief the incredible labours of scientists would be without hope. It is this instinctive conviction, vividly poised before the imagination, which is the motive-power of research—that there is a secret, a secret which can be unveiled."[1] Every secret is potentially capable of being unveiled by methods within the capacity of the human mind: this is the principle which scientists almost universally accept; and in this acceptance is foreshadowed the dichotomy in science which we have dimly foreseen. A key-question is raised which merits our deep reflection. If the acceptance is not true, there must be an underlying division in science which is of fundamental importance. The question must be postponed until we have considered the ways in which applied and pure science have affected humanity.

Science in action presents a spectacle of dazzling success—so dazzling that many are captivated by it and are unable to see beyond it. Radiating from western Europe, the achievements of applied science spread over the world in a remarkably short period. Space and time have been conquered; neither oceans nor mountains any longer offer barriers to travel; the human voice can be heard across the globe; medicine and surgery can now perform what our ancestors would have regarded as miracles, and have gone a long way towards eliminating disease and the results of accident; food from every climate in the world regularly reaches the great centres of population; information, cleanliness and sanitation have replaced, over large areas, the ignorance and squalor of the past; the weather can be foretold, and the first attempts are being made to control it. By the achievements of science in action, the nations of the world have been brought into close contact with one another and their economies woven into a single pattern.

All this is a marvellous achievement and cannot be too highly applauded. But it is not the whole picture; and a glance at the whole shows that these achievements are not simple steps to Paradise. They are blessings: but they have repercussions. For one thing, they have so accelerated the pace of life as profoundly to disturb our mental habits.

They make life too complex for peace of mind. They increase the speed of living to such an extent that there is no time to look beneath the rapidly moving surface and to reach firm foundations. In our complicated and divided society, individuals are by an intensive round of special duties fenced off from reality. Many live artificial and unsatisfying lives, so that

[1] *Science and the Modern World*, p. 15.

some even welcome the advent of war as a release from boredom. Problem after problem has been solved by science only to raise fresh problems in their train. Inoculation, sanitation, the prevention of famine, the fighting of floods are some of the blessings which have been handed to the populations of the Far East; but, in proportion as these have been put into practice, fresh problems have arisen. Suffering has been alleviated; lives have been saved; but the result has been an increase in population which the land cannot support. Success in fighting the malaria-mosquito in British Guiana threatens to over-populate that country. In an article entitled "The Spectre of Malthus", Sir John Boyd Orr wrote: "The fact that with 200,000,000 more people to feed we are not yet back to the pre-war food position should be a grim reminder to those in power that the rising tide of population and the falling reservoir of food-producing resources are a more serious problem for human society than the conflict of political ideologies."[1]

Again, the advances made by the scientific age in sea-transport enabled the peoples of Europe to emigrate to the unfilled continents of the world, there to live on the products of virgin soil. But this gift of scientific progress, has had its counterblast and has raised the gigantic problem of continental soil-erosion. So serious is this that Sir John Boyd Orr wrote, in the same article: "Of those who have studied this problem, some think the position is hopeless. Our western mechanized civilization, which has destroyed the resources of the earth with accelerating rapidity, is, they say, doomed. The two world-wars and feverish preparation for a third are its death-throes. We must look forward to a long, dark age during which the earth will have a chance to recover from its wounds, after which a saner civilization will begin to evolve, probably in Asia." Although some say this, others take a brighter view: but it is clear that the achievements of science in action are not simply an unmixed blessing.

Modern education, again, is an advantage which we owe to science: but it, also, has its reverse side; for much of the education so widely spread is superficial, over-specialized or merely technical. It is plain to see that universal education does not raise all minds to a single, elevated standard; nor does it automatically increase mental capacity. "It has", as Sir S. Radhakrishnan has said, "become more easy to get into a college and more difficult to get educated. We are taught to read but not trained to think." Even the lax standard of education which prevailed 150 to 200 years ago had a compensating advantage. G. M. Trevelyan remarks that: "the product of genius per head of the population in eighteenth-century England seems, by comparison with our own day, to have been in inverse

[1] *Observer*, January 9th, 1949.

proportion to the amount of education supplied." And again: "The old-fashioned Grammar School for farmers' sons at Hawkshead would not have borne modern inspection, but it allowed the shy and tender plant of Wordsworth's genius to grow naturally and in its own queer way, as would not have happened if the boy's every hour had been mapped out for organized athletics and instruction."[1] Progress in knowledge and its applications is not a single forward path. It plunges us into an ever more complex pattern of events.

It is not only, however, that the practical problems, so brilliantly solved by applied science, have given rise to further problems. When we look at scientific achievement as a whole, it becomes clear that there are two sides to the scientific balance-sheet. There is a debit side as well as a credit side. Since the object of science was to apply knowledge for the benefit of mankind, how is it that a debit side has arisen? That there is a debit side cannot be denied, for the discoveries of science are used for good and evil purposes alike. The reason for the debit side is not far to seek. When we examine the credit-items, we see that each of them makes certain *demands*, which must be met if the credit-item is to remain a credit-item only. If these demands are not met, the credit-item will appear in the debit-column as well. It is true that the credit and debit sides of the scientific balance-sheet are not quite as simple as they are in a ledger-account. Real situations are seldom perfectly clear-cut. The balance of advantage and disadvantage in any country at any particular time may vary according to the kind of government in power. The evil effects of the debit-column can, to a certain extent, be restrained by law, as, for example, by the restriction of the sale of dangerous drugs. Or, to take another example, the inventions of science benefit both the criminal and the police; but in a well-governed state, the advantage lies with the police. In an ill-governed country, on the other hand, the police themselves become a menace and the debit-column swells to immense proportions. But if we allow for these variations in the balance-sheet, the credit- and debit-columns of science remain an outstanding feature of the scientific era and a problem of momentous importance.

Take, for example, the motor car, which offers a convenient and enjoyable means of travel as well as an excellent mode of distributing goods. It is a tremendous asset; but it also makes very stringent demands. It calls for a high degree of responsibility, thoughtfulness, good manners, careful attention and self-control on the part of all who use the roads, if it is to be used with safety. Since the introduction of the motor car, these demands have been met to a certain extent, but not to anything like a

[1] *History of England,* p. 523.

sufficient degree. Consequently there are between one and two hundred
thousand road casualties annually in this country alone. This is the debit-
item. It is the same with the other inventions of science: some lean more
to one side: some to the other; but on the whole, each makes demands
which must be rigidly met if the invention is to remain a blessing and is
not to become a curse as well. The crux of the situation is that the demands
often involve a radical change in human nature: yet human nature has
changed very little, if at all, since civilization began, and shows no
appreciable tendency to do so now. On this matter, a well-known historian
has said: "Till this earth ceases to be physically habitable by man, we may
expect that the endowments of human beings with original sin and with
natural goodness will be about the same, on the average, as they always
have been so far as our knowledge goes. The most primitive societies
known to us in the life or by report provide examples of as great natural
goodness as, and no lesser wickedness than, the highest civilizations
or religious societies that have yet come into existence. There has
been no perceptible variation in the average sample of human nature
in the past; there is no ground, in the evidence afforded by History,
to expect any great variation in the future either for the better or the
worse."[1]

This important fact profoundly affects every application of science as
well as every description of social planning. It should prevent us from
regarding science as a universal panacea for human ills; and it should
especially prevent us from placing the Golden Age in a future Utopia,
built on scientific achievement: also from looking back, as the Greeks
did, to a Golden Age in the past, or from seeing it, as some do to-day, in
the medieval "age of faith". With regard to the latter, G. M. Trevelyan
reminds us that "it is an error to suppose that the mediaeval world was
safe and peaceful because its inhabitants were theoretically conscious of
the unity of Christendom. It was indeed free from our modern dangers of
race-hatred and war organized on the national scale, for the low level of
organization and transport prevented France and Germany from conceiv-
ing the idea of racial patriotism and making war on one another as nations;
but they were both in a state of internal war between the petty feudal
powers composing them, wars conducted with the utmost ferocity,
though for purely personal motives. In the feudal world, the hand of
neighbour was perpetually raised against neighbour, and death, in-
justice and outrage were the daily lot."[2] Human nature is much the
same under a dominant church as it is under dominant science. Internal

---

[1] *C.T.*, p. 248.
[2] *History of England*, p. 107.

change in the individual is the only thing that can bring about a real alteration.

Human nature may fluctuate in some degree in different times and in different places, but, on the average, it remains about the same. If this were not so, we should long ago have been plunged into heaven or hell. But the black and white threads are interwoven and apparently will always continue to be so. The tares and the wheat will grow together until the harvest. Nothing could be truer than this; and it is on this basis that we must plan for the future of the world. We may be sure that every invention of science will be used in the future, as it is in the present and has been in the past, by the regenerate and unregenerate sides of human nature alike. "We have invented the motor car—and Caliban has climbed into it and Europe flares red in the wake of Panzer armies. We have invented the aeroplane—and Caliban soars in it, dropping on our clever heads the two-ton bombs we have likewise contrived for his amusement. We have invented the wireless and from it Propagandaministerium comes —the voice of Caliban. For his are the Kingdom, the Power and the Glory."[1]

Whatever science achieves, it will not exterminate Caliban. The motor car was mentioned as one of the minor illustrations of an item which appears on both sides of the scientific balance-sheet. But the international problems, which science has created, or at least magnified, also appear in the double columns. The world food-shortage might be solved by the credit-items of science if the demands made were fully met. "This could be done", said Sir John Boyd Orr, in the article previously quoted, "if the nations would arrange a political truce and co-operate in a World Food Plan. It can scarcely be done with every country acting independently on its own national plan." The demand is for international co-operation on a basis of mutual trust and for the abandonment of nationalist ways of thinking. Science, in fact, demands a single World-government—not a dictatorial régime, but a sane, wise, democratically minded body of rulers, beloved and trusted by all. Central planning and control is what is demanded because of the interlocked complexity of the world-situation. But the demand is impossibly high; for only men of superhuman knowledge, understanding, integrity and spiritual development could make such a ruling body a success.

Nationalism shows no sign of declining because science has produced a situation which demands that it should. Ingrained patterns of thought and feeling do not change in order that they may adjust themselves to external conditions. International co-operation succeeds only when no demand is

[1] F. L. Lucas, *Critical Thoughts for Critical Days*.

made for a radical change in human nature. Human institutions, social, political and religious, adhere to their established lines like growing plants, changing only with extreme slowness. Their innate pattern persists whatever new situations may arise, whether due to science or any other cause. The extent to which social planners and scientific sociologists ignore this patent fact is extraordinary. It is widely assumed that humanity will adjust itself to any situation that is planned for it. "The advantages of international co-operation are so great that they must come."[1] What does a mother do when she sees her baby playing with a knife? She takes it away from him. She does not say: The advantages of handling the knife carefully are so great that my baby is bound to do it! Why are we so extraordinarily blind to the factors which exist within ourselves? Why do we expect that people will change because it is to their advantage to do so? Mr. Winston Churchill was reported as saying in a speech at Zurich in 1946: "The process is simple. All that is needed is the resolve of hundreds of millions of men and women to do right instead of wrong and to gain as their reward blessing instead of cursing." This is perfectly true. It has always been as simple as that; but the rational demonstration of the fact that it is more advantageous to do right than wrong will not alter the heavy fixations that go to make up human character; for these are largely founded on instinct. They do not change in response to the logic of the conscious kind. This has been the perennial problem of the teacher and the priest since civilization began.

It is evident that science, in its capacity of dealing with practical problems, has created an extremely complex and dangerous situation because it is always looking outwards at the external world and takes no account of the human being. Even in psychology this same outward-turning method is pursued. Man does not realize that he himself is an essential part of every situation that arises.

Science cannot control the human factor. One who took part in the making of the peace treaty after the First World War wrote as follows: "The contrast between the success of modern European minds in controlling almost any situation in which the elements are physical bodies and the forces physical forces, and their inability to control situations in which the elements are human beings and the forces mental forces, left an indelible mark on the memory of everyone concerned with it." The truth is that no government can be efficient so long as it retains a false idea of human nature and of the constitution of the human individual.

[1] From a review of *Your World To-morrow*, by Professor A. M. Low in *The Times Literary Supplement* for October 11th, 1947.

Science in action has affected human society in another way. The profusion of its productions and their unlimited exploitation keep the mind always moving from topic to topic like a grasshopper. There are so many distractions that nothing sinks in; people rush hither and thither without pausing to obtain a firm grip on anything. This debit-item is the result of an unfulfilled demand. The demand in this case is for restraint in the use of new inventions, which would keep them on the credit side. If these are not used wisely and sparingly, they become a dazzling screen which prevents people from appreciating the serious aspects of life and adjusting themselves to them. The demand is not met because "no improvements in science or knowledge make the world one jot the wiser". As soon as modern transport is available, vast crowds run hither and thither at the greatest possible speed. The aeroplane appears, but it is not reserved for special purposes or for emergencies; it is thrown into international competition for faster and faster air-traffic. Every effort is made to exceed the speed of sound; and of course the principal application of the aeroplane is for war. The radio is used to maintain programmes of broadcasting for sixteen hours a day and the available wave-lengths are filled to the point of overlapping. Modern methods of printing emit an immense flood of largely unnecessary literature, while the advantage of increased leisure, which might accrue from mass-production, is thrown away by encouraging people to consume or to waste as much of the mass-produced goods as possible. Again, the gifts of science and the characteristics of human nature come into collision. The increasing complexity which science has introduced into life renders it more than doubtful whether man can any longer control the machine he has created. Economics is certainly a field for the specialist; but who can escape the pressing doubt as to whether modern economists understand this subject in the modern, complex world, or whether governments have the power to control it.

It is not suggested that restraint should be imposed by governments or forced upon mankind. It is not likely that the demands made by scientific inventions can be met. Only a complete revolution in human nature could meet them. We have no panacea to offer. We are merely looking at science in order to appreciate the situation that has been created. The credit and debit sides of the scientific balance-sheet will always be there and the question which is vital to our time is whether the two columns can continue to mount up side by side without destroying the civilization that has produced them.

The significance of human life does not, however, lie in the solution of this problem. It lies in the perennial struggle between good and evil

—not in the hope of eliminating evil from this world and of substituting for it only good; for the ideal of Utopia in this world is no more than a carrot dangled before the donkey's nose. Even if human beings were, by some miracle, to attain such a Utopia as materialistic humanists and scientific sociologists imagine, they would be living under conditions false to the inmost nature of a world such as this. They would be out of touch with reality. There would be no vent in such a state for forces which are part and parcel of the human being. Not only is Utopia in this world unattainable; if it were achieved, human beings would revolt, would form themselves into opposing factions and would destroy it. Normal human life in this material world is set in a framework of continual turmoil, tossed back and forth between the pulsations of the Mighty Opposites. Good and evil, side by side, are continually present and always will be. Without the contrast of darkness, how should we recognize the light? Strife is the key-word of life in this world:

> *The troubles of our proud and angry dust*
> *Are from eternity, and shall not fail.*[1]

It is true, however, that the world could be a better place than it is if each one of its inhabitants were to rise to a condition of wisdom, and right-eousness and self-improvement. "The soul of all improvement is the improvement of the soul." But the improvement of society can only be achieved through the improvement of the individual, not by political mechanisms or mass-schemes or by anything imposed on mankind from without. The changes that do come about are of a superficial nature and are rather adaptations to circumstances than genuine alterations of character. Highwaymen nowadays seldom hold up traffic on the roads; but this is not because everyone has become too virtuous to rob, but because the modern police-service has rendered it not worth while. We must not mistake adjustments of this kind for genuine improvements in character. It is the human being which lies at the core of every problem, while science turns its eyes only to the external world.

The most dangerous item on the debit side of the scientific balance-sheet is, however, the immense power given to modern dictators or oligarch-ical groups. These owe their power to science in action. There is of course nothing new in tyrannical government. Indeed, the very spirit of the modern totalitarian state, with an added dash of the philosophy of Omar Khayyám (which also is widely prevalent to-day), may be found in the second chapter of the *Wisdom of Solomon*. The most menacing features of

---

[1] W. Macneile Dixon, *The Human Situation*, Chapter 10.

the dictator-state are, however, new. Autocracy is traditional in Russia and it is not surprising that it should still continue in the form of the Soviet Régime. States alter little. But "there is this of novelty in the Soviet system. A living religion is enforced by the massed large-scale propaganda of a scientific age, by machine-guns and aeroplanes, telephone and telegraph, printing press and film, broadcasting and the regimentation of all the arts. A hundred and sixty million human souls are by a gigantic system of governmental pressure hermetically sealed against the invasion of unwelcome truth. All previous experiments in tyranny recorded in human annals pale beside this colossal achievement."[1] To-day a handful of ruthless and determined men can hold an entire nation in its grip because the devices of applied science have given them unprecedented power and opportunity. The result is substantially the same whatever ideology the ruling group may profess and enforce. It is through the perfection of modern means of transport, communications, modes of propaganda and so forth that the police-state and the perpetual "cold war" have become possible. Underground strategy is a major weapon in the hands of every aggressive ruler now that applied science has made this form of aggression possible. " 'Our strategy,' said Hitler, 'is to destroy the enemy from within, to conquer him through himself. Mental confusion, contradictions in feeling, indecision, panic . . . these are our weapons.' "[2]

Napoleon is said to have remarked: "Whereas the advent of cannon killed the feudal system, ink will kill the modern social organization." If for "ink" we substitute scientific propaganda, it would seem that nothing could be truer. So astonishing is the power of propaganda to-day that a dictator can not only force his subjects to obey him: he can persuade them that by so doing they are performing a noble duty. This, and psychological methods of forcibly coercing the mind are perhaps the most insidious of scientific achievements.

The driving force of totalitarian states, whatever ideological colours they may fly, is lust for power. Power and the intoxication it produces has indeed always been the principal incentive to war. The gifts of modern science in the hands of a ruling group to-day offer power on a scale never before dreamed of. Ideologies also can swell to gigantic proportions and their mental fixations are an incalculable danger to peace and mutual understanding. Closed to reasonableness and to the perception of truth, the ideologist is in the grip of fixed *clichés* and his mind has become fossilized in a doctrinal creed. Lysenko decried the laws of inheritance

[1] H. A. L. Fisher, *A History of Europe*, pp. 1215-6.
[2] Kenneth Walker, *Meaning and Purpose*.

discovered by scientists because "genetics is contrary to Marxism-Leninism and is therefore a heresy"! This removes at a stroke the principle of free inquiry upon which science was founded. If this kind of mentality gains in influence, it is difficult to see what but disintegration of society can lie ahead. *Quem deus vult perdere dementat prius.* The human being, static in character and therefore unable to meet the demands of science in action, has given rise to the gigantic problems of the present day.

But behind all this can be seen the slow working out of a historical pattern. This also is visible in a bird's-eye view. Eastern Europe may long have been prepared by fate to be the rival and antagonist of the West. Russia, having turned her face to the west in ironical fashion and taken from it the most dangerous of its inventions—Marxism—is now using it as a weapon of fratricidal war. Arnold Toynbee generously calls it "a leaf torn from the book of Christianity and misread," but may it not be the charge of explosive which is destined to destroy modern civilization? Russia, with her Byzantine inheritance, is in part a legacy of the ancient world; and perhaps we are now witnessing the fruition of seeds sown in the long distant past. It may be that the division of the Roman Empire into East and West was fraught with more ominous consequences than anyone realized.

What lies behind the present pattern of events so fraught with distress and bewilderment? Is the whole significance written on the surface? Or is there a deeper pattern which we are not able to fathom? On the surface we can see that the demand inherent in scientific weapons of war is for a universal agreement to abolish war. But human nature is incapable of meeting the demand and scientific methods of war therefore pass into the debit column.

In any case, the crushing burden of preparation for war must go on and it is difficult to visualize a competitive race in armaments which will continue indefinitely without ever resulting in their use. The fact which stands out with the utmost clearness is that we can form no true estimate of the world-situation if we insist on merely looking outwards at what science has done in the external world. It is absolutely necessary to take *ourselves* into account as an integral part of that situation and we must see ourselves from a point of view other than that of the scientific specialist. For the specialist always tries to approach inward things from an external point of view.

This chapter is not a sermon nor does it urge any particular course of action. It is a comprehensive glance at one of the two aspects of science, in which its exclusive interest in the external world and its disregard for the human factor appear. Natural as this at first sight seems to be, there is behind it the subtle factor with which we are dealing. The outward turning is *urged* upon us. So is the refusal to look within. In this a trace of the dividing line between science in action and science in discovery comes into view; but in order to see it more clearly, we must turn to science in discovery.

CHAPTER IV

SCIENCE IN DISCOVERY

THE effects of science in action, important as they are, are not our main concern. We are chiefly interested in the effects produced by science in discovery. The latter has played a double role. In the first place it has passed on the knowledge acquired in the laboratory to those engaged in applied science; but secondly it has built up a general picture of the universe and of man, which has taken a firm hold on the contemporary mind; and this has led to practical effects of a different kind from those brought about by science in action. It has influenced human society by creating values and motives. But this second effect of science in discovery has not been deliberate: it has happened rather than been planned.

Although science has been a principal factor in forming the modern outlook, it has not been the only one. Philosophy also has played its part; and science and philosophy have acted and reacted upon one another. While earlier science, for example, was influenced by the views of Descartes, later philosophy has been influenced by the positive methods of science. In matters of values and morals, the modern world also owes much to Christianity. But the intellectual outlook of to-day is predominantly a scientific product, which has grown up around scientific discovery and is permeated by the scientific way of thinking. Yet, it is based less on specific facts than on tacit assumptions. This outlook has changed considerably during the last century. In Victorian times, it was dominated by a belief in inevitable progress, which then seemed to be a law of nature. This belief has by no means died out; but in the nineteenth century everything seemed to support it. In Great Britain, the population was increasing; practical science was advancing by leaps and bounds; coal and iron, in close proximity, facilitated the application of science to industry; colonies and countries overseas were ready to exchange food and raw materials for manufactured products made at home; national power was on the increase; social reform had begun; the standard of living was rising and everything seemed to be undergoing a steady improvement. Then, as if to confirm the belief in progress, Darwin's theory of evolution arose and showed that all life had arisen from the smallest beginnings and had progressed by successive stages to the supreme product of man.

Seen in retrospect, the rise of Britain to power and prosperity was clearly due to special circumstances produced in the nineteenth century (although the intensely interesting question remains as to whether there may not be a profounder pattern in history beneath the tangled pattern of surface causes). But organic evolution was later discovered to be something very different from a story of uninterrupted progress. Yet the idea of a continual uprising from the lower to the higher—an amelioration leading towards perfection—haunted and still haunts the scientific imagination. Progress really did occur in organic evolution and this led to the assumption that it must continue in human society; and there is still to-day a tendency to exalt it into a cosmic principle. In the form of progressive emergence, progress is made to unify the organic and inorganic realms, as can be seen in the works of C. Lloyd Morgan and in the philosophy of S. Alexander.

This view does not accord very well with another which is widespread to-day, namely the conception that the material universe comprises everything within itself and is completely governed by the laws of physics and of chance. On this view, the human mind arose in quite inexplicable fashion out of mechanical relations; but it nevertheless became the supreme focus of law and order and the sole creator of values. It thus falls to man to take over the course of evolution where nature abandoned it and to mould himself by the light of science according to his own design. He must also control, by the exercise of his reason, the irrational chaos out of which he arose. Progressive emergence on the one hand and the universal potency of physical law on the other are not easily compatible with one another.

The Victorian idea of perpetual and inevitable progress (not, however, held by a minority even in Victorian times), is now known to be illusory in the simple form in which many held it in the nineteenth century. But we, in the twentieth century, are addicted to a view which is equally out of focus with reality. This is the view that the scientific age marks the real beginning of human progress. It is thought that science has brought to the human race genuine enlightenment for the first time. This view may be attributed partly to the sense of finality which always attaches itself to the latest achievement. We do not yet see the scientific age as future generations will probably see it, as a phase in human thought and not as the absolute starting point of human civilization. The view, so often expressed by psychologists, anthropologists and others that pre-scientific man was no more than an ignorant and superstitious child, will no doubt pass like the Victorian idea that evolution means inevitable progress. It is helpful to try to see the scientific epoch in its true historical perspective, which is brought home to us in such a sentence as the following of

Arnold Toynbee's: "Western Christendom is merely one of five civilizations that survive in the world to-day; and these are merely five out of
nineteen that one can identify as having come into existence since the first
appearance of this species of society about six thousand years ago."[1]

Civilizations pass and with them their modes of thought. The idea
that there must be progress towards a future terrestrial goal is characteristic
of the modern era; but it is the product of a way of thinking and not a
discovery. Should we then reject the idea of progress? Not altogether;
for nature seldom presents a clear issue. There *has* been progress throughout the development of life: Darwin's discoveries were sound. There has
been progress also during the course of human civilization; but neither
the one nor the other has consisted of unadulterated progress. Organic
evolution was full of halts and backslidings. Human civilization has
progressed, but in a one-sided manner, which has consisted mainly in the
accumulation of knowledge; and this has not resulted in a pure advance
but, as we have seen in the last chapter, has given rise to a very complicated
combination of advantages and dangers. Progress, or at any rate, change, is
there; but it is superimposed on a static background. The two blend, and
make a picture of reality which frustrates the attempt to state it as a
single, clear-cut issue. Disappointing though it may be, we have to learn
not to form a rigid conclusion which we accept as final. To do this is to
draw reality into the pattern of our own thought instead of extending our
minds sensitively to catch the impress of things as they are. Thought must
be kept fluid: fixation tends to the fossilization which is characteristic of
ideologies. We have to remember the fate of the dinosaurs, who encased
themselves in rigid armour and became extinct. Fluidity of thought will
save us from the illusion that man became rational only with the birth of
science and the dawn of the Enlightenment.

No doubt the uses of applied science will not be forgotten, whatever
fate the future may have in store for the world; although the generations
to come may employ them differently; but what we have called "the
scientific outlook" is likely to prove a phase of thought belonging to this
particular epoch. This outlook began at the time of the Copernican
revolution. Before Copernicus, it had been accepted that the earth
occupied the centre of the universe and provided, with heaven above and
hell beneath, the habitation for a unified human and divine family. It was
a naïvely anthropocentric view, not necessarily wrong in emphasizing the
importance of man, but wrong in its conception of the nature of the
physical cosmos and of man's physical position in it. After the time of
Copernicus, the physical universe expanded beyond the wildest dreams

[1] *C.T.*, p. 155.

of medievalism until man and his planet shrunk to infinitesimal dimensions. Our picture of the scale of the physical universe to-day is as follows: "If a model of the universe were constructed on such a scale that the distance travelled by light in one year is represented by one mile, then the stars would be on the average four or five miles apart, and would be represented by spheres no larger than grains of sand."[1]

Our earth would be a microscopic speck revolving round one of these grains of sand, and that not the largest. (It will be remembered that the velocity of light is approximately 186,000 miles a second.) Thus seen, the size of the physical universe dwarfs man under a feeling of utter insignificance. Also the number of stars that have been counted runs into unthinkable numbers of millions. But this is only the size of the universe in space. It embraces also inconceivable vistas of time. Medieval man gave it a life-history of some 4,000 years. Now we are told that, "on the whole, we should be justified in assigning to a typical star a life of between 10^{10} and 10^{11} years"; while the age of the earth is estimated at something like 3×10^9 years. (The index-figure gives the number of zeros after the one, so that the age of the earth would be about three thousand million years. The modern picture of the expanding universe is on a still more terrific scale.)

There is also another direction in which the ground seems to have been swept from under our feet. The scientist has been busy with the microscope as well as with the telescope; and here, too, an unfathomable abyss opens before us. "Drawn to a proper scale, if the hydrogen atom, i.e. the orbit of the electron, were of the same diameter as the earth, the diameter of the electron would be about a hundred yards, and the diameter of the nucleus about two inches."[2]

Had the universe a beginning? Will it come to an end? Is space-time finite or infinite? Is there a limit to the infinitely small? The human mind indulged in some speculation in the past; but the positive discoveries of science have brought such questions to a head. Some, no doubt, will say that ordinary people do not trouble themselves about things of this kind, and that science, for the man in the street, means the work of clever people who provide hot water in the home, motor cars for week-end travel, the cinema for evening entertainment and wireless to enliven the drudgery of the housewife. But the climate of opinion which science has formed at upper levels inevitably descends and permeates all levels of thought in the course of time. It presents itself to every class of mind in a hundred different ways, through literature, the press, broadcasting and in the conversations which take place in every sort of gathering. Indirectly,

[1] B.E.W., p. 59.
[2] F. Soddy, Evolution in the Light of Modern Knowledge.

people become impregnated with the scientific thought of the time although they may not necessarily know anything about science. It is true, as Radhakrishnan has said, that: "a scientific frame of mind has become part of the mental equipment of even ordinary men and women."[1] For those who pause to reflect, it is scarcely surprising that these discoveries should have had a marked effect on the current conception both of nature and of man; and this conception inevitably spreads until it affects the whole of society. Again, Radhakrishnan has well expressed it: "In the known universe the Milky Way is a tiny fragment. In this fragment the solar system is a speck, our earth is an infinitesimal dot. On this dot mankind is crawling about desperately struggling to effect his own destruction. Even if he escapes this fate, the history of man is but a brief episode in the life of the solar system, which is itself doomed to destruction. While myths of creation are repudiated by the sciences of astronomy and geology, conceptions of mind and soul are revolutionized by biology and psychology. Historical events on which religions are based are explained in a different way by anthropology and history. Supernatural phenomena are given natural explanations. Secular education leads men to think that there is no rational or moral meaning in the universe, that all is mechanical or amoral, that values have no validity apart from accidents of time and place, that things dictate to a man the law of intrinsic development, that the individual *per se* does not count, that men are accountable only to themselves, that spiritual life is wishful thinking, and when this earthly journey is ended it is all over with man. We sweep the skies with the telescope and find no trace of God, we search the brain with the microscope and find to sign of mind. However much religion may have served humanity in the infancy of the human race, in an age of reason like our own, it is said that there is no longer any need for it."[2]

This outlook has been built up, not as a logical conclusion based on scientific fact, but as a picture which has formed itself as the result of preoccupation with *selected* facts seen from a *selected* standpoint. Numbers of intellectual and cultured persons to-day accept this view of man and of the universe as if it were scientifically sponsored and irrefutable. For example, Dr. Julian Huxley writes: "The purpose manifested in evolution, whether in adaptation, specialization or apparent progress, is only an apparent purpose. It is just as much a progress of blind forces as is the falling of a stone to the earth or the ebb and flow of the tides. It is we who have read purpose into evolution as earlier men projected will and emotion into inorganic phenomena like storm and earthquake."[3]

The reiterated expressions of this outlook, now so often to be found,

[1] *The Hibbert Journal*, July, 1946.   [2] *Ibid.*   [3] *Evolution*.

suggest, when examined, that they arise from exclusive preoccupation with physical things; that is to say from the building of a cosmic outlook solely on data supplied by the senses. If you keep your attention turned always in one direction, in the course of time you will come to form a philosophy based solely on your restricted observations. You will assume that there is no other direction in which you can turn and so come to believe that what you are observing embraces everything. One who does this will have a ready answer to the objector who asks why he does not widen his range of vision. I cannot, he will say; all the information I can possibly acquire comes to me by way of my bodily senses. My conclusions are based on all the data there is. No other source is possible. The fallacy here, and the cause that prompts it, is hidden from him. One or two quotations from a small book by the eminent philosopher Lord Russell (Bertrand Russell), who has in addition a comprehensive grasp of science, throw some light on the way in which the scientific outlook has arisen. "There are some who maintain that physiology can never be reduced to physics, but their arguments are not very convincing and it seems prudent to suppose that they are mistaken. What we call our 'thoughts' seem to depend upon the organization of tracks in the brain in the same sort of way in which journeys depend upon roads and railways. The energy used in thinking seems to have a chemical origin; for instance a deficiency of iodine will turn a clever man into an idiot. Mental phenomena seem to be bound up with material structure."[1] The facts of observation on which this last conclusion is based are, indeed, facts. But they are derived solely from observations of what the senses present without any reflection as to whether this base is broad enough to support the conclusion. The conclusion is accompanied by no critical examination of the observational or experimental methods employed and no critical examination of the observer. It is typical of the scientific attitude that it makes no allowance for the selection and limitation inherent in its methods; and it is under such unrecognized selection and limitation that the general scientific outlook has been built up. The scientific picture of mind arises from concentrating solely on the physical correlates of consciousness. "All the evidence goes to show that what we regard as our mental life is bound up with the brain-structure and organized bodily energy. Therefore it is rational to suppose that mental life ceases when bodily life ceases."[2]

Pope, in the early eighteenth century, could write:

> Expatiate free o'er all the scene of man
> A mighty maze! but not without a plan.

[1] *W.I.B.*, p. 12.   [2] *Ibid.*, p. 15.

But to-day the existence of a plan is precisely what is doubted, and often emphatically denied.

As seen through the spectacles of modern science, the universe is wholly an inanimate structure. An excellently succinct and pungent summary of this modern view appeared in *The Atlantic Monthly* for September, 1948, in an article written by Professor W. T. Stace of Princeton University. The article is entitled "Man against Darkness", and the author discusses what it is that has killed the belief in religion in so large a section of the modern world. "You can draw a sharp line", he says, "across the History of Europe dividing it into two epochs of very unequal length. The line passes through the lifetime of Galileo. European man before Galileo—whether ancient pagan or more recent Christian— thought of the world as controlled by plan and purpose. After Galileo, European man thinks of it as utterly purposeless. This is the great revolu- tion of which I spoke. It is this which has killed religion. . . . Religion can get on with any sort of astronomy, geology, biology, physics. But it can- not get on with a purposeless and meaningless universe."

Perhaps the revolution was not quite as sudden as this passage suggests; but it has come about, and the purposeless universe is widely accepted. Professor Stace himself accepts it; yet he deplores its discovery. "The Catholic bishops of America recently issued a statement in which they said that the chaotic and bewildered state of the modern world is due to man's loss of faith, his abandonment of God and religion. For my part I believe in no religion at all. Yet I entirely agree with the bishops." Man, in the scientific outlook now so widely prevalent, has been elevated to a position of lonely grandeur. "Since the world is not ruled by a spiritual being, but rather by blind forces, there cannot be any ideals, moral or otherwise, in the universe outside us. Our ideals therefore must proceed only from our minds; they are our own inventions. Thus the world which surrounds us is nothing but an immense spiritual emptiness. It is a dead universe."

We may compare this with Dr. Julian Huxley's statement that man "stands alone as the agent of his fate and the trustee of progress for life".[1]

In that case, what trustworthy standards to live by can there ever be? As Professor Stace remarks: "Hobbes saw at once that if there is no purpose in the world there are no values either. 'Good and Evil', he writes, 'are names that signify our appetites and aversions; which in different tempers, customs and doctrines of men are different. . . . Every man calleth that which pleases him good and that which displeases him evil.' " Man, on this modern view, is the measure of all things. He must create his own

[1] *Man the Trustee of Ethical Goodness*, p. 159.

values; and they will be pragmatic; he must create his own standard of morality. He is an extraordinary accident—a short-lived freak, which the dead universe has produced by chance. Professor Stace inserts the following condensed quotation from Bertrand Russell's book, *A Free Man's Worship*: " 'Such an outline, but even more purposeless, more void of meaning, is the world which science presents for our belief. Amid such a world, if anywhere, our ideals henceforward must find a home. . . . Blind to good and evil, reckless of destruction, omnipotent matter rolls on its relentless way; for man condemned to-day to lose his dearest, to-morrow himself to pass through the gates of darkness, it remains only to cherish ere yet the blow falls, the lofty thoughts that ennoble his little day . . . to worship at the shrine his own hands have built; and to sustain alone, a weary but unyielding Atlas, the world that his own ideals have fashioned despite the trampling march of unconscious power.' "

"We can create our own values", says Dr. Julian Huxley. But when he adds: "Society must make rational use of an irrational mechanism in order to create the system of values that it wants", one cannot help feeling that this whole point of view is based on a very queer assumption, which requires a great deal of examination before it can be accepted. If the mind is the product of irrational mechanism, how can its rationality have come into existence? Is that rationality, logically, a thing to be trusted? It is important to realize that it is not a question of whether this outlook of science must be accepted or else rejected together with the validity of science as a whole. Nor is it a case of choosing between this outlook and the entire traditional system of institutional religion. The question is: What does a synthesis of the whole range of experience point to when looked at from a balanced standpoint?

According to the scientific outlook, nothing exists beyond matter and the ex-irrational rational human mind. Belief in any further extension of existence beyond these is held to be an illusion. Illusions, Professor Stace thinks, are necessary for us; and there are minor illusions which we still can cling to. "But without the Great Illusion, the illusion of a good, kindly and purposeful universe, we shall *have* to learn to live."

Truth, on this view, as presented by science, is inimical to human well-being. It is a pity we have discovered it; but now that we have, we must grin and bear it until final darkness overwhelms us for ever.

Professor Stace's view that the scientific outlook is injurious to mankind is supported from quite a different quarter. "It seems to me", writes C. G. Jung, "that, side by side with the decline of religious life, the neuroses grow noticeably more frequent. There are as yet no statistics to enable us to prove this increase in actual numbers. But of one thing I am sure, that everywhere the mental state of European man shows an alarming lack of balance. We are living undeniably in a period of great restlessness, nervous tension, confusion and disorientation of outlook. Among my patients from many countries, all of them educated persons, there is a considerable number who came to me, not because they were suffering from a neurosis, but because they could find no meaning in life or were torturing themselves with questions which neither present-day philosophy nor religion could answer."[1]

That peculiarly versatile European, Albert Schweitzer, said a long time ago: "Only when we are able to attribute real meaning to the world and to life shall we be able also to give ourselves to such action as will produce results of real value. As long as we look at our existence as meaningless, there is no point whatever in desiring to effect anything in the world."[2]

Thus the scientific outlook has given rise to a new view of man. It has elevated him to the position of the one and only existent thinker; it has placed his future development entirely in his own hands; it regards his intellect as in principle omnipotent; yet it sees him in the light of a psychological and physical machine. A President of the British Association said on one occasion: "Most important of all, our attitude to ourselves has changed. We now think of human beings, not from a theological or philosophical, but from a biological standpoint."[3] The assumption is that all that lies in man can be discovered by examining his body. This is one example of the axiom on which science is based, that all knowledge must have its source in the external world. But this viewpoint is really the result of drawing the human being into the scope of scientific method-ology. The specialist is comfortably blind to the fact that he is always selecting; but the non-specialist is in a position to notice this. Thus blind-ness is one of the factors which has helped to build up the scientific out-look. The scientific conception of the human being owes much to the limitations which hedge in the scientific experimentalist; but the latter never seems to realize that limitations, passed over without being allowed for, introduce a subjective factor into what the scientist supposes to be purely objectively acquired knowledge. So the new attitude arises. Professor Stace describes it further: "We hear of economic determinism, cultural determinism, historical determinism. We are not responsible for what we do because our glands control us or because we are the products of environment or heredity. Not moral self-control but the doctor, the psychiatrist, the educationist, must save us from doing evil. Pills and injections in the future are to do what Christ and the prophets have failed

[1] *M.M.S.S.*, pp. 266–7.   [2] *The Decay and the Restoration of Civilization*, p. x.
[3] Sir Edward Poulton, 1937.

to do." This is the human being as seen from the biological standpoint.

The more we ask on what valid foundation this new outlook stands, the more we see that it is, in reality, a foregone conclusion resulting from the way in which the scientist thinks and from the limitations by which he is restricted. The scientist takes efficient causes into account, but dismisses final causes because they are beyond his scope. In consequence, the scientific method has the effect of distorting the real perspective of things. Efficient causes are those which we immediately perceive and can deal with. Final causes are the deeper influences in the background whose presence is revealed only when we think more deeply. In science, efficient causes are supposed to be responsible for everything and to reach rock-bottom. To put it slightly differently, the scientist builds on the assumption that the explanations which lie within his scope are all-inclusive and reach to finality. He *assumes* this without definitely stating it. He does not say: Whatever I cannot deal with does not exist. But he reasons in such a way that this is implicit in his arguments, and in the end it leads to general conclusions which scientific facts are supposed to, but do not, support. These general conclusions are also immensely strengthened by the prestige which science has gained from its success in action; so that people come to regard this outlook, which has loosely formed itself, as being the logical outcome of indisputable facts.

Thus conviction that the universe is purposeless and meaningless does not arise merely from the feeling of human insignificance: it owes a good deal to the tendency of the mind to seek for all knowledge in the external environment of matter and to do so as a matter of course and unreflectingly. Science fosters this mental characteristic; but so also does any intellectualized state of society. A tendency towards the modern outlook can be seen in ancient Greece and also at a later period in Roman civilization. The mind, when it becomes civilized, tends to foster the leaning towards materialism, which is innate in it. It is interesting to inquire how this tendency arises. We can see something of its origin by noting that science concentrates exclusively on the data of the senses and fails to take into account the limitation of these senses or the specialized viewpoint that is inseparable from them. But the intellect, whether its activities be called "scientific" or not, always tends to do this. It turns in the direction which nature has marked out for it and seeks all its illumination from a single source. Two questions to which this gives rise are very important. One is to what extent this sole reliance on the data of the senses is inevitable. The other is, whether it is inevitable or not, what is the consequence of failing to allow for it?

It will probably be said that these matters lie within the province of philosophy and have been there dealt with and that it is useless to raise them from the standpoint of the amateur. But it is not a case of pitting the views of the amateur against those of the professional. We are looking at the whole field from a standpoint which is quite different from that of the professional, and the claim here put forward is that we are consequently able to perceive certain things which the professional or specialist is very likely to miss. This claim will probably be rejected by the majority of specialists and it cannot be substantiated at this early stage of the present argument. The reader who pursues the argument to the end must judge for himself. As non-specialists, surveying the field of specialists, we shall trespass as little as possible on matters on which the latter are admittedly the supreme authorities. We shall rely for our data largely on what they themselves have said. The suggestion that there is an unrealized division in science, which is of the greatest consequence—unrealized because of the universal limitations imposed by nature on the human being—is at present shadowy and vague. Indeed, the present author would not have ventured to put it forward had it not been that his eyes were opened by the experience which will be recounted in the next chapter.

CHAPTER V

WHAT PSYCHICAL RESEARCH DISCLOSED

TO turn to the subject of psychical research, in order to follow the clue dimly seen in our bird's-eye view of science, will probably shock the reader, who will regard it as a descent to a banal level. But I am bound to narrate the following experience because it is relevant to all that follows: and, since it is a personal experience, it will be convenient to write about it in the first person. I may perhaps say at once that it will not lead to the kind of discussion that the word "psychical" probably suggests. I myself, though interested for a long time in psychical research of a scientific order, did not dream of the disclosure that this subject was destined to make to me.

Anyone who writes about psychical research and expects to be taken seriously is usually obliged to make an excuse for leaving the beaten track of the recognized sciences. My excuse is that a small group of people, whose ability and intelligence were beyond question, initiated the study of this subject on a scientific basis when they founded the Society for Psychical Research seventy years ago: and there is no reason why the careful records accumulated by this society should not be as seriously studied as those of any other scientific body. The critical faculty and methods of research brought to bear on the matter were of a very high order and I became much interested in the evidence because, for these reasons, it was clearly valid. If it were valid there was no doubt that it brought to light matters whose value, for giving insight into the structure of the human being, could scarcely be exaggerated.

One thing particularly impressed me about this evidence: I found that nearly everyone looked upon it as referring to something entirely apart from all familiar phenomena—to a group of white elephants. Having thus mentally sequestered them, they refused to take them seriously. People would use them to give colour to fiction, to make an exciting or bizarre story, or to create entertainment-programmes for broadcasting; but they would not treat the evidence of psychical research as they would treat evidence in psychology. The former was labelled "paranormal" and placed in a separate compartment from the "normal". Now, my examination of paranormal material did not lead me to endorse this view. I could not see that there was any intrinsic distinction between what was called "normal" and what was called "paranormal": the distinction, to my mind, was artificial and was due to the way in which people thought about these things.

Two simple cases which occur in the records of the Society for Psychical Research will illustrate this. The first is a normal case and does not surpass the province of psychology. A lady received a letter from her solicitor stating that a cheque was enclosed in it. Being busy at the time, she peered into the envelope containing the cheque and letter, and looked at the former, noting as she did so the handwriting on it and the marbled colouring of the paper. She put the envelope away in her bag with a sense of satisfaction. Next morning she looked inside the envelope, but the cheque was not there. She searched for it in vain. Then another letter arrived from her solicitor containing the real cheque and apologizing for having omitted to enclose it in the previous one. This we may call the "cheque-case": it is typical of quite a large class of similar cases of sensory hallucination due to expectation or some other cause classed as normal.

In sensory hallucination, experiences of seeing, touching, hearing, etc., occur when there is nothing in the external world to cause the experience and the sense-organs do not participate. It is a commonplace of psychology and is not particularly rare in everyday life, although, under waking conditions, it is nearly always partial and transient. If it were not, it would obviously be extremely dangerous. Yet *potentially* it is capable of creating the appearance of complete surroundings.

The second case is similar. A lady received a letter from her daughter which she read aloud to her sister. In the letter occurred the sentence: "Nanny is in bed with bronchitis." Nanny was an old family nurse who had retired and was living alone. She had actually been in bed with bronchitis, but, in order to avoid upsetting the family, had refrained from telling anyone of her illness, though she wished very much that the lady who received the letter could know about it. After a visit to Nanny and a second reference to the letter, it was discovered that the above sentence was not in the letter at all. It was a case of visual hallucination similar to that in the cheque-case. (The latter was, however, tactual as well as visual.) We may call this the "Nanny-case". It, too, is representative of a class: but it is paranormal because the cause of the hallucination originated in someone else's mind. In both cases the mechanism was the same. Whatever the psychological machinery consists of which causes hallucinations of the senses to occur, it operated in both these cases. The only difference between them is the *cause* which set this machinery in action. In the cheque-case, apparently, this was expectation produced by reading the solicitor's letter. In the Nanny-case it was a suppressed wish in Nanny's mind telepathically conveyed to the reader of the letter.

The mechanism itself is not regarded as paranormal. Very similar mechanism must operate in the production of dreams. The only reason for segregating the Nanny-case into the white-elephant category called paranormal is the element of telepathy in it.

Now I could not see that the attitude which accepts the cheque-case and others of its class as psychological commonplaces, but sets aside the Nanny-case and others of its kind with raised eyebrows and a sceptical smile, was in accordance with the facts as nature presents them. Sometimes the telepathic cause and the expectation cause combine in one single dream or other experience. They operate indifferently and I could see no reason for separating them into two widely differing categories. I became convinced that this difference is not innately present in the phenomena themselves but is subjective in the sense that it is provided by the way in which our minds work. But it was a long time before I saw the importance of this.

Psychical research revealed to me another thing which increased in significance the more I reflected upon it. All the phenomena called "paranormal" evidently originated somewhere in the personality outside the conscious boundary. Those attributes of the human being studied by psycho-analysis are also located there. But there is no more reason why everything outside the boundary of consciousness should be of the same type than there is that the Bay of Biscay should resemble the Pyrenees because both are outside the British Isles. Telepathy clearly takes place *outside* consciousness, otherwise the subject would be conscious of the telepathic process. But so, for that matter, do sense-perception and memory. We are consciously acquainted only with the products of these functions and not with the processes involved. Sensory hallucinations are unconsciously caused also. If, in the cheque-case, expectation caused the vision and feel of the cheque, it was because the expectation had sunk below the conscious level and had there set the machinery of hallucination in action. All the paranormal phenomena of which there is evidence act *vertically*, the centre of origination being beyond or below consciousness, the messages rising to the conscious level. These messages are by no means always literal reports but often convey an idea symbolically. Many spontaneous cases of telepathy show this. If someone has had a visual hallucination of a friend or relative about the time when he was drowned, for example, the figure might appear wet and dripping in order to convey by symbolism what had happened.

Telepathy is thus not "thought-transference" in a literal sense: the source of the information is not the *conscious* mind of the sender or agent but some source beyond consciousness which lies outside our ken. If, however, the idea happens to be conveyed literally and not symbolically, it might *appear* very much as though it were direct thought-transference from one conscious mind to another. This is a pitfall in the interpretation of the evidence to be avoided. The evidence also showed me that the region beyond consciousness from which telepathic information originates is not a mere insignificant annexe of consciousness: it is something very large exceeding our power of comprehension. The extraordinary faculty of precognition shows this. There is a considerable quantity of evidence, some of a very cogent kind, which shows that future events can be foreseen under conditions which preclude inference. This is extremely important because it indicates a situation which is completely baffling to our intellect. It reduces our ideas of freedom, determinism and causality to an incoherent medley. It reveals a state of affairs, that is to say, in which the pattern of events is quite different from that which obtains in our familiar world. Could anything be more important than to investigate this state of affairs further?

The great piece of enlightenment which psychical research had in store for me was, however, yet to come. For a long time it had been assumed by workers in psychical research that there was evidence for two types of paranormal faculty in this branch of the subject, that of "telepathy", understood in the sense of thought-transference, and that of "clairvoyance", understood in the sense of paranormal perception of physical objects or events. Either faculty might refer to the future or to the past as well as to the present and so might be precognitive or retrocognitive. These faculties together were given the name of "extra-sensory perception". For myself, the distinction between "telepathy" and "clairvoyance" seemed to rest on superficial observation and to be out of accord with the view, to which all the valid evidence seemed to point, that paranormal matter rises vertically *within* the self from the subconscious to the conscious level.

During recent years, the study of extra-sensory preception had largely taken the form of quantitative experiment based on the principle of guessing cards or some other simple event which was amenable to statistical treatment. It was an excellent way of showing that *something* apart from perception by the senses occurred. It had the advantage of dealing statistically with success by chance and of affording a repeatable experiment—that is to say an experiment that was repeatable in the sense that if any investigator were prepared to spend a great deal of time and trouble in testing a number of subjects, he would probably achieve positive results in the end. These experiments were perfectly "objective" in the scientific sense of being controlled in all *external* factors. It was only

necessary to devise conditions under which no normal leakage of information was possible and to deal with the results by the standard formulae of
statistics and the result of the experiment was clear. Numbers of persons
when tested obtained only chance scores and those who obtained scores
above chance did so in a sporadic manner. But even a small deviation from
chance-expectation becomes highly significant if the experiments include a large number of trials. The positive results that were obtained in
some cases were astronomically above the point of significance. I had
carried out experiments myself, not with cards, but with a self-recording
machine which was so made as to be automatically proof against error and
I had obtained such high superchance scores that I was quite convinced
of their genuineness. Others, using cards or pictures, had done the same,
so that it was quite clear to me that extra-sensory perception could be
demonstrated by an objective, laboratory test in spite of the uncertainties
and delays which attended the experiments.

Those who had done this many times naturally wished to proceed
further and to find out something about the nature of the extra-sensory
faculty. Carrying in their minds the ideas of telepathy and clairvoyance,
they tried to devise experiments which would differentiate between
the two. Now quantitative experiments, on the lines of card-guessing,
lend a superficial support to these hypotheses. If A looks at a card while
B proves that he knows what it is (chance being eliminated), it is strongly
suggested that the idea of the card in A's mind has been directly transferred to B's mind. Similarly, if a pack of cards is shuffled so that no one
knows their order, and B proves that he knows what some of them are
(chance again being eliminated), it is strongly suggested that B has
perceived the cards as physical objects by means of some faculty akin to
paranormal sight. The experimenters tried to devise purely mental
experiments in which no cards were used and nothing was written down:
they assumed that if these were successful, telepathy in the sense of thought-
transference would be proved. Similarly, knowledge of cards shuffled
in an unknown order they took to be direct perception of the cards. In
both cases it was assumed that successful results would prove that the
source of knowledge drawn upon lies in the spatio-temporal world. Had
experiment shown that success was *never* achieved unless the agent was
consciously thinking of the card, or, conversely, that success was *never*
achieved unless physical cards were used, that would indeed have shown
that one or other of these conditions was essential to success. But that was
not shown by experiment so far. There had been on some occasions
success and sometimes failure under either condition; and this suggested
that the real source of the phenomena was not being controlled.

D

But the qualitative evidence pointed in another direction. It pointed to the "vertical" view—that is to say it indicated that the source of the information lay outside the spatial world and beyond the reach of experimental control. Very likely it also lies outside the reach of our comprehension. If knowledge of future events can emanate from this source, it is obviously very unlikely that it would be the kind of source we could control or reason about. It seemed to me that the reason why experiments in so-called "telepathy" and "clairvoyance" are controllable, in the sense that they sometimes succeed in a sporadic fashion, is that *the passage to consciousness, and not the source of the message*, is influenced by the will and interest of those engaged in the experiment. Thus, success in "telepathy" is not due to the flashing of a conscious thought from one conscious mind to another: and success in "clairvoyance" is not due to the ability to peer through some pieces of cardboard and to perceive in something akin to visual fashion the face of another. In other words the agent, and perhaps all concerned, play a *directive* and not a *generative* role. The common view seemed to me to be similar to the assumption that the driver of a motor car, because he controls the mechanism, must necessarily be providing the power.

There are many cases of spontaneous "telepathy" in which the agent is unaware that he is taking part in telepathy at all. There are also cases in which the percipient gets to know what the agent knows, but also proves that he knows more about the same matter, although the agent does not know it. It was obvious to me that the statistical type of experiment should not be planned or interpreted in isolation, but should be both planned and interpreted in the light of the qualitative evidence. In fact, before formulating a hypothesis for test, it seemed clear that the general evidence should be studied.

But I found that those engaged in the quantitative experiments showed no inclination to do this. It was this point that struck me forcibly. I therefore suggested to one of them that it might be advisable to study the general evidence before drawing conclusions from the prolific number of card-experiments which he was carrying out. His reply took my breath away. He said that the general evidence was unscientific because it was observational rather than experimental; that the card-guessing type of experiment alone was scientific and was the only one to be relied upon. The experimental method, because assumed to be "objective" and because in a sense repeatable, was, in his eyes, sacrosanct. It was infallible because it followed the traditions of natural science. Not to accept it as an infallible method would be a scientific heresy! Conclusions drawn from this hallowed method, *must* be true: there was no need to bring reflection or criticism into the picture. He seemed to regard the quantitative method as a kind of machine which, fed with any material, would grind out truth as soon as the handle was turned.

It was at this point that my study of psychical research began to have its major effect upon me. I felt illumination creeping over me. The scientifically trained mind tended to regard science in an ideological fashion. There was surely significance in this. I looked round and saw that others engaged in statistical experiments shared the view of my correspondent; and a sarcastic remark, attributed to Anatole France, floated into my mind: "The sciences are beneficent. They prevent men from thinking!" I now began to connect the attitude of these scientifically stereotyped experimentalists with something else that had engaged my attention for a long time—the general attitude of scientists, philosophers and the educated public towards paranormal phenomena. Why was their attitude, not merely one of caution, but one of avoidance and escapism? The evidence that had been collected so carefully and, in a general sense, on scientific lines was more than enough to constitute a *prima facie* case. The significance of the evidence was immense. Yet, only a very small minority showed any real interest in the things to which this evidence points or manifested any enthusiasm to increase it. The Society for Psychical Research, when it began to investigate the subject sixty-seven years ago, found itself faced by bitter opposition, especially in scientific circles. Although positive opposition has to a considerable extent died down, indifference and refusal to treat the subject seriously remain.

Various reasons for this indifference have, at different times, been given. It has been said that occultism has at all times been a stronghold of superstition and that what is now called the "paranormal" has, in popular hands, become a semi-religious movement called spiritualism, in which is to be found a mixture of credulity and charlatanism from which nothing definite emerges. Another is that busy people have no time for such a nebulous subject; and yet another that the evidence for the paranormal is not strong enough to be convincing. At first I looked upon these reasons as being merely weak; but gradually I began to take more interest in them; for I saw with ever increasing clearness that they were charged with escapism. Whatever the unqualified public might do with the subject, there was no reason why scientific men should not approach it seriously and extract the grain while winnowing away the chaff. In the course of more than half a century, *someone* must surely have had time to deal with matters of such intriguing significance. Even if it were true that the evidence is not strong enough, that is no reason why an effort should not be made to strengthen it. The alleged reasons for avoiding the subject were evidently excuses. But why? Was it because evidence of the paranormal pointed to the existence of things which lie off the scientific map? Is it a scientific heresy to suggest that there are things which lie outside the pattern which scientists recognize? Professor C. D. Broad, one of the eminent philosophers who have recognized the significance of the paranormal for philosophy, says in the preface of his book, *The Mind and Its Place in Nature*, that he expects to be blamed by certain scientists for having taken into account the alleged facts which have been investigated in psychical research. "I am wholly impenitent about this," he continues. "The scientists in question seem to me to confuse the Author of Nature with the Editor of *Nature*; or at any rate to suppose that there can be no production of the former which would not be accepted for publication by the latter. And I see no reason to believe this."

I was coming to see that this is precisely where the crux lies. It is not that the paranormal *contradicts* the normal or impugns the discoveries of science. It does not. But it challenges the claim that the scientifically recognized pattern of the universe includes all there is. This is what scientists resent.

As time went on, I saw more and more clearly that it is the *attitude* adopted towards the subject which is the key-factor and that behind this attitude really important matters were waiting to be revealed. Whether in this or in any other country, serious work in this subject is carried on by only a tiny group of workers, whose efforts are always curtailed by lack of funds. This is itself a reflection of the attitude of withdrawal and the lack of general interest. Instead of stimulating curiosity, the evidence accumulated by psychical research has had the effect of killing it. In a previous book dealing with psychical research, I had devoted two chapters to examples of this tendency to escape from the evidence, and had suggested that some psychological cause must be at work behind the scenes.[1] I was now coming to see that this psychological cause is not individual but general.

After the quantitative experiments with cards etc. had been going on for a good many years, and positive results under good conditions, rising to figures enormously greater than chance-expectation, had been obtained again and again, I came across the following statement: "After the symposium on extra-sensory perception held by the American Psychological Association in 1938 at which there was no effective criticism of the well-done experiments, it became clear that mere card-calling could not convince most psychologists of the reality of extra-sensory perception. Card-calling experiments demonstrate an anomaly in nature and few

---

[1] *The Personality of Man*, Chapters 26 and 27.

psychologists will accept an anomaly of such momentous implications."[1] This showed where the root of the attitude lies. For these psychologists, it was not a question of whether or not experiment shows that extra-sensory perception *does* occur. It was a question of whether, according to their *a priori* judgment, extra-sensory perception *can* occur. Their attitude was that of the theologians who refused to look through Galileo's telescope. I found this extremely interesting. Whether or not people accept the evidence for anything outside the type of phenomenon they expect depends on the constitution of their own minds far more than it depends on the evidence. If Freud's theories about dreams had been regarded as being initially highly improbable, they would all have been explained away and Freud and his theories would have been treated as a joke. One might have expected that a scientific experiment based on mathematical technique and successfully repeated over and over again, would have settled the question of the existence of extra-sensory perception once and for all. But, not at all: all kinds of arguments were raised in order, if possible, to explain the successful results away; and, in spite of individual exceptions, the general attitude of indifference and escapism remained. Even figures, showing huge odds against chance, were not regarded by some as finally ruling out chance, *when the alternative was the paranormal*. It was frequently argued that something *must* be wrong with the chance-calculations, though these were calculated on standard lines; but it was not shown what was wrong. Also arguments frequently took the form, both with regard to the qualitative and the quantitative evidence, that chance could account for far more when faced with the paranormal as an alternative than it could account for in normal cases. Dr. S. G. Soal, who had accomplished a great deal of quantitative work in this subject, wrote: "A distinguished mathematician known to me as a hard bitten materialist remarked a few weeks ago that 'even though Soal has obtained odds of 10^{35} to 1 against chance he is not justified in claiming that the effects are not due to chance'."[2] This is tantamount to saying that if extra-sensory perception is the only alternative to chance, then chance can explain anything!

I had come to see that if one discounted these tendentious attempts to explain away paranormal evidence, while still demanding evidence as good as one would demand in a normal subject, the possible scope of psychical research was fairly evident. By the combined use of qualitative and quantitative methods, it could be shown—indeed it had already been shown—that there is in the human being an uncomprehended hinterland

[1] *Journal of the Society for Psychical Research*, June-July, 1948, p. 242.
[2] *Ibid.*, January, 1948.

beyond the boundary of consciousness, in which the phenomena called "paranormal" originate. The methods used by natural science are capable of showing this; and psychology has already impinged upon a corner of it. These methods can also show that the character of this extra-conscious region is quite different from the character of the familiar world. Its relations to both space and time are different. The cut and dried methods of science can get so far. But whether the extra-conscious region is to be regarded wholly as an individual self or as consisting of something independent as well is a question that is very difficult to answer. In order to answer it we should probably have to grasp new ideas about the relation of subject to object. It did not seem to me likely that psychical research, by using a scientific technique, could answer these questions. It could demonstrate that the paranormal exists; but it could not, as far as I could see, make a great deal of progress in exploring its nature. Also, the more strictly the scientific method was adhered to, the less was the chance of progress. I saw that there were two principal reasons why the strictly scientific method could not make much progress towards exploring the nature of the paranormal. In the first place, there was no general agreement as to the value of the evidence. When assessing the value of evidence, two factors are involved, (i) the intrinsic strength of the evidence, and (ii) the degree of improbability attaching to the conclusion to which the evidence points. In ordinary science, there is general agreement on this second point; but in psychical research opinions differ widely. Hence, in ordinary science, a body of generally accepted evidence can be built up: but in psychical research, this is much more difficult, if not impossible. The estimate of the antecedent improbability of the paranormal is the key-factor in psychical research, and it seemed to me that it should be given first attention. I found that most people regarded the attitude towards psychical research as being merely composed of different grades of credulity or scepticism; but I did not think that this was the right way to look at it. It was not merely that a credulous person accepts evidence for the paranormal too easily while a sceptical person demands a higher standard of evidence because he is more cautious. The sceptical person might be as cautious as you like: he would still, if he had a balanced mind, treat evidence according to its intrinsic value. But the sceptical person, because his scepticism is based on an unreasoned conviction that the paranormal is next door to impossible, will find a means of explaining almost any evidence away.

Secondly, the more definite and the more ostensibly objective an experiment in psychical research is, the less informative it becomes. That is why the card-guessing type of experiment is an excellent way of demonstrating that *some* unexplained mode of acquiring information without the use of the senses exists; but the events used are too restricted to shed much light on the question of what the procedure actually is. Thus, the lack of agreement about the improbability of the phenomena, and the lack of a method of research which has at once the objectivity of natural science and the power of reaching the hidden causes beyond the boundary of consciousness is likely to prevent scientific methods from progressing very far. Private research in the subject might, nevertheless, progress a good deal further than public research. But it would not convince all.

An idea was slowly forming in my mind. I was beginning to see that, whether or not psychical research was capable of shedding much light on another world, it was capable of shedding a very important light on this one. It was becoming more and more evident to me that the psychological factor in the background had a very high importance; and I decided to survey the different types of attitude towards the subject.

There was first the popular attitude. Many people would probably call it an attitude towards the "supernatural". When I came to think of it, I realized that this attitude consists of two contradictory elements, scepticism and fear. It might be described by the phrase: I don't believe in ghosts, but I am afraid of them! It suggests more belief under the surface than on the surface. There is a third factor also in the popular attitude. Sometimes the paranormal is accepted fairly easily, as when, for example, tradition supports it or when it becomes habitual, as in the case of a perennially haunted house. In such cases, the phenomena are too persistent to be denied, so they are drawn into the everyday world and, as far as possible, normalized. The habitual ghost is looked upon as a human being, stereotyped in its habits and tenuous as to its body, but still a human inhabitant of the normal world. When one comes to think of it, to deny, to flee from and to normalize are three ways of *escaping* from the paranormal; and each can be used in the appropriate circumstances.

Spiritualists appear, at first sight, to extend whole hearted acceptance to the paranormal and I asked myself whether this did not contradict the view that there is something innate in the human mind which tries to push the paranormal away. But, when I considered their attitude more closely, I saw that they include in their outlook a good deal of the last item of the popular attitude. To a considerable extent they escape from what is genuinely paranormal by *normalizing* it. The messages which come through mediums contain little enough that is paranormal in a strict sense. They are homely and familiar messages, redolent of this world. Descriptions of the other world are thoroughly terrestrial and often commonplace.

There is little in the spiritualist's *milieu* which wrests his mind away from this world. Spiritualists do not go out to meet the paranormal to any great extent; rather they draw it into this world.

The attitude of rationalists and of those trained in science contains, as I saw it, mainly the first element of the popular attitude—scepticism. It differs from popular scepticism chiefly in the ingenuity shown in explaining the paranormal away. I found this attitude particularly interesting, because those who adopted it were evidently unconscious that they were deviating at all from perfect poise and balance. I noticed three or four techniques that they employed (probably largely unconsciously) when dealing with paranormal evidence. Sometimes they greatly overstressed unlikely explanations of a normal kind—chance, for example, being frequently endowed with extraordinary powers. Sometimes the witnesses for paranormal cases would be assumed, without any evidence, to be pathological and therefore untrustworthy. Sometimes the weaker parts of the evidence would be stressed and made much of, while the stronger parts would be lightly skated over and dismissed. Or else a technique of inuendo and suggestion would be used, by means of which an impression would be created that there was something wrong with the evidence somewhere, though it was not clear exactly where. A university professor, after reading a paper by someone who regarded himself as an evenly balanced critic, remarked that if criticism of this kind were applied to science or even to history, there would be little science or history left! It did not seem to me likely that minds of this type would make much progress in psychical research beyond the initial stage in which the standard scientific methods are effective. My interest in such critics was, however, rapidly increasing. I was coming to regard them as self-exhibitors rather than as critics; and, as I observed them, I felt inclined to take off my hat to the psychologists who had brought to light the faculty of "rationalization", which, I suppose, might be defined as the "finding of bad reasons for what we believe on instinct". There were certain types of mind which seemed to be unable to accept any evidence for the paranormal at all; and yet were unable to leave the subject alone. They would always pursue it and always strive to reject it in favour of some kind of normal explanation, thus illustrating a saying of Hazlitt: "Prejudice is never easy unless it can pass itself off as reason."

Another difficulty which the paranormal presents to scientific method arises from its lack of uniformity. This also appears to some extent in biology and psychology. Occam's convenient maxim that hypotheses should not be increased unnecessarily, becomes difficult to apply as soon as we come into contact with the phenomena of life and mind. It is a maxim which admirably suits our natural way of thinking; but Nature plays ducks and drakes with it outside the inorganic realm.

Progress in science, when it is carried far afield, and leaves the familiar world behind, is apt to have its smooth generalizations disrupted by a welter of brute facts. As F.C.S. Schiller put it: ". . . all the subjects of scientific interest are turning out to be immensely more complicated, individual and· unique than anyone suspected: the simple sweeping affirmation of universal 'laws', 'eternally' prescribed to all things, is being more and more plainly revealed as a convenient postulate of method. . . ."[1] This is the kind of thing to which specialists close their eyes if they can. Subjective factors creep into psychical research sometimes, ironically enough, for the very reason that the scientific mind endeavours to make its experiments as "objective" as possible. It was indeed this that finally opened my eyes to the disclosure which forms the subject-matter of this volume. It was the persistent refusal of those engaged in statistical experiments to interpret them in the light of the general evidence that made me realize that there was an unconscious urge behind it. Perhaps it was not altogether logical; but it was this that gave me the thought which proved to be my great awakening. I saw, with a flash of illumination, that the attitude adopted by most people towards psychical research was not confined to that subject. It did not concern only what people class as "paranormal": nor was the urge behind it merely personal. *Those in its power were subconsciously afraid;* but they were not afraid of being drawn *towards* something: they were afraid of being drawn *away* from something. *I was being supplied with evidence which showed that the human mind is in the grip of an unconscious urge which makes it cling desperately to the world of familiar things and resist all that threatens to tear it away from its moorings.*

I now saw why workers in quantitative experiments in extra-sensory perception cling to the hypotheses of "thought-transference" and "clairvoyance". It is because these hypotheses keep the paranormal within the limits of space and time and so have the effect of drawing the phenomena into the familiar world. They refused to compare their experiments with the qualitative evidence because the latter takes the explanation too far away from this world. It leads away from the neatly comprehensible to the vague and uncomprehended; and this draws forth an unconscious resistance. Their contention that they were adhering to these explanations in order to be scientific was a piece of unconscious camouflage. The attitude of these workers, as well as the attitude of indifference and escapism shown by the educated public at large and by many scientists and philosophers, was due to an unconscious impulse to cling to the world of

[1] *Must Philosophers Disagree?*, p. 217.

familiar things and to keep everything within its orbit. Such an impulse must, I saw, lie deep beneath personal idiosyncrasies and complexes of the psycho-analytical type. It must be something broadly human—something racial. I asked myself whether such an idea was plausible. Would not anthropologists and psychologists have discovered such a racial factor if it existed? C. G. Jung had indeed dealt with the "racial unconscious", supplying, in a sense, a locus for such a factor as this. What, I wondered, would academic psychologists have to say about it? As far as I could gather, they thought very little about such things or about any general and far-reaching principles. They seemed to be immersed in the detailed work of the laboratory. I had already been much impressed by the lack of any general outline supplied by specialists from their own work. There seemed to be no available light on an idea such as this. Why should I not follow up this disclosure in my own way, which would be to look at the whole question from the non-specialist point of view? Any universal factor in the mind, which tended to conceal itself from consciousness, would presumably have originated during the course of biological evolution. That would be the direction in which to turn. A factor such as this must have originated during the mental adaptation of man to his environment. It was, then, to evolution that I must turn, viewing it, if possible, in bird's-eye fashion and with non-specialist detachment.

CHAPTER VI

HOMO FABER

WITH the idea of adaptation in mind, it is worth while to take a brief glance at some of the details of biological evolution in order to realize the extraordinary thoroughness with which organic life has been adapted to its environment. When discussing evolution, people are usually more concerned with its causes than with its effects; and it is questionable whether the full consequences of mental evolution in man have ever been thoroughly studied.

In the first place, we may note that the adaptation of human beings, as well as of all other living creatures, to their environment, is a fact which is independent of any evolutionary theory. It can be established by contemporary observation without any theory at all; and it would have been just the same if the living world had resulted from an act of special creation.

All living things may be said to reflect the character of the planet as a whole. However widely animals may differ in structure and form, each detail is correlated, for example, with the force of gravity at the earth's surface, and would have been different had the force of gravity been different. At the same time each organism is adapted to special conditions, which vary on the same planet—fish to the water, birds to the air, etc. But no one doubts to-day that this process has been gradual and has occupied millions of years. "To-day, after half a century, there is no longer room for doubt that the fitness of organic beings for their life in the world has been won in whole or in part by an almost infinite series of adaptations of life to its environment, whereby, through a corresponding series of transformations, present complexity has grown out of former simplicity."[1]

A glance at the case labelled "Mimicry" in the South Kensington Museum is sufficient to impress one with the extraordinary efficiency of adaptation. On a piece of tree-trunk are moths so coloured and patterned as to be invisible without a careful search: there is a tiny creature, clinging to a rose-stem, coloured and shaped exactly like a thorn: there are insects which resemble green leaves in shape, surface, veining and every detail: there are others which resemble dead leaves: there are insects which resemble others in order to gain some advantage—a harmless fly, for

[1] *F.E.*, pp. 4-5.

example, striped to look like a wasp. One insect exactly resembles a flower, so that when flies approach it, deceived by the resemblance, it seizes and devours them.

But adaptation goes beyond bodily colouration and form. Behaviour also is adapted. The stick-insect not only resembles a twig: it behaves like one, sticking out at an angle from the stem and remaining perfectly rigid. The chameleon, as is well known, adapts its colour to its surroundings: also the sole adjusts its tint to match that of the sand on which it lies, and it obscures itself by raising a cloud of sand in the water above it. The Squinado Crab carefully covers itself with seaweed; and the Grayling butterfly, not content with alighting on a brown background which matches its colour, folds its wings together and inclines them at an angle to the sun so that they cast no shadow!

The behaviour of the insect-catching plant has been described as follows: The properties of the trap are, "briefly, a water-tight door, snap-action on actuation accompanied by an inrush of a column of water carrying with it the prey responsible for the actuation, the immediate return of the door to its original position, and the subsequent exhaustion of the water from the limen of the trap resulting in resetting it."[1] Behaviour is therefore adapted even in plants.

Behaviour, which has been adapted in the course of evolution, is quite different from intelligent purpose in human beings. It can make what, from our point of view, we should call the stupidest of mistakes; yet it can achieve results which, if intelligently planned, would require a high level of thought and understanding.

"No case of this kind is more wonderful than that of the Sitaris beetle which begins life by attaching itself to a bee which has afterwards to provide for it. Does one ask how the larva knows the bee? The reply is, it does not."[2] The larva attaches itself to any hairy object; and large numbers probably perish by attaching themselves to the wrong insect. Instincts are not always perfect from the beginning, but may improve with practice.

For all their apparent stupidity, instincts can exhibit what we should regard as extraordinary foresight. "The caterpillar of the emperor moth spins at the upper extremity of its cocoon a double arch of stiff bristles, held together above only by a few fine threads. The cocoon, i.e., opens at the very least pressure from within, but is able to resist quite strong pressure from without. Auten Rieth writes of this in his *Ansichten über*

[1] Dr. F. E. Lloyd. From an address to the British Association, 1933, reported in *The Times* of September 12th, 1933.
[2] *The Mind in Evolution*, p. 69.

Natur-und Seelenleben: 'If the caterpillar acted from reflection and with understanding, it must, on human analogy, have pursued the following train of thought: that it had reached its chrysalis stage, and would therefore be at the mercy of any unlucky accident, without possibility of escape, unless it took certain precautionary measures in advance; that it would have to issue from its cocoon as imago without having organs or strength for breaking through the cover it had spun as caterpillar, and without possessing any secretion, like other insects, which would, if emitted, eat through the threads of silk; and that consequently, unless it took care to provide as caterpillar a convenient exit from its cocoon, it must certainly come to a premature end in imprisonment. On the other hand, it must have clearly recognized during its work upon the cocoon that, in order to have free egress as imago, it would only be necessary to construct an arch which could resist attacks from without while opening easily from within; and that these conditions would be fulfilled if the arch were made of stiff threads, inclined together in the median line, and with their ends left free. At the same time it must have realized that the plan could be carried out if the silk employed for the construction of the other parts of the cocoon were employed with special care and skill at the other end. Yet, it could have learnt nothing of all this from its parents.' "[1]

Complicated instincts can therefore be manifested in lowly creatures such as insects. Some butterflies, like some birds, are migratory, and find their way in the same mysterious manner. That instinct is not confined to a mechanical routine is illustrated by the following case. The caddis larva *Molanna,* studied by Dembowski, which builds for itself a case of characteristic shape and structure, was found to adjust its behaviour to many new situations artificially imposed upon it. When its case was damaged or cut about in various ways, the larva dealt with each situation appropriately. "It is noteworthy also that in responding to these operational defects, the larva has to deal with unusual contingencies which are unlikely to have presented themselves in its individual or its racial history; its power of effective response is therefore something fundamental and primordial, not to be accounted for by selection."[2] We cannot therefore suppose that the caddis larva had, in the course of evolution, behaved in an infinite number of ways at random and that all the wrong ways of behaviour had been eliminated by natural selection, leaving the right behaviour surviving by chance. For in that case the right behaviour would be fixedly adjusted to the normal circumstances and would not vary as the circumstances were varied artificially. In any case, since the right behaviour is extremely complicated, it is not *one* behaviour but a complex of many behaviours

[1] *The Mind in Evolution,* p. 71. [2] *D.O.A.,* p. 22.

adjusted to one another, which renders the hypothesis of chance incredible. Even the most insignificant creatures respond effectively to their
needs. Speaking of the *Arcella*, a little shelled rhizopod, E. S. Russell says:
"When the dissolved oxygen in the water in which it lives is reduced
below a certain point, its invariable response is to secrete gas-bubbles of
oxygen in its substance, which reduce its specific gravity and float it to the
surface, where oxygen is normally plentiful."[1] These are only a few
random examples of instinct, or whatever we choose to call the directive
factor which permeates the whole of life. Instinct is hard for us to grasp. If
we include it in the definition of "mind", then mind has been as minutely
adapted to the conditions of life as has body. And from this, there seems no
reason to exempt human beings. In the case of plants, we prefer to speak
of a directive agency rather than of instinct; but it is merely a matter of
terminology.

The human mind must have been adapted to the conditions of life just
as the human body has been. Psychologists speak of fundamental race-
instincts, the instinct of self-preservation, the instinct of sex, the social
instincts, etc. But there are instincts of a less obvious kind by means of
which the mind has been adapted to the conditions under which it lives.
C. G. Jung, contrasting the mentality of African natives with that of white
men, shows how the mind adapts itself to the conditions which are
important for any particular kind of life. "I once showed some native
hunters, who were as keen-sighted as hawks, magazine-pictures in which
any of our children would have instantly recognized human figures. But
my hunters turned the pictures round and round until one of them,
tracing the outlines with his finger, finally exclaimed: 'These are white
men.' It was hailed by all as a great discovery."[2]

These natives had, on the other hand, an incredibly accurate sense of
locality and could find their way in a forest where a white man, without
instruments or special precautions, would have been hopelessly lost. On
the other hand a palaver of more than two hours, in which they had only
to answer questions in a desultory way, was too great a strain on their
attention: yet when hunting, or on a journey, they could keep their
attention concentrated for many hours at a stretch. Clearly the mind is
adapted to its circumstances as well as to the world in general.

What are we to say about human power of reason? Has the rational
faculty of man been untouched by the hand of evolution? Did reason
descend on mankind from the gods, like the gift of Promethean fire?
or has it, too, been through the evolutionary mill? This is a question of
great importance, and one would have expected it to be a central theme

[1] *D.O.A.*, p. 51.   [2] *M.M.S.S.*, p. 147.

of psychology. But psychologists, like other scientific specialists, seem to be more concerned with detailed laboratory experiments than with broad principles, and it is not easy to discover what they think about this. We can see at once that it is not an easy question; for, in order to answer it, reason has to sit in judgment on itself. We are apt to think of man as possessing the same sort of instincts as the animals; but as having quite a different faculty, that of intelligence, over and above these instincts: and we think of his intelligence as having grown while his instincts have dwindled. The rudiments of intelligence appear in some of the higher animals, particularly in the ape-genus; but, apart from this, intelligence is looked upon as a purely human endowment. It is questionable however whether instinct and intelligence can be easily separated.

There appears to be no water-tight compartment between them. Instinct and intelligence interpenetrate one another. "There is no intelligence," says Henri Bergson, "in which some traces of instinct are not to be discovered, more especially no instinct that is not surrounded with a fringe of intelligence."[1]

Now, speaking teleologically, we can see that the whole aim of evolution was pragmatic. Mental and bodily functions were both evolved to give their possessor practical advantages in life. Was the rational faculty, which is almost uniquely the possession of man, alone an exception? Human intelligence, since the beginning of pre-history, has been applied to practical ends, to outwitting man's brute-competitors and to making serviceable use of natural laws. Can it, during this long apprenticeship in the struggle for survival, have escaped the pragmatic tendency which generally developed man's faculties into useful tools? This is a question fraught with momentous consequences; and it is a question to which we can scarcely expect to find a pat and ready answer.

Bergson says in another passage: "If we could rid ourselves of all our pride, if, to define our species, we kept strictly to what the historic and pre-historic periods show us to be the constant characteristic of man and of intelligence, we should say perhaps not *Homo sapiens*, but *Homo faber*. In short, intelligence, considered in what seems to be its original feature, is the faculty of manufacturing artificial objects, especially tools to make tools, and of indefinitely varying the manufacture."[2]

Again T. H. Huxley, the great protagonist of evolution, expressed the same idea by saying: "The great end of life is not knowledge but action."

Human intelligence is surely a specialized product, for it is concentrated on the external world as presented by the senses; and is adapted to work with the senses. It is fitted to them as hand to glove. Bergson emphasizes

[1] *C.E.*, pp. 142-3. [2] *C.E.*, p. 146.

this also: "When we pass in review the intellectual functions, we see that the intellect is never quite at its ease, never entirely at home, except when it is working upon inert matter, more particularly upon solids." And again: "Our intelligence, as it leaves the hands of nature, has for its chief object the unorganized solid."[1] This has been noticed by others besides Bergson. There is a passage, for example, in which F. H. Bradley says: "With regard to the normal mind we are bound to add 'what there is of it', for our waking mind is narrowed, and it is essentially the result of narrowing in a certain interest. . . . Our waking mind is bounded and contracted first for practical purposes, since it has to maintain itself against a special environment."[2]

That the human mind has been adapted and specialized would probably be admitted by many. But we have in it a first hint of a very illuminating idea. Possibly what has been adapted is not the whole of the mind, but rather a specialized abstraction from the whole. How, otherwise, did *Homo faber*, in progressing along the path towards *Homo sapiens*, reconquer his unabstracted self? The journey has been slow and painful and perhaps even now has been scarcely more than begun. *Homo sapiens* can scarcely claim to be wise? He is rather the man who *knows*—the man who has attained a certain degree of awareness and is struggling to attain still more. Yet in every upward step towards free and balanced reason, *Homo sapiens* is dogged by *Homo faber* and his instincts. If instinct followed man out of the animal world, as it surely must have done, by what stages did he cast it off? Has he, indeed, wholly cast it off now? If not—if instinct still penetrates intelligence—what influence has it had upon reflective thought? What influence is it having upon science and philosophy to-day? It will be worth while to consider these questions more closely.

[1] *C.E.*, p. 162.   [2] *Essays on Truth and Reality*, p. 463.

CHAPTER VII

NATURE'S PROBLEM

ONE of the advantages of the non-specialist approach is that it enables us to make use of metaphor. Nothing is more abhorrent to the man of science or to the modern philosopher than metaphor, for it is presumed to lead the mind away from clear thinking into vagueness. And it is perfectly true that, as long as the ideas dealt with can be completely and adequately expressed in abstract language, the greater the precision with which words are used the better. But it is possible for the mind to obtain a partial grip on ideas which *cannot* be exactly expressed in words; and in that case metaphor may be a help and not a hindrance. Specialists would probably dismiss this with the remark that, if you do not use expressions which have an exactly definable meaning, you do not know what you are talking about. But this is to neglect the intuitional factor in thought by means of which ideas grow slowly in the mind without the use of words, like a photograph in the developer. It is possible at first to have only a vague idea of what a metaphor stands for, but to gain a clearer idea as you go on using it. In the following chapters, at any rate, we shall speak in a highly metaphorical manner of Nature, as though she were a motherly person charged with the task of bringing mankind into the world. This is by far the most convenient way of putting things. The reader may, if he pleases, substitute for the word "Nature" whatever forces or influences were responsible for organic evolution.

Although the word "Nature" is freely used by writers on all subjects, it is not easy to define. A philosopher gives the following definition of it: "I should myself regard the word 'Nature' as a good word to indicate whatever is, or could be, sensibly experienced together with the occasions and conditions of what can be sensibly experienced and the modes of their interconnections."[1] According to this definition, consciousness would seem to lie outside Nature and so would presumably have to be classed as supernatural.

A wider, if looser, definition of Nature is given by Dr. C. S. Lewis: "Nature seems to be the spatial and temporal as distinct from what is less fully so or not at all. She seems to be the world of quantity as against the world of quality: of objects as against consciousness: of the bound as

[1] *P.P.*, p. 115.

against the partially or wholly autonomous: of that which knows no values as against that which both has and perceives value: of efficient causes (or in some modern systems of no causality at all) as against final causes."[1] According to these definitions, Nature is limited. The term does not apply to all there is, so that the question naturally arises: What lies beyond Nature? Are there two Natures, one limited to the sense-perceived world and the other consisting of what lies beyond the sense-perceived world?

The truth is that we use the word "Nature" in a vague way as a convenient term to cover the causes which are responsible for the world we experience. Something innate in us prompts us to regard the world we sensibly experience as comprising the whole of reality; and so we think vaguely of "Nature" as a universal power. Closer examination of our experience shows, however, that there is much that our senses do not reveal and this we are disinclined to include in the province of Nature. So a dichotomy arises. We shall here speak principally of "Nature" as the power behind organic evolution.

Nature, as we shall use the word, was faced with a difficult problem when she set out to fashion man for life in the physical universe. How was man, with his limited intelligence, to possess knowledge of the universe which, if not infinite, was at any rate incomparably vast in relation to his tiny mind? Man must either be fitted to grasp the entire universe in principle; or else he must be acquainted with only a part of it. The first alternative being impossible, Nature had to adopt the second; and the part with which man must be acquainted had obviously to be the material patt because man has a material body. Even so, there had to be restrictions; for Nature's scheme was pragmatic, and only the useful properties of matter needed to be perceived. The principal means of limiting man's acquaintance with the universe to that which was necessary for practical purposes was by specialization and limitation of the bodily organs of sense, so that they should present to the mind only the knowledge required. But a little reflection is sufficient to show that restriction of the sense-organs alone would not be enough: the *mind* would have to co-operate with the senses in order that the portion of the universe presented might be reduced to manageable form. Sir Arthur Eddington, for example, remarks that: "The element of permanence in the physical world which is familiarly represented by the conception of substance is essentially a contribution of the mind to the plan of building or selection."[2]

Of course the whole man was adapted to his environment—muscles,

---

[1] *The Abolition of Man*, p. 34.   [2] *The Nature of the Physical World*, p. 241.

nervous system, sense-organs and mind as one integral system. But a point arises which is well worth thinking over. If the adapted man (*Homo faber* as we shall call him), is to *act* efficiently in his world, he must be made to feel at home in it; that is to say he must be convinced that he understands it and that he can rely on it to produce the results he expects. This is very important; for confidence is a *sine qua non* for any intelligence that has to fight its way against difficulties.

A double problem arises here. Man's surroundings must be intrinsically simple, if he is to have confidence in them, in the sense that they must react simply to his activities. And secondly, any puzzling features that the world may contain must be concealed from him. The first condition was met; and it brings to light a fact which we rarely think about. Matter has characteristics which fit it to be the home of life; for it responds to *Homo faber's* elementary activities in such a way as to inspire him with confidence. We take it as a matter of course that it should; but there is really no matter of course about it. This strikes us at once if we leave the rut in which our mind tends to run. Man can hunt, fish, fight, make tools and weapons, till the soil, build, launch out on the waters and, in fact, do anything which lies in his power without being met by circumstances which cause him embarrassment. Nothing that he can do causes the appearance, for example, of high-tension electricity or starts a chain of atomic fission or results in things catching fire without obvious cause. We are inclined to say: Of course they do not: why should they? But these things *can* happen. The fact that man cannot bring them about until he has become highly sophisticated and has taken a great deal of thought is a provision of Nature without which human evolution would have been impossible. It is one of the many ways in which the physical universe has somehow been fitted in advance to be the nursery of life.[1]

Certain events likely to cause terror in the mind of early man do occasionally occur spontaneously, such as volcanic eruptions and earthquakes, and, very rarely, the descent of a large meteor. But these events are sufficiently rare and localized to leave the confidence of the human race undisturbed on the whole.

The second condition called for action on Nature's part. The world revealed by the senses had to be made to appear *simple*. It is a tribute to the efficiency with which this was done that we, thinking beings, unless we acquire an unusual frame of mind, do not see that there was any problem to be solved. Is the world simple? Ask the physicist or the biologist. After three and a half centuries of inquiry, we are still struggling with the complexities of the world in science; and the most interesting thing about

[1] See Chapter XIV.

this inquiry is that the complexities increase rather than diminish as the inquiry proceeds. If the aim of the physicist is to reduce the world to a state of thorough intelligibility, then his goal was at his starting-point. One wonders how such a far-sighted physicist as Sir Arthur Eddington could have written: "Broadly speaking, the familiar world is the problem, and the physical world is the physicist's solution of it." It would surely be truer to say: The physicist's world is the problem and the familiar world is Nature's solution of it. The two are diverging. Max Planck says: "The physical world has become more and more abstract"; while Eddington continues: "It is well known that for a long time the physical world and the familiar world have been becoming more and more dissimilar, but it is only in the present century that the difference has become radical. As the result of two great theories—the relativity theory and the quantum theory —the familiar world and the physical world have become entirely distinct."[1] The progress of science shows that the fundamental character of the world continually escapes us and retreats indefinitely the further we pursue it. But for *Homo faber*, the complexities and difficulties discovered by scientists do not exist. His world is so simple that "the wayfaring man, though a fool, cannot err therein". Had it been otherwise, he would never have gained any confidence at all, but would have slunk back, cowed and defeated, and would never have mastered his environment in the way he has done. We are apt to think that there is no reason why fatal difficulties should have intruded into the world of *Homo faber*; but a little thought shows that they *would* have intruded if Nature had not kept them out.

It was the *mind*, on the level of the perceptual consciousness, and a little above it, working in conjunction with the sense-organs, that constructed for *Homo faber* an artificially simplified picture of the material world; and Nature achieved this apparent but specious simplicity, partly by limiting the scope of the human senses, but largely by instinctive indoctrination of the mind; though it is important to realize that this indoctrination had nothing to do with belief or judgment. It is not easy at first to realize how an appearance of specious simplicity could have been produced in this way. Let us take an example. Physical objects are given as being intrinsically coloured. Are they; or does the colour arise in the mind of the observer? We regard the latter suggestion as academic and think that it could only have arisen as the result of philosophical argument. But it *could* have appeared obvious without any argument at all. It *could* have been made to appear unquestionable, at an elementary level of consciousness, that colour is dependent on the observing mind and its relation to

[1] *Philosophy*, January, 1933, p. 31.

what is observed; but it *was* made to appear unquestionable that colour is a property of material objects in an intrinsic sense, that it is entirely objective and is independent of any perceptual situation. Indeed, phenomenalism *could* have been made to appear instinctively obvious: but there was a very good reason why it should not be. Any disclosure of such a complex situation would have presented the world as a puzzle; and it was a primary principle of mental adaptation that puzzling aspects of truth should not appear at *Homo faber's* level. Even the puzzle of all puzzles—Time—was simplified for him so that it should offer no difficulties to his practical mind. When we are in an *active* state of consciousness, we speak of what we are doing, of what we have done, and of what we are going to do without the slightest sense that there is anything in this that is difficult to understand. Time is bereft of all its difficulties and mysteries for the level of mind which engages in action. Directly we rise to a reflective level of thought, however, time becomes unintelligible. The future is non-existent because it has not yet come into being: the past is non-existent, for it has ceased to be: only the present exists. But what is the present? A mere dimensionless point-instant without extension. Into this apparent nonentity is crowded the whole of reality! Even if we postulate a specious present, this idea, too, raises difficulties when closely examined. Time, at the reflective level of thought, is a problem which increases our bewilderment the more we think about it. Time, at the practical level of thought, offers no difficulties at all because the mind at that level has been pre-adapted to think of it in a particular way. When the mind rises from the practical to the reflective level, puzzles pile themselves one on top of another. Time, to the pre-relativity physicist, was represented by an infinite straight line. But, according to the relativity theory, space and time constitute a four-dimensional manifold. If space-time is finite, how can the universe have had a beginning *in* time? How can it end *in* time? Yet finiteness seems to imply a beginning and an end. We need not, however, enter into these difficulties. The point is that time, for the practical level of consciousness, is completely simple; while time for the reflective level of consciousness is an ever-growing puzzle. This state of affairs could not have existed unless Nature had pre-arranged it. She contrived to render the practical consciousness of man blind to all these difficulties in order to provide him with a simple nursery in which to develop unalarmed. We do not see this: we do not realize that the external world, as presented to us, has been simplified for us, because it is part of Nature's scheme that we should not see what she has done. We are urged to accept it uncritically. No better device could have been employed for concealing unmanageable truths than that of *suggesting* simplicity at a lowly level of the mind. The simplicity which time, and other things, have for us in practical life is not the result of a *belief* into which judgment enters, but of an unthinking *acceptance*, which has been inserted into the mind before judgment comes into play. This was part of the method by which the human mind was adapted to its environment in the course of its evolution; and it was the mind of *Homo faber* which was thus worked upon. It is here that instinct and intelligence intertwine.

We must not think of *Homo faber* as a historical personage; he is a level of awareness in *ourselves*. If he ever was a historical person, he must have lived a very long time ago, probably soon after man parted company with his simian ancestors. We must remember that we include in ourselves all that has gone before; for life is not represented by the series *a, b, c,* etc., but by the series *a, a+b, a+b+c,* etc. The mind becomes hierarchical by retaining the rungs of the ladder by which it has climbed. The simplicity of *Homo faber's* world exists for us, therefore, only when we are on *Homo faber's* level, which we occupy while our attention is fixed on practical action in the outside world. At first sight it may, perhaps, seem as though we could deny that the mind of man is influenced by innate suggestions, which it unconsciously takes for granted. There is the human critical faculty. Is not this capable of dispersing any assumption that the mind may have instinctively accepted? But this is to overlook the fact that we flit up and down the levels of awareness comprised in us with such rapidity that we do not notice the differences between them. This rapid passage integrates them and causes the lower and higher to interpenetrate. At a sufficiently high level we *can* criticize what lies below: but we seldom attain a sufficiently high level to admit of our criticism being more than partial.

It is not, of course, true, even when our minds are on the practical level, that they encounter no difficulties; but the difficulties they then encounter are of a special kind. They are difficulties which, in principle, are capable of being completely solved in a final and satisfactory manner. We might call them "convergent difficulties"; and the questions which arise on this level "convergent questions". The difficulties we encounter when we ascend our grades of awareness to the reflective level can be of a very different kind. Some of them are "divergent" difficulties and questions; and these Nature had, at all costs, to keep out of *Homo faber's* sight. Convergent difficulties stimulate the mind and inspire it with confidence when they are solved; and they are all, in principle, soluble. Divergent difficulties paralyse the mind and dishearten it. The practical man works in a self-contained world of convergence which has been freed from the latter kind of difficulty.

The convergent nature of the problems which arise in practical life is the chief reason for the immense success of the industrial arts and of applied science. It accounts for the confidence which science has everywhere inspired. The secrets of the convergent world are secrets which *can* be unveiled.

It would be satisfactory if we could draw a sharp line between this region of convergent problems and the region of divergent problems: also if we could clearly distinguish between the practical mentality of *Homo faber* and the reflective mentality of *Homo sapiens*. But the distinctions we find in the real world are rarely clear-cut; if we "discover" something which appears to be completely clear-cut and mentally satisfactory through and through, which lies *outside* the world of practical affairs, we have probably provided it. States of consciousness are not separated from one another like the leaves of a book: they interpenetrate. So it comes about that when we leave the practical state of awareness for the reflective state, we do not leave the former entirely behind: it pursues us and influences our reflective thought. This is the gist of Bergson's remark: "It is the philosophers who are mistaken when they import into the domain of speculation a method of thinking which is made for action."[1] But the philosophers do not know that they are importing anything: nor do the scientists, nor does anyone else. The importation is insidious: it is veiled: it slips into the reflective mind unperceived, before reasoning begins. It is the micro-organism which passes through the filter. Surely few things could be more important than this unconscious factor, which has the power of unconsciously influencing reason. Why does not every thinking person recognize that Nature, in the course of evolution, has indoctrinated the human mind for practical purposes and that this indoctrination has had certain effects on human thinking of which the mind remains unconscious, unless it makes a special effort to perceive it?

How did Nature achieve this? A little reflection will show that she must have brought off a double achievement. She not only presented the external world as being far simpler than it really is; she also presented it as being *universal*. After all, the one involves the other. Man could not be cognizant of the universe as a whole. He could know only a fragment of it—the fragment which was of practical use to him. *But he must not be aware that the fragment is only a fragment or its simplicity will be gone.* His world must be apparently autonomous and without external context if he is to feel at home in it. It must be intelligible and convergent; it would never do to allow it to shade off into the unintelligible and the divergent. Being a fragment, it must in reality possess a boundary; but it was absolutely essential that the existence of this boundary should be concealed.

[1] *C.E.*, p. 146.

Where is the boundary of the world we live in? Most people, if asked this question, would probably look for it *in* the world which is presented by the senses. They would ask such questions as: Is space-time finite or infinite? Is there any limit to the size of the ultra-microscopic? Nature is already standing behind them when they ask these questions: she has jockeyed their minds *into* the space-time world before they have had time to gain any independence of thought. The specialist is particularly liable to follow Nature's prompting in this way (which is the point of Bergson's remark), because he adopts a kind of mental methodology which plunges him at once into analysis and screens from him the possibility of looking round and of asking seemingly irrelevant questions, as the non-specialist is free to do. The truth is that the boundary of our world is *subjective* and is determined by the nature and limitations of our organs of sense, of our bodies and of our minds. Like the horizon at sea, it has no intrinsic existence, but simply marks a limit to our capacities. But this fact had to be concealed if the world was to appear to be the whole and not a fragment; and there was only one way of concealing it, namely by indoctrinating the mind of *Homo faber*, so that the all-inclusive completeness of his world would be taken for granted by him. To me, the primary importance of psychical research is that it has clearly revealed the existence of this subjective boundary and has shown the instinctive resistance to all evidence which threatens to expose it.

It is to be noted that, because of the subjectivity of the boundary, we are not here involved in any controversy about philosophical idealism and realism. That is a discussion which considers the nature of the world from an ontological angle: nor, in speaking of a boundary and of what lies beyond, are we drawing a distinction between phenomena and noumena. I do not know how Kant regarded these as being related to one another; nor do I know whether he himself was altogether clear about this relation. All that we are saying is that man can only grasp a fraction of what is real by means of his senses, and that his mind has been so conditioned by Nature that he accepts this fragment as the whole. Man thus assumes that he can grasp the entire universe in principle because Nature has instilled into him a suggestion which causes him to assume this. She has succeeded in making him mistake a parochial world for the cosmic whole. This psychologically achieved illusion is quite compatible with the principle of philosophical realism, though not with naïve realism.

But how did Nature succeed in instilling this acceptance into the mind of man and in hiding from him the fact that she had done so? Perhaps in more ways than one.[1] But she did it in one outstanding way. She did it by

[1] See p. 179.

making the external world appear to be entirely objective. We must remember that Nature was able to influence man, as well as all other living creatures, *from within*. She had done this throughout the realm of animal life: what else is instinct? Instinct is "innate impulse", according to the dictionary definition. What is this but inculcated suggestion?

When we sit in the theatre watching a play, we are conscious that the story which is being unfolded on the stage is artificial and not part of the real world. We are also conscious that we, as observers, are watching it. Very occasionally this sense of independence may be lost, as when some unsophisticated play-goer loses his grip of the situation and shouts a warning to the hero, who is about to be trapped by the machinations of the villain. But this is rare: almost invariably the spectator is conscious of himself and realizes his independence. When we are out in the everyday world, however, it is different. There we are in an *active* state of consciousness and are *doing* things, and then we lack this sense of independence and become so intensely aware of the external world that we lose our sense of separate selfhood. We are unified with our surroundings and are so absorbed in them that they alone appear to exist. Of course it is true that the physically active man is aware of himself in one sense, for he protects himself from danger, as also do animals. But this is not due to conscious separation of the self from its surroundings, but rather to consciousness of the body as a special object among objects.

As an example of the innate unconsciousness of the subjective factor in sense-perception, we may point to the difficulty which many persons encounter in understanding the nature of an hallucination of the senses. If a human figure is seen standing in a room, looking entirely natural, when in fact no person is there, people feel instinctively that some cause for it *must* exist in the external world. They will go on searching for such a cause and they will invent theories about "immaterial matter" in order somehow to find an objective cause in space; but the one thing they often cannot get hold of is the idea that the phenomenon is entirely subjective. Instinct is in operation here; for, on the level of sense-perception, Nature has flatly eliminated all consciousness of the role played by the percipient.

In truth, our material surroundings, as we perceive them, owe much to ourselves: philosophers and psychologists know this well. And there is no reason why this should not be obvious to the percipient in each and every act of perception. But it has been deliberately concealed from him by Nature. When we see, hear, touch, etc., we are made to *feel* that we are in direct contact with objects and that these are, in an ultimate sense, exactly what we perceive them to be and possess all their properties in complete independence of ourselves. We are so absorbed in our surroundings when we are in the state of consciousness which is wholly absorbed in action, that the sense of being fused with the external world is complete. As soon, however, as we leave the active state of consciousness (and we scarcely realize when we do leave it) and become reflective, this state of affairs no longer holds in anything like its former completeness. We can then become aware that there *is* a subjective element in sense-perception and that we and the objective world are separate and inter-related. But, even in reflection, Nature's device still dogs us. Pursuing us from the lower level of consciousness to the higher, it causes us instinctively to turn to the objective world as the sole source of any reliable information and the sole avenue to truth. Though we then realize our independence, and that it is *our* experience rather than anything independent of us that is of fundamental importance, we still have little idea of how powerful a part subjective factors are playing in determining our conception of things. Scientists believe, for example, that the more objective they make their methods the nearer they will get to the truth. This is true enough in applied science; but it is far from true in pure science. Their belief is founded on the instinctive conviction instilled into *Homo faber*.

Clearly the sense of a wholly objective world makes for efficiency in action: it clears the decks and renders the situation simple. But it does more than this. *It conceals the boundary of the world.* It is Nature's device for making the world of action appear to be the whole universe and not a fragment of it—a world that is self-sufficient, autonomous and all-inclusive. Of course the everyday world is not presented as being complete in one sense: we do not at once perceive the geographical whole. It can be explored internally—within the subjective boundary—and there is plenty to be discovered in that way. But however much we explore it geographically, it still remains simple, self-sufficient and complete in principle. It still presents itself as the all-in-all.

We will postpone for the moment the question of what the world is for the reflective consciousness. Our present point is that awareness of the subject-object relation had to be suppressed on the active level of consciousness in order to attain an apparently simple, autonomous world: for, if it had been allowed to appear, the observer would have been aware of himself as standing apart from his world, perceiving it and acting upon it *ab extra*; and then his world would have been no longer complete in itself. Its autonomy would have been destroyed through the door which his own self had opened. His world would have been seen to be but a fragment and, with this, its specious simplicity would have disappeared. If the observer had not been blotted out, he would have appeared beyond the boundary, thus revealing the latter's existence. The boundary, being subjective, would have appeared with the recognition of himself; and the boundary had at all costs to be concealed. With the boundary in view, there would be a beyond; and with a beyond, the world of *Homo faber* would no longer have been a closed system. Questions arising in it would have led to no satisfactory answers, but would have wandered off into the blue. The world, seen as a fragment, would have had ragged edges. Signposts would have appeared, pointing to an uncomprehended beyond. The world would not have been such as *Homo faber* could cope with: he would have shrunk back from it, bewildered and dismayed. It was essential, therefore, that the external world should appear to be completely objective and all-inclusive.

That the world presented by the senses includes everything had to be made to seem so obvious as to offer no hold for doubt or question, so that the indoctrinating factor *could* only be instinctive; and when this instinct permeates upwards and in some degree influences the reflective level of thought, it will necessarily continue to resist facts, suggestions or reasonings that threaten to expose the boundary of its world. It will instinctively reject or explain away anything that comes from beyond the boundary and shows through into the ordinary world. It will also resist anything that suggests that the external world is not wholly objective. It will sponsor the philosophy of common sense and of naïve realism and will try to force all facts into their mould. When it inserts itself into philosophy, it will encourage positivism. This factor is a fundamental characteristic of the human mind and is still strong even at the reflective level of the intellect.

When we look at *Homo faber's* world from a standpoint of relative mental freedom, which we can acquire by avoiding the specialist's groove, we see that nature has forced man to accept an absurdity. She has presented him with a world so simple that the meanest mind can grasp it and can feel at home in it; and yet a world so comprehensive as to include within itself the be-all and end-all of existence. The two propositions are so utterly incompatible that the attempt to unite them would be regarded as a joke had not Nature rendered us blind to the absurdity. But, indoctrinated as we are, we accept the combination with perfect gravity and see nothing inconsistent in it.

When *Homo faber* rises to the status of *Homo sapiens*, his powers of geographically exploring his world increase. More than that, he acquires new ideas about its nature, though these are not fundamentally removed from ideas originated by the senses. But still, allowing for this expansion, the world as Nature presents it to the senses is still the entire universe for

Homo sapiens as it was for *Homo faber*. Unless a very high level of intuitive awareness is reached, the indoctrinating instinct does not wholly lose its grip; and *Homo sapiens* assumes as axiomatic that the entire universe is submissive to his understanding. He sees nothing absurd in the assumption that all its problems are convergent. Although his senses are palpably limited and his understanding has been forged in the evolutionary mill, he still believes that he can grasp the all-in-all. We *can*, by attaining a higher level of awareness, partially free ourselves from this powerful illusion; but we rarely rise high enough to escape from it altogether.

How did Nature achieve the illusion? The answer is that she used instinct in an extraordinarily subtle way. Biologists have dealt with animal instincts and psychologists with human instincts; but the latter have concerned themselves with the more obvious examples; such as sex-instinct, social instinct and the like. Perhaps it is because scientists are specialists that they tend to pass over the subtler manifestations of instinct without noticing them. That instinct provides Nature with a means of indoctrinating the mind in ways that are hidden from consciousness may be demonstrated by an illustration.

Suppose that we are looking at any scene, say a red-brick house with white window-frames and a patch of green creeper growing up the wall. The *bare data* which the eyes convey consist of a medley of coloured patches of different shapes and sizes. They are, like the bits of glass in a kaleidoscope, just a pattern; and if our sense of sight conveyed no more than this pattern, the world of vision would be just a shifting maze of coloured patches which would leave us bewildered. But the sense of sight does not leave matters like this. The house we see is not a mere pattern of red, white and green shapes, which change and move, kaleidoscope-fashion, as we walk about: it is more; and also it is simpler. It is a *single object*—a house. One glance tells us that it is a complete house, which includes data that we do not see; for the house is *given* as possessing, not only a front, a portion of roof and possibly one end, which are included in the visual pattern, but also a back and another end and even an inside, none of which we see. We become aware of an entire *object* and not of a kaleidoscopic medley. This feat is achieved, not by our eyes, but by our *mind*. Philosophers call this step from the bare data of sense to the perception of an object "perceptual acceptance". It is a synthesizing process: perhaps one might call it a *gestalt* process. And Nature achieves it by the use of what may legitimately be called instinct. At the low level of perceptual consciousness, the mind comes in this way to the assistance of the eye. Instinct causes the mind unconsciously to take the necessary acceptance for granted at a level of awareness too low to be capable of judgment or question. The suggestion is accepted in much the same way as a hypnotic suggestion is accepted.

If Nature can so work upon the mind by instinct as to cause objects to be presented to the perceptual consciousness in a synthetic and useful form, why should she not use the same device in order to make the world appear simple and self-complete? Such an instinct would have to operate on a mental level somewhat higher than that of the perceptual consciousness; but there is no reason why it should not. The fact that the observer exists independently of what is observed can be hidden by blotting out self-consciousness and by hedging in the perceived objects, as it were, with a wall. The complexities of a complex world can thus be hidden by the suggestion that everything that is presented is obvious and everything that happens *must* be so.

Any niche which might offer a hold for questions is concealed. In this way an extremely puzzling universe, which in reality stretches away from man's standpoint to infinity and whose characteristics diverge in every direction and pass into unintelligibility, is converted into a cosy, self-contained nursery. Within this nursery everything (provided it is not too closely looked into) is "obviously" simple and easy to understand: and yet the nursery apparently contains everything! Instinct, together with the limitations of the body and the senses, has thus secured a fit world for *Homo faber* to live in.

We may not altogether like the idea that Nature fitted out our nursery by operating on *us* rather than on *it*. It is true, however, that Nature operated on both; for the nursery for unconscious life did depend on very fortunate external conditions, as described in Chapter XIV. We probably do not like to think that we were made comfortable and confident by being provided with illusions. We spend our time in trying to avoid illusions and to find out the truth. We are inclined to say, with the bucolic philosopher, Josh Billings: "I honestly believe it iz better tew know nothing than tew know what ain't zo." But Nature's motto is different. She goes on the principle: "Better a dish of illusion and a hearty appetite for life than a feast of reality and indigestion therewith."

In one sense, however, Nature has presented us with the truth; for she has put us in touch with the real world and not with a world of fantasy; only she has trimmed the real world as presented to *us* into a form best suited for action. The world with which we are acquainted when we are acting upon it *is* the real world, only it has been specially edited. It contains illusions in the sense that we are made to see reality in a specially prepared form, which does not agree, in many respects, with the world viewed from a different standpoint. It is like a child's first history-book, which is very different from what actually happened in the past, and might, in one sense, be called fiction; but which is, nevertheless, ultimately founded on what actually happened.

Reflection should convince us that this editing of reality was absolutely necessary. Man, and indeed all life, had to be brought up in a nursery; and how could this have been achieved except by mutual adaptation? We readily accept the adaptation of man's body; but we boggle at the adaptation of his mind. We boggle because the adapted mind is at work in ourselves, urging us to accept our own mental omnipotence and the universal intelligibility of all things.

We have spoken of the boundary of the world, which is subjective and hidden from view, as if it were fixed. It would be simpler and more convenient to explain if it were; but it is not fixed because the human mind is not fixed or definitely bounded. The boundary of the world is relative to the human state of consciousness. For *Homo faber*, who is the active level of consciousness in ourselves, the boundary is close at hand, being determined by the scope of the unaided senses, and the instincts which collaborate with them: but, as higher states of awareness are acquired, the boundary of the world recedes. Within this boundary, the problems which arise are convergent and can be completely solved by the human mind in a satisfactory manner. Outside this boundary, problems diverge and are not amenable to the powers of the intellect. But the boundary is elastic and expandable because, when a higher degree of awareness is attained, the mind works less in the groove dictated by instinct and becomes freer and more capable of asking questions and hence of forming genuinely new ideas, the possibility of which it could not have seen at a lower level of awareness. Problems which were divergent and insoluble at the lower level may thus become convergent and soluble at a higher level. The progress of modern physics is a good example of this expansion of the boundary. The expansion has, however, given rise to the false view that science can progress for ever. It is thought that the progress of science is potentially limitless and that the methods of science are omnipotent. The boundary of the world has, indeed, been pushed outwards by science; why, then, should it not be pushed outwards indefinitely? The answer is that it cannot be pushed outwards indefinitely because man is tied to his body, his senses and his indoctrinating instincts. Although he can reinforce his senses with instruments and can partially free himself from the grip of instinct, so as to reason more or less freely, he is yet tied to his anchorage and in the long run can only move away from it to a limited extent. Thus, science is doomed for ever to work inside a ring-fence, although the ring-fence can be thrust outwards until it reaches a final limit. We might illustrate this by a simple metaphor. Imagine an island surrounded by vertical cliffs. Can its area be increased? Yes; for cantilevers could be thrown out from the cliffs all round the island and covered with a platform. Perhaps some theorist, who knew nothing about practical engineering, would hold that the area of the island could, by this means, be increased indefinitely. But practical people would know that a limit must soon be reached. When scientific research passes beyond the scope of familiar words and images and is obliged to rely on mathematics, the cantilevers are becoming thinner. "Both upward and downward, both in the large and in the small, science seems to be reaching its limits. It is thought that the universe is of finite extent in space, and that light could travel round it in a few hundred millions of years. It is thought that matter consists of electrons and protons, which are of finite size, and of which there are only a finite number in the world, but proceed by jerks, which are never smaller than a certain minimum jerk. The laws of these changes can apparently be summed up in a small number of very general principles, which determine the past and the future of the world when any small section of its history is known. Physical science is thus approaching the stage when it will be complete, and therefore uninteresting."[1]

Physical science may be approaching this stage; but if it becomes complete and uninteresting it will not be because it has discovered the inmost nature of the universe but because it has reached the end of its tether and has gone bankrupt. What is happening in science at its points of greatest advance is that the illusion of the pure objectivity and self-completeness of the world is thinning and the part played by the observer is coming more and more into view. This is the early stage of the fundamental lesson that the road to any far-reaching advance in knowledge lies *within* the human being and not in the external world.

This discussion of Nature's Problem has brought us to the following conclusions: (1) that the mind of man was adapted during its evolution as thoroughly as was his body to meet the demands of practical life in the material world; (2) that this adaptation was effected, partly by the limitations inherent in the human body and sense-organs, but partly also by the play of instinct within the mind, which caused it to accept unconsciously the world before it as simple and all-inclusive; (3) that this instinct was applied to consciousness at the level concerned with active life, but that its effects penetrate into higher levels of consciousness to a greater or less extent and influence the course of thought and reason in matters which are far removed from the familiar world. Instinct acts, not

[1] *W.I.B.*, pp. 9-10.

as an innate idea, but as an innate *tendency*; it is an important factor in the reflective mind: (4) that the degree to which thought is influenced by instinct depends upon the level of conscious awareness attained. This is an individual and not a public matter. At a very high level of awareness, the power of instinct to influence thought disappears and thought becomes entirely free: (5) that the world revealed by the senses is not the whole universe. In the first place, what is completely intelligible to the human intellect could not be the whole, for the lack of proportion involved in such a proposition is so great as to be grotesque. Secondly, there is much evidence for the existence of things which originate beyond the boundary of the sensible world, and the vigour with which the adapted mind seeks to reject these things stamps them as being extra-terrestrial and therefore inimical to it. Thus there are two arguments against the widely accepted view that the world presented by the senses includes everything.

These conclusions show that the human being is, in reality, looking at the general from a special standpoint; whereas it believes that it is looking at the special from a general standpoint. But the conclusion we would particularly emphasize at the end of this chapter is that *the world revealed by the senses, even when expanded by science, is not the whole.*

CHAPTER VIII

THE INTRUDER

IF we can bring ourselves to criticize the assumption that the human intellect is, in principle, capable of comprehending all that exists, and also to criticize the view that intellect is a discrete, homogeneous faculty which does not shade off into grades of awareness, we shall begin to see that the investigation of all far-reaching problems involves the simultaneous investigation of the mind which essays to solve them. That the intellect is not homogeneous, that thought is not all of one kind is not, after all, very hard to discover. Professor C. D. Broad writes of thinking as follows: "Now it seems to me that we must distinguish between what I call 'fluid' and 'crystallized' thinking. We must recognize that, whilst the greater part of any so-called process of 'thinking' is of the latter kind, it must also contain short spells of the former. And we must recognize that the latter presupposes the previous occurrence of the former in the same mind or in some other mind. Anyone who considers what happens when he solves some problem for himself will recognize the difference. He would commonly be said to be 'thinking' about the problem during the whole course of his work. Now, during the greater part of this period, he is certainly only manipulating symbols almost mechanically according to rule. But (1) at the beginning of the work, and at isolated intervals during the course of it, he must cease to do this and must contemplate face to face the actual abstract objects with which he is concerned and their actual relations to each other. When he does this he is performing acts of 'fluid' thinking and no facility in manipulating symbols is any substitute for this. The power to perform acts of fluid thinking constitutes that difference between a man and a well-trained parrot which the Behaviourists (doubtless from excess of modesty) are so loth to admit. (2) I can now manipulate symbols blindly according to rules and can feel confident that the result will accord with the real relation of things, only because I or my predecessors directly contemplated these things and their relations and made up a symbolism whose rules of operation were seen to accord with the relations of the things symbolized. Thus the symbolism is just the 'crystallization' of the past fluid thinking of myself or others; and, if it were not, there would not be the faintest reason to treat these operations with symbols according to rules as anything more than solemn trifling."[1]

[1] *M.P.N.*, pp. 334-5.

From our present point of view, we should say that the passage from crystallized to fluid thinking involves the passage from a lower to a higher grade of awareness. Crystallized thinking we should regard as specialized thinking, brought into line, perhaps with difficulty, with physical events spread out in space and time. Fluid thinking would be thought which is less highly specialized, and more spontaneous and intuitive.

Another eminent philosopher has written as follows about the function of reason, perhaps rather surprisingly considering his outstanding contributions to logic: "But in fact the opposition of instinct to reason is mainly illusory. Instinct, intuition or insight is what first leads to the beliefs which subsequent reason confirms or confutes; but the confirmation, where it is possible, consists, in the last analysis, of agreement with other beliefs no less instinctive. Reason is a harmonizing, controlling force rather than a creative one. Even in the most purely logical realm, it is insight that first arrives at what is new."[1] Intuition feeds reason from above while instinct directs and sometimes misleads it from below. Insight, or direct awareness, is thus the primary factor in thought. Afterwards thought descends to the level of the vocabulary and the rules of logic. But the question naturally arises as to whether instinct, intuition and insight can all be classed together. Is direct insight a faculty of the same kind as the instinct which controls the behaviour of animals? This instinct has curious properties, seeming to be intelligent and unintelligent at the same time. It shows extraordinary foresight; yet it sometimes dictates a routine-behaviour which does more harm than good. Insight, as the genetic factor in human thought, is surely very different from animal instinct. We have held, also, that instinct in the human being can create illusions if the circumstances demand it. Surely insight in higher thought is not like that.

Why do we tend to class instinct and insight together? Apparently for the negative reason that both lie outside the province of the intellect. This is the result of the perspective with which we start. Intellect we assume to be the central function; while instinct and insight are lesser elements which lie on the fringe. Being in our eyes secondary and comparatively trivial, we class them together. But if we take a different view of the intellect, we need not do so. If we regard the intellect as a specialized function evolved for a special purpose it does not follow that what is not included in intellect is merely a residual, marginal function.

Human mentality takes on a different aspect if we regard *awareness* and not intellect as the primary datum. The conception of awareness is admittedly difficult to fit with a dictionary definition. It may be regarded

[1] Bertrand Russell, *Mysticism and Logic*, p. 13.

as a synonym for selfhood or being. But our way of thinking demands a distinction between awareness and awareness *of*. Yet it is difficult to draw this distinction; for awareness is apt to merge into self-awareness or awareness *of* the self and so to obliterate the distinction by making the self an object of awareness, which it can never be. We cannot define awareness: yet we *are* aware. It is also a matter of experience that there are degrees of awareness and these degrees are not rigidly separable from one another. What we call the intellect includes grouped awarenesses, variable in degree and extent, and specially adapted to the conditions of life. Fluid and crystallized thinking take place at different levels of awareness: the former is able to seize what is new while the latter can only churn over the old. It is on the former that progress in thought depends; for important truths are not discovered by applying the rules of logic but by attaining a level of awareness at which they are directly seen. When seen at this height, they may be gradually assimilated at lower levels and may take shape on the public level of thought like a developing photograph. "Two thousand years of logical reflection have left logic impotent to account for novelty in thought."[1]

There is a great deal of evidence in support of the view that original ideas are not created by the intellect as it exercises its rational function, but enter into it from some source which is outside. R. G. Collingwood testifies to this: "I have always been a slow and painful thinker, in whom thought in its formative stages will not be hurried by effort, nor clarified by argument, that most dangerous enemy to immature thoughts, but grows obscurely through a long and oppressive period of gestation, and only after birth can be licked by its parent into presentable shape."[2] Argument does not help thinking of the fluid or intuitional kind: it obstructs it: it cannot be applied until the fluid process is complete. Again: "The highest creations are evolved, not as the result of thinking according to a pattern, but as the outcome of insight, hard reflection, and solitary meditation of men who are lifted above the common groove."[3] A consensus of first-hand testimony from poets, authors, artists, musical composers and even scientists that all their original creations came to them in this supra-rational way is to be found in Dr. Rosamond Harding's interesting book, *An Anatomy of Inspiration*.

In plants, the lowly trickle from the universal and nameless river adjusts, co-ordinates and directs their development in an astonishing manner. No detail is overlooked. The organic world of unconscious life has a character that is alien to our ways of thinking. The pattern baffles us because it is

[1] *Must Philosophers Disagree?*   [2] *An Autobiography*, p. 107.
[3] S. Radhakrishnan, *Kalki*, p. 31.

acting into our world from without. Its beauty strikes us as being at odds with its pragmatism: its ways appear sometimes as if they were purposeful in the human sense and sometimes as if they were purposeless: its infinite diversity offends our predeliction for grouping things under general laws; its prodigal combination of creativeness and destruction strikes us as being incredibly wasteful. Its whole essence is out of agreement with our adapted ways of thought because it does not take its rise within the boundary of our world. We seek, therefore, to draw it into our world and to force upon it explanations of the kind we understand.

Instinct shows by its character that it originates beyond the boundary. There are two types at work in the animal world, one of which acts in conjunction with the senses while the other short-circuits the senses. Both are frequently met with and are probably often combined. The behaviour of the cuckoo illustrates them. Instinct, acting through the senses, urges the adult cuckoo to look for another bird's nest in which to deposit its egg. Instinct, dispensing with the aid of the senses, urges the young cuckoo to migrate to the appropriate place abroad without previous experience and without instruction. In the latter case, the background of awareness, which in its essence is beyond our understanding, brings forward into the ordinary world its uncomprehended powers and specializes them as an adapted instinct. Hence the young cuckoo relates its action to a situation of which it has no normal knowledge. A similar thing happens to the human being in the case of telepathy or extra-sensory perception: but there it is fitful and sporadic, whereas when it appears in the animal world it has been harnessed by nature and rendered dependable. It is another example of the lack of any real difference between the "normal" and the "paranormal". The paranormal is so called because it originates beyond the boundary of our world and brings uncomprehended features into it: the normal belongs to this side of the boundary; but both in reality inhabit a single world. The boundary is subjective: there is no intrinsic separation.

It may, perhaps, seem as if the thesis of mental adaptation is inconsistent with the fact that the human mind, in relation to ordinary life, has expanded and the intellect has grown. How could civilization have progressed if the human mind were bound by the chains of instinct? The answer is to be found in the Intruder: in other words in the unadapted factor in man, which joins itself to the adapted factor. At what epoch the Intruder first appeared it is hard to say. Animals are wholly adapted; and at one time man, or his immediate progenitor, was no doubt wholly adapted also. The Intruder must have made its first modest appearance when our ape-like ancestors earned the name of *Homo*. When that occurred it is for anthropologists to say. The essence of the Intruder was a heightening of awareness—a movement away from instinctive fixation and towards mental freedom. Instead of simply reacting to the data supplied by the senses, man began to form concepts and to be influenced by them. Language was a powerful instrument of advance; but it was the result and not the cause of growing awareness. As time went on, the faculty of wonder arose. What lay behind the phenomena with which man was surrounded? It was natural that early man should imagine that living agents stood behind the forces of nature. He did not have to invent this idea; for living agents actually controlled the material bodies of animals and of his fellow men. Those who maintain that savages and primitive men have no conception of natural law but attribute every phenomenon to the agency of spirits, surely exaggerate. So likewise do the psycho-logists who maintain that these ideas are solely projected fears or repres-sions or arise from other factors dealt with in psycho-analysis. These may indeed have played their part; but the factor in man which carried him upwards and along the path towards *Homo sapiens* was the steady expan-sion of the power to *realize*. This was the primary factor; and it was this which expressed itself symbolically in the various beliefs of the conscious mind. The unadapted Intruder was entering into and modifying the adapted mind. Early man dimly realized that more lay behind the world of his senses than the senses delivered; and this realization expressed itself in various kinds of anthropomorphic symbolism. As man grew through the long period of proto-civilization and afterwards of civilization, the awareness we have called the Intruder expressed itself in divination and prophecy and inspired testimony. " 'On the subject of inspiration,' wrote Mr. Walter Scott in his edition of the *Hermetica*, 'Egyptians, Hebrews and Greeks thought much alike, from the earliest times to which we can trace back their thoughts; and in the time of the Roman Empire, pagans, Jews and Christians spoke of it in similar terms.' We have, in fact, a belief which goes back to primitive man all the world over, and persists in the various civilizations which have grown out of primitive society. . . . Right through the history of all peoples, from their savage origins to the last attainments of civilization, this belief runs like a thread, which has, no doubt, at the savage level a cruder form than later on, but is nevertheless, in spite of modifications, essentially a continuous tradition."[1]

The progress of man, in other words, was marked by an influx from without rather than by a growth from within: that is to say it was not the mind of man, adapted by nature to his world, which provided this growing sense of something beyond that world; it was an inspirational

[1] *S.S.*, pp. 13-14.

influx of awareness which had not been adapted. It was something that intruded upon man as Nature had evolved him. This inspirational awareness, coming to the adapted consciousness from a wider range of the being, expressed itself in various forms as it entered that consciousness. Some of these forms no doubt appear to us primitive and childish, but their source is a wide, unadapted region of the being. On the modern outlook this view would be rejected; for it is to-day taken as axiomatic that nothing we experience can owe its origin to a source outside the sensible world. The religious beliefs scattered throughout history, the belief in divination, etc., must, according to the present outlook which owes its origin to science, be found in characteristics of man as revealed by the senses. They must be put down to neuroses or repressed wishes or fancies belonging to man in his racial infancy. The general belief in a world of spirits is held to be merely a substitute for the total lack of any conception on the part of early man of natural law. But this is not a balanced reading of the facts: it is a characteristic forcing of the facts into our contemporary frame of thought.

The view that savages have no conception of natural law, and that their belief in spirits is a substitute for it, will not bear examination. Edwyn Bevan quotes a passage from Lotze's *Mikrokosmus* which exposes this contention, showing it to be academic and unrealistic: "Only a dream-state, confined to vision without activity, could go on happily in the imagination of an animate life which penetrated all provinces of nature with free and arbitrary impulse."[1] Man, early or late, savage or civilized, has always had to deal with inanimate things; and he could not possibly have done so if he were in a state of illusion about the laws that control them. He was bound to recognize their regularity and calculability and to see that there is a necessary connection in them which can be known beforehand. In order to build a shelter, to hunt, to make weapons, primitive and savage men must have been aware of the elementary laws of mechanics. For them, the world must have been largely governed by uniform law. But they were confronted by a dual world in which certain lumps of matter obeyed inanimate laws and other lumps of matter were governed by desires, emotions and impulses. In the latter, "spiritual causation" was given as a fact of experience: there was no need to invent it. "Since the world of consciousness is inaccessible to sense-perception, since you cannot see your neighbour's desires or emotions, but only the bodily movements to which they give rise, you cannot tell by looking whether elsewhere desires or emotions are in existence or not."[2] They made the mistake of allowing the world of life to invade the background

[1] *S.S.*, p. 14.   [2] *S.S.*, p. 17.

of inanimate things; but surely it was a more sensible mistake than that of the Behaviourists, who do the opposite.

The conception of the Intruder is inevitably not a precise and clear-cut idea. It is not something that can be sharply defined. It would be absurd to expect it. The assumption that everything that enters into human experience can be sharply and clearly conceived and definitely put into words arises from the natural instinct to assume that all questions and problems are convergent. The Intruder enters into our lives from outside the area of convergent questions, as also does everything that comes by inspiration. It is for us to adapt our minds to such conceptions if we can; not for the reality to adapt itself to our minds. If we cannot expand our minds to accept it, we must expect to be faced by intellectual puzzles and apparent contradictions. To ask what is meant by the attainment of a higher state of awareness is to raise such a difficulty. What is the source of an inspiration? How does it enter consciousness? Is it from ourself? If so, how does it appear to normal consciousness to come from another source? How can the source be at once the self and not the self? Probably the only answer we can give is that we have no conception of what the self is. We cannot define it or state its characteristics or make it an object of thought. The contradiction is due to our mental incapacity to conceive selfhood. If we feel inclined to throw all this aside and to take refuge in the clarity of words, believing that whatever is verbally clear *must* correspond with reality, we cannot escape from the fact that by so doing we are evading contact with the kind of reality that lies beyond the boundary of our intellectually conceivable world. To retreat into a verbal fastness is to act like a mountaineer who takes refuge in a rest-camp instead of facing the difficulties of the climb.

Fixity and verbal definition will not do. Introspection shows that the normal consciousness is not fixed but variable and that the intellect is therefore an arbitrary standard. Consciousness expands and contracts; and when it contracts it raises a problem. Is that which is "I" in the expanded stage, still "I" in the contracted stage, where it seems to have been left behind by the contraction? "In point of fact we are never aware of all the experience we are having", says a psychologist.[1] This expresses the crux between the "I" and the "not I". Which road shall we take? Shall we draw the "I" and the "not I" into the Procrustean bed of verbal polemics? Or shall we endeavour to overcome the apparent logical contradiction by expanding our consciousness until it gains some intuitive grasp of the situation?

Perhaps it may help us a little to think of the dreaming self. It is "I"

[1] F. Aveling, *Personality and Will*, p. 226.

who am awake: is it also "I" who dream? In a perfectly good sense the
dreamer is "other" than the waker. Yet in another perfectly good sense,
the dreamer and the waker are the same. And who creates the dream
which often surprises us? Is it one's self or another? So it is in the case of
different grades of awareness. We can seize, as it were, a piece more of our
complete self. What we seize adds in some sense to ourself; yet in another
sense, it was ourself all the time. Perhaps we would do well to use the
words "potential" and "actual"; but clearly they do not go to the root of
the matter. In actual life, our consciousness is perpetually on the move,
at one moment sinking, at another, rising to the stage of intermediate
thought and occasionally rising to the heights of comparative freedom
which we call "intuitive".

Increasing awareness is the means by which we can go forward to meet
new ideas, expanding ourselves towards them instead of drawing them
down into our lower grades of awareness. Increasing awareness is in
reality the fundamental principle which lies behind the growth of
intellect. Using the word "awareness" in its widest sense, we may say that
increasing awareness is the principle that lies behind all life. It is the
parent stem which underlies organic evolution. From the lowest living
cell, through plants and animals up to man, growth in awareness energizes
every process. This growing awareness is a principle in the uncomprehended background and has entered the physical world and has become
specialized and fixed in the forms and habits of plant and animal life. In
plants, every imaginable device is used to make the degree of awareness
that there is effective in reaching its various goals. The word "awareness"
is, indeed, stretched in application to plants; but there is no adequate word
by which to indicate that which underlies the goal-seeking and directing
activity. Yet in plants there is the same primal and underlying something
which, in the animal world, reveals itself in the form of specialized
instincts, and in man reveals itself again in the form of his specialized
intellect. Behind all the evolution of life there is that which acts into the
material world from without in a myriad ways, although the acting
inwards from without is only an appearance, because the whole of existence is one. We endeavour to explain the functions of life and mind in
terms of causes which lie on *our* side of the subjective boundary; but that
is clearly because Nature has succeeded in making us believe that what lies
on our side of the boundary includes everything.

We have maintained that the growth of man's intellectual powers
was the result of the attainment by a few individuals of a higher state of
awareness; that what they grasped in this way was true, and they gave it,
or part of it, verbal expression and transmitted it to a sufficiently large

minority to transform it into public knowledge. Heightened awareness is the indispensable prerequisite of the power to ask questions; and on the power to ask questions, the growth of intellect depends. At a low level of awareness, the mind is almost completely under the sway of instinct, which causes it to accept everything as obvious in a hypnotic manner. At this level there is no possibility of asking questions. The world is a simple place to live in and there is nothing questionable about it. But the influx of higher grades of awareness loosens the hold of instinct and reveals the world as possessing niches or holds on to which questions can be fastened. With every question, the simplicity of *Homo faber's* world retreats and the boundary of *Homo faber's* world is thrust outwards. Man, in the ordinary phrase, grows in intelligence. The process is in fact, a movement from the limited, the specialized and the compelled towards freedom. But it is not a move to freedom in one step, for instinct still attempts to insert itself into the reasoning process and to deflect it towards foregone conclusions. It is because of this that science makes enormous progress on the mediocre level that is required for practical achievements, but comparatively little progress in forming a picture of the universe on a higher level.

That intellectual advance arises from enhanced awareness, and the attainment of partial freedom from the grip of instinct, can be illustrated by an example. Everyone knows the story of Newton and the apple. The following conversation, which occurred in 1726, was recorded by Newton's friend William Stukeley: " 'After dinner, the weather being warm, we went into the garden and drank tea under the shade of the apple-trees, only he and myself. Amidst other discourse, he told me, he was just in the same situation, as when formerly, the notion of gravitation came into his mind. It was occasion'd by the fall of an apple, as he sat in contemplative mood. Why should that apple always descend perpendicularly to the ground, thought he to himself. Why should it not go sideways or upwards, but constantly to the earth's centre? Assuredly, the reason is, the earth draws it.' "[1]

The natural line of thought which this story induces is first of all admiration for the genius which was set pondering by the fall of an apple, and secondly interest in the subsequent development to which this thought led, that is to say to the formulation of the mathematical law of gravitation. No doubt the genius of Newton was required to arrive at this law; and the view here suggested does nothing to minimize it. But if we look at this story from a non-specialist angle, it strikes us very differently. The remarkable thing about it then is not that Newton asked why the apple

[1] *A.I.,* p. 109.

fell vertically to the ground, but why thousands of people had not asked this question before. Some, no doubt, had done so; but the idea had not gone home and the questions did not lead anywhere. What is absolutely astonishing, if we consider this incident with a free mind, is that it was not until late in the seventeenth century A.D. that this question was asked with effect. Why was this? Why had not every intelligent child asked this question before? Century after century, human beings had watched bodies falling to the earth: they had struggled with heavy weights: they had used the force of gravity to weigh their goods: rocks had come hurtling down the cliffs, and some had remained so firmly glued to the ground that they could not be moved. But nothing in all this caused the slightest surprise to millions of human beings. That, surely, is the point about Newton's story that ought to strike us with amazement. Gravity, sheltered behind instinct, was at work everywhere, but so "obvious" that it offered no hold for questions. Individuals here and there had probably wondered about gravity from time to time; but they soon dropped back into *Homo faber's* unquestioning frame of mind. For humanity in general, gravitation presented no problem at all; for everyone saw it through a mind which had been adapted by instinct to take it for granted. Instinct hid the niche which offered the hold for Newton's question.

Evidently Newton's mind, as he sat in the orchard in contemplative mood, rose to a state of higher awareness sufficiently free from instinct for the phenomenon of gravitation to appear questionable. From that height, the simplicity of *Homo faber's* world was broken through. Newton was looking through the relatively clear glass of a liberated mind at what the masses of people saw through the darkened glass of instinct. Nature had to keep the possibility of such questions as gravitation hidden from the minds of workaday men, or the simplicity of their world would have been ruined. As it was, Newton's question led to a divergent problem out of which arose two opposing factions of thought, one of which maintained the theory of action at a distance while the other did not. In the end it led to the still more remote conception of relativity; and who shall say what the final solution will be, if there ever is one? (Hoyle seems to have asked a question which goes beyond the relativity theory.) By instilling instinct into the mind in such a way as to convince its owner that gravitation offers no problem and no hold for questions, Nature avoided all the puzzlement and confusion that arise in the problems of modern science. Had these been visible, they would have produced, in the primitive mind, something akin to dismay.

We suggested that the human intellect grew by moving away from the instincts implanted by Nature and by gaining states of freer awareness—

by moving further from the adapted self towards the unadapted self. But it is not the intellect only that can grow in this way. The character also rises by moving from adaptation towards freedom. Character and awareness are subtly interrelated. Aldous Huxley points out that "knowledge is always a function of being"[1] but the relation is not simple, for knowledge on the intellectual plane can be independent of character or state of being. The possibility of genuinely intuitive perception does, however, depend on what we are, and in this way direct awareness differs from the intellect. A man may be a brilliant thinker within the range of publicly expressible ideas, and yet not possess a character on the same level as his intellectual attainments. But with the kind of intuitive awareness which illuminates the whole man it is different. With it, balance, insight, vision and a right sense of values are linked together. To *perceive* on a high level and to *be* on a high level mutually involve each other. Without this kind of awareness the mind may be patchy; it may be completely at home within a certain range of ideas and completely lost outside that range. Even direct awareness, however, has its levels. That at which insight is gained into such a phenomenon as gravitation involves character to a much less degree than does the kind of insight called "spiritual". The question of the adaptation of human character to its environment by the process of evolution, as the mind has been adapted, and of the ways in which it can free itself from that adaptation is however too large a subject to be entered into here. It diverges from the main issue that we are discussing. In the next chapter, however, we shall touch briefly on some practical examples of it.

A word may be said with regard to one point which would seem to be raised by the conception of direct awareness. Is it a means by which we can directly and infallibly know what is true—is it omniscient? This question involves difficulties which we cannot fathom. Awareness does not seem to be necessarily a form of cognition. It is rather a state of being mentally alive and awake to possibilities. At the same time we have evidence in the instincts shown by animals, and in what we call telepathy or extra-sensory perception among human beings, that facts can be in some way directly apprehended. What the limits of this faculty are we do not know; but it is certain that, however great the knowledge it could potentially supply, very little infallible truth enters the normally conscious mind and, in the process of entering it, often becomes distorted.

We may sum up by saying that with regard to life in our present world the incarnate self may be looked upon as an abstraction from the total self. Normal awareness is focused on the senses and its mode of acquiring

[1] *Ends and Means*, p. 287.

information is restricted to them and to inferences from the data they supply. Although the incarnate self is adapted to its world, it is not completely enclosed by the domination of matter. It is possible for this abstracted self to reintegrate with the self from which it has been abstracted in greater or less degree by withdrawing from its ordinary sense-fixation and by seizing and assimilating something of the greater self through the vague and shifting boundary of normal consciousness. But in order to do this, it must free itself from the instincts which have of necessity been implanted in the adapted man. These instincts tie the self to the senses and the body and automatically resist any attempt to break away from them. This view of man is entirely at variance with the picture of man as he normally sees himself. In the latter view, man is to all appearances a piece of psychically endowed organic matter—an atomic entity complete in itself. Our natural instinct urges us to accept this sense-given picture as the entire man just as it urges us to accept the sensible world as the entire universe. Both are acceptances necessary for practical life; but both are none the less delusions. Man, as we see him, is no more a complete entity than is the sense-presented world. He is given in his totality neither within our sense-field nor within our comprehension. Selfhood is rooted in the infinite: it cannot be destroyed: its nature cannot be conceived. From time immemorial the intruding enlightener has stood behind the processes at work in men. It has been the messenger of the "Perennial Philosophy", whose truth only those who are under its influence can see.

The point which is emphasized at the conclusion of this chapter is that *the normally conscious man is not the whole.*

CHAPTER IX

ADAPTATION IN ORDINARY LIFE

NOW that we have reflected on the idea of mental adaptation, which psychical research at first disclosed, we have realized how necessary a factor it is in the evolution of man. It is time to look for further evidence of it in other departments of life.

Do human beings show by their behaviour in ordinary life that they are adapted to this world in mind as well as in body? In order to see man related to his world as Nature has made him, it is best to leave towns and crowded areas and to go out into the open. There we can not only see our fellow men as Nature made them: we can ourselves become at one with Nature. With the keen air blowing, perhaps with a hand on the tiller of a sailing boat, or with the lake and the mountains spread out in their beauty, we human beings are in our natural setting. The mind and the whole man then melts into unity with its surroundings. We are projected into the outside world. Self-awareness vanishes, and we and our surroundings become one. A feeling of confidence inspires us; we are at home. We can, indeed, leave this natural state of mind and ascend, if we wish, to a reflective level of awareness. If we do, we look down on the practical self and reflect upon it. We realize that our own practical self is blended with its surroundings, and that this is a necessity without which no primitive or wild life could be in a state of ever-readiness to make quick reactions and to act upon external things in the efficient way on which its existence depends. The practical being is not a detached onlooker or an actor operating on the world from without. That would be too clumsy a relation. It is integrated with the world about it; it is suffused and absorbed into it; it is not merely *in* it but *of* it. Reflection shows us how essential it is that the external world should, for any mind engaged in practical living, appear to be absolutly simple and appear to be the whole. Puzzles and difficulties would prise apart the observer and the observed and would create a fatal dichotomy. For *Homo faber*, the mind, the muscles, the senses and the external world must be fused into a single whole.

Another thing strikes us as we reflect: the senses blended with the mind could tolerate no rival. Instinct is widely diffused throughout the animal world. It is also at work in ourselves; it plays a leading role in adapting our own minds to their surroundings. Could not this mysterious power, we wonder, if it had been further developed by Nature, have helped man immensely to gain the practical ends towards which he struggles with so much difficulty by trial and error? A cat, taken to a strange place in a basket, and then released, is able to find its way home. But no such instinct helps man when he is lost in a forest. In a thousand ways, instinct could have enabled man to take short cuts to his goals. Man does indeed possess certain instincts; but, in comparison with animals, they play a minor role.

But once we have grasped the hierarchical nature of the human personality, which was discussed in the last chapter, it becomes clear that any such assistance from instinct would have prevented the influx of the higher awareness, which has been responsible for the growth of intelligence. We see that instinct on any large scale would have been destructive to the development of reason. Nature's choice for man was the development of intelligence. His growing mind was focused, like a searchlight, on the external world. It was linked with the senses and its development was founded on the spatio-temporal. Thought and the senses form a highly specialized combination. This we see on every hand if we examine ourselves and our fellow human beings. The sailor is a good example. He is a very actively minded person, for ships and the sea need watching. He projects himself into his surroundings completely, thought and eyesight acting together like a single instrument. This fusion is only possible because the external world has been made to appear attractive to the practical mind by its apparent simplicity and objectivity. In the world thus prepared by Nature, the sailor is confident: he feels completely at home. So it is with all those engaged in practical tasks, the builder, the plumber, the garage-mechanic are equally confident in their work. They are never perplexed by incorrigible problems. They master every situation that arises: they take in at a glance all its principal features: they see how the job can be done with the maximum economy of material and labour: they foresee future contingencies and make allowances for them: they make difficult and intricate estimates and all with an air of serene ease and confidence. No one at work in the practical world is permanently hesitant, confused or baffled; for the belief which Whitehead tells us is the key of success in science is everywhere justified in practical life—the belief that every secret is a secret that can be unveiled. Because experience justifies this belief, confidence, *savoir faire* and assurance of success are the characteristics of the practical man. The booking-clerk puts down tickets and change with the rapidity and accuracy of an automatic machine: the train runs at sixty miles an hour over a tangle of points and crossings. All have been oiled and properly set, nuts have been tightened, tyres and axles examined, human eyes and brains have mastered the difficulties and have dealt with them all. In these matters there is no sense of bafflement, no insoluble puzzles arise, nothing causes men to hang back.

No doubt people will say that there is nothing remarkable about this. These men, they will say, have learned their work and they do it: that is all. But in the very saying of this we exhibit the bias of our own minds. All this to us is obvious and has no significance. But if we take tight hold of ourselves and become critical, we see that these apparently common-place things are, in reality, highly significant. People behave in this way only when mind and body are acting in unison as Nature designed them to do. Take the mind away from its physical interactions and it will behave very differently. At once it loses this facile ability and self-confidence, this wonderful power of achieving success. "We see men frequently dexterous and sharp enough in making a bargain, yet, if you reason with them about matters of religion, they appear perfectly stupid."[1] It is true that Locke goes on to say: "I am apt to think that the fault is generally mislaid upon nature." But surely not; for it is Nature's skilful adaptation for the purpose of action which lies at the bottom of it. Nor is it only that mental efficiency, with the majority, is far greater in practical than in abstract matters: the mind refuses to admit the existence of diver-gent problems which cannot be provided with answers that the intellect can grasp. Confronted with a divergent problem, people at once ask: What is the explanation? If they are told that the first steps in a solution can be followed but that after that the problem lapses into unanswerable questions and becomes unintelligible, because it involves that which lies outside our experience, the questioner rebels. There *must* be an explanation, he insists, only we have not yet found it. He will not recognize that the familiar world is limited and that some problems go beyond and elude our intellectual grasp for ever. Problems connected with the nature of time, especially that raised by the evidence for non-inferential fore-knowledge afford an example. They are assumed to be, in principle, soluble by our intelligence; and the tendency of the mind is to seek for the solution in some hypothesis of a geometrical or mathematical kind in-volving additional space-dimensions or something of the kind. That is to say the mind endeavours to pull the problem into the region of things which it recognizes and understands and assumes that the solution *must* lie there. As Bergson said: "All the operations of our intellect tend to geometry as the goal where they find their perfect fulfilment." Geometry would naturally appeal to the mind that is always dealing with solid objects located in space. But we do not see that the kind of solution we offer depends upon *our* mental structure.

[1] Locke, *The Conduct of the Understanding*.

We may be inclined to ask why the questions and problems which arise in practical life are simpler than those we meet with in reflective thought. They would not be simpler if Nature had allowed the practical mind to pursue them into the background; but she compels the practical mind to stop short by providing it with apparent finality. Thus the mind acts like a glass through which we see everything. In matters concerning the world of practical life it acts like a lens bringing the whole scene into a clear focus and making it appear self-complete. In remoter matters it acts like a distorting glass. But we are able to leave the adapted level of consciousness, at least partly, and to rise to higher stages of awareness. The poet and the artist do so, though not of course completely or consistently. Their relations with life are often far more strained and difficult than those of human beings who are immersed in the practical world. The mechanic, whistling at his job, as he masters his surmountable difficulties, exemplifies man adapted to his world. The poet, reducing his thoughts to words in stress and pain, exhibits a mind at grips with things that will not easily enter the human nursery. The truly sensitive artist is distraught in the very same circumstances in which ordinary people feel most at home; for he is at work in a region in which adaptation hinders rather than helps him.

Another significant feature in the human mind is that it prefers argument to raw contact with reality. It feels at home when arguing within a set of fixed rules, and following a chain of deductive reasoning. But it does not like having to appeal to unfamiliar experience. While it is true that science owes its existence to the partial overcoming of this tendency, yet scientists, when faced with empirical experience that they do not expect, show a preference for *a priori* argument rather than empiricism with which to deal with what is new. Logic, mathematics and analysis appeal to the mind far more than contact with brute fact. But argument, unless constantly checked by appeal to experience, tends to degenerate into a kind of game in which the object is not so much to arrive at the truth as to score dialectical points against an adversary. The mind, in other words, is guided by its own innate tendencies rather than by facts which are independent of it.

The adaptation of the human mind, and, indeed, of the human being as whole, to its world is reflected by the channels in which human interest naturally flows. Physical adventure exercises a strong attraction because, in it, the body and the mind work together in unison, as Nature fitted them to do. Geographical exploration, mountain-climbing, sport of all kinds, political intrigues and rebellions, war—these and similar occupations call forth from the average man the highest pitch of effort and produce the maximum of mental as well as physical efficiency. Enthusiasm, time, energy, money and skill are readily forthcoming for projects of this kind. It is a mass-characteristic. Millions will spend their money, will travel long distances and stand for hours in queues to watch a football match; for here physical and mental excitement are combined.

It is not the intrinsic value of what is achieved which calls forth the heroic efforts spent on these things: it is the satisfaction which they afford to the natural man. Why were Scott and his companions willing to sacrifice everything in order to penetrate the frozen wastes of the Antarctic? Why was Lawrence unable to resist the call of Arabia? Why did Whymper risk his life to stand on the peak of the Matterhorn? Why did Columbus spend years of wearisome effort in collecting the tiny fleet in which he sailed out into the unknown West? It was not the desire for fame: for fame is uncertain and comes only to the few; whereas millions respond to the call of adventure. There is the call of the sea, which offers a life of hardship and danger: yet how hard it pulls. We must remember, too, the fleet of miscellaneous craft which willing hands drove into the jaws of death at Dunkirk.

These examples, however, reveal something further besides the working of Nature's adaptation in human beings: there is more here than the satisfaction of *Homo faber*. There is an element of idealism. Such adventures elicit self-sacrifice, even to death; and this shows that more is involved than the psycho-physical man. Idealism comes from above and dips down into the psycho-physical; or the psycho-physical rises to make contact with idealism. Whichever way we look at it, we can see that something more is at work than the adapted personality of *Homo faber*. It is true that man is firmly interlocked with his environment: but it is also true that there is an element in him which is not thus interlocked. After all, if the interlocking were complete, man would be an automaton like the ant. We obtain a glimpse here from practical life of the fact that man is hierarchical and that it is the interaction of different levels of consciousness which makes the human being so puzzling. Adaptation from below combines with the Intruder from above.

The mind of man is thus partly a tool, pragmatic in its construction, yet partly more than a tool. Looking again at active human beings in the world, we see the adapted level of their minds imposing short-term views over long-term views. The prize that glitters in the foreground stimulates immediate effort: the long-term objective is eclipsed by it. It seems worth a great risk to plant a national flag on some barren rock or frozen waste, to win an international competition, or to travel faster than sound.

G

But it does not seem worth while to put forth much effort to gain light on human questions which are of fundamental importance. The ultimate nature of the human being and its destiny would, if seen from a standpoint aloof from the practical world, appear to be worthy of the most strenuous investigation. We could find out much more about these things by making a concerted effort. Hindu and Sanscrit scholars could marshal the written wisdom of the ancient East and possibly obtain access to unwritten sources. This they could place at the disposal of philosophers and theologians for careful comparison with the knowledge of the West; while Greek and Hebrew scholars, collaborating with them, could compare the study of the Bible and the origins of Christianity with these. The records of mysticism in East and West could be collected and placed in comparative form. The evidence of psychology and psychical research could be put in proper relation to these studies; and the ancient religions of Europe and the Near East could be considered in conjunction with the whole. Thus the wisdom of East and West, together with modern science, could be combined into a synthetic whole. If this were done without distorting prejudice, our outlook on the world and on humanity would be very different from what it is to-day and much would have been done to bring our perspective into line with reality. Its effect on the social conditions of the world might well be incalculable; for the human individual would be seen in its true light instead of only from the limited standpoint of science. Government and the structure of society depend, in the long run, on the conception formed of the nature of man. Probably if this were done with whole-hearted zeal, and the results digested by the world at large, the new conception of man and of the universe would profoundly alter the political and religious structure of the world and would bring the dreams of social reformers nearer to fruition than could be effected by any other means. To collect and correlate this information might cost as much as a couple of battleships; but it certainly will not be done, for the constitution of the human mind stands in the way. It is the mind, as it is adapted to the world, which decides the relative importance of different objectives in human eyes. War, political intrigues, economics, sensebound ideologies loom large, and the efforts of the majority is poured into these; while the cosmic perspective is dismissed as academic trifling. Thus, adaptation is the main factor which dominates the human situation.

It is not suggested that mankind should be urged to place fundamental considerations of this kind first. Such a proposal would be ineffective. The important point is that we should be, and we can be, *alive* to the situation. We ought to realize what it is that controls our affairs and assigns value to our various objectives. Humanity will not change its nature because it is in its interest to do so. That is an illusion which many ideologists accept with facile lack of criticism. Such people preach their doctrines and strive to put them into practice without realizing what the human being is and without knowing that they themselves are thinking in the grip of *Homo faber*. But it is possible for those who are able to survey the human scene from a comparatively untrammelled point of view to realize how matters stand. If they do so, they are in a position to provide a chart and compass, which others, in time, may be persuaded to use and which may be extremely useful in the difficult times which undoubtedly lie ahead.

The adapted character of man shows itself in yet another direction. Consider how we distribute our sympathy. The whole personality, up to a certain level, has been adapted. Emotion has been encased by adaptation in an armour-plated shield. If it were not so, we should be quite unfitted to live in this perilous world or to meet its shocks and horrors. It is not that human beings are devoid of sympathy, but that the expression of sympathy has to be overlaid and restrained. We bear the troubles of others with remarkable fortitude; but that is largely because we have acquired a stiff emotional resistance. We are also courageous in bearing our own troubles. When tragedy occurs, the appropriate response would be to reel back, stricken with grief and horror. We do not do this: we react in adapted fashion. Stubbornness, coolness, tenacity, fortitude, courage, determination—these are the qualities which it is necessary to encourage and push to the fore. Moreover, we must always be ready for *action*. We must not allow ourselves to be ousted from our position of control. If news arrives that an acquaintance has ended a life of tragedy with suicide, the ordinary man will respond to it with: So-and-so's had a raw deal, while he picks up his golf-clubs and goes out. This is the normal, sensible reaction to tragedy. We accept it uncritically and therefore we do not realize that it is *adapted* reaction. It would be a most inappropriate reaction if it were not for the peculiar conditions of life in a material world. The behaviour we accept as "normal" is, in reality, highly specialized behaviour; but we do not see it. The same specialization assigns to matters their relative importance. Ask an average man some large and general question, such as whether he thinks our present civilization is likely to last another twenty years. Lighting a cigarette, he will say: Tough problem, that! But ask him about something smaller and more immediate, such as a question about contemporary politics, and he will take the cigarette out of his mouth and begin to talk seriously. Yet our complex life has, in reality, transcended the level of the adapted mind and needs judgment and control from a higher level of the personality. As Albert

Schweitzer wrote some time ago: "The spirit of the age drives us into action without allowing us to attain any clear view of the objective world and of life. It claims our toil inexorably in the service of this and that end, this and that achievement. It keeps us in a state of intoxication of activity so that we may never have time to reflect and to ask ourselves what this restless sacrifice of ourselves to ends and achievements really has to do with the meaning of the world and of our lives. And so we wander hither and thither in the gathering dusk formed by the lack of any definite theory of the universe like homeless, drunken mercenaries, and enlist indifferently in the service of the common and the great without distinguishing between them."[1] We need more help from our supra-adapted selves.

Most of the subordination to instinct, which is necessary for practical survival, is inevitable; yet we *can* struggle and in some degree succeed in understanding how to plan our lives from a higher level of insight with greater freedom and more light.

Again, the influence of the adapted part of man shows itself in the effects produced by different kinds of knowledge. Some kinds of knowledge are geared to action while others are not. Everyone *knows* the futility of war and the appalling suffering and loss which are its only results to-day. In one sense this has been known for centuries. I believe that Virgil uses the phrase: *Scelerata insania belli* (The criminal madness of war). Even dictators know it, but this does not restrain them from making military war when they feel strong enough to do so and from waging a "cold" war of nerves when they do not. An intelligent being, unadapted to our world and viewing it from without, would assume that human beings, with their past experience, would no more dream of making another war than of thrusting their hands into fire. Yet, in this matter, knowledge and past experience have so far counted for nothing; wars and preparation for wars have gone on just as if no one knew anything about its disastrous consequences. Preparation for war and actual war of a non-military kind are in full activity to-day, although it is well known that if military war breaks out again our civilization is unlikely to survive. But the combative tendency in man is strong and instinctive and operates on one level, while this knowledge is held at a higher level of consciousness, which has much less influence on action. It is because the instinct for conflict, for power, or for material gains transforms itself into *immediate action* that war fills the pages of human history; while enlightened knowledge that these things lead to disaster struggles feebly to moderate the force of instinct; but it works on a higher and less effective level. The knowledge that war is

[1] *The Decay and the Restoration of Civilization.*

madness has inspired the few to construct institutions which they hope may render this knowledge effective, such as the League of Nations in the past and the United Nations Organization in the present; but the instinctively inspired actions of the majority have so far wrecked their efforts. Reason is clearly no match for instinct ingrained into the roots of the mind even when the victim of instinct "knows", at a certain level of consciousness, that he is bringing about his own destruction. If one nation discovers that another has stolen a march on it with regard to some military weapon, this knowledge produces immediate action. Brains and enthusiasm are poured into the task of catching up with the rival; everyone concerned works with readiness and a maximum of ability; for knowledge and action are in gear.

Another example of knowledge rendered ineffective, because instinctive impulses at a lower level of consciousness oppose it, is the well-known fact that if everyone were to give up his habits of grasping selfishness, of jealousy and self-centred vanity, etc., and were to treat his neighbours with self-sacrificing generosity and good will, the world would be transformed into a comparative paradise. Christian and other teachers have tried to instil this into mankind for centuries; but the knowledge thus disseminated has not resulted in action on any considerable scale. The majority of mankind continues to behave according to its lower-level characteristics, as it always has done, and so keeps up its supply of self-created misery and relegates the hope of a happy and contented humanity to the world of dreams. All this shows that human actions, as they appear in the records of history, are more *caused* than *willed*. Yet they *can* be willed by any individual who succeeds in rising to a state of awareness which is relatively free from the influence of instinct. On the whole, however, willed action is interwoven with caused action.

Another example of belief which is not geared to action, because it does not refer to anything which is important for physical life, is the intellectual acceptance, which was general in medieval times, that sinners would go to hell. The hell presented was of such an appalling nature that one might have supposed that all who believed in it would have spent every minute of their lives in trying to avoid it. But their lives were neither better nor worse than those of human beings who did not believe in such a hell; for this belief occupied a level of consciousness too far removed from the adapted being to be geared to action. Again, people know that they are going to die; and this knowledge inspires actions of a terrestrial kind, such as the making of wills. But it is not powerful enough to deflect interest from this world to another. Up to the last moment of life, the interest of this world absorbs the ordinary person entirely. Death does not come home to realization in the way in which the things belonging to practical life come home to it. The human being is not only *in* this world; he is emphatically *of* it. Professor J. B. S. Haldane says, for example: "I am far more interested in the problems of biochemistry than in the question of what, if anything, will happen to me when I am dead."[1] This shows how Nature has succeeded in concentrating the mind on the world of the senses and in belittling the things that are of real importance. With many people golf, or bridge or sport, rather than biochemistry, occupy the field of principle importance. But in any case it is *this* world that claims the attention of man who has been adapted to it and sets his standard of values. Yet he is blind to his bias towards it.

The relations between the adapted and unadapted regions of the self are very complicated and no hard and fast line can be drawn between them. A man who has led a selfish and perhaps even a criminal life may, in a crisis, perform a noble act of self-sacrifice. Again, a man who is intellectually a materialist, believing in no religion, no absolute values and no future life may yet lead a life of kindly and moral virtue. This fact is often interpreted as meaning that morality needs no support from religion. But the truth is much more complicated. The materialistic beliefs are an intellectual profession which does not penetrate deeply into the self. But there is a deeper level of the self behind the superficial consciousness from which inspiration and insight and all that is truly original emanates. This deeper self has a grasp of the true situation whatever the intellect may decide; and it can also reach down, so to speak, from above and influence action, though not with the potency of adapted instinct. It is from this source, and not from intellectual beliefs that this kindness and morality spring, thus bringing the intellectual profession of the materialist into contradiction with his actions. But human behaviour is full of contradictions, and the human being is a patchwork of unreconciled elements. Behind the working of our rational mind lie forces which rise up to it from the instinctive level and also forces which descend to it from the unadapted level. Both can influence the mind unconsciously. An example of the latter kind is provided by the building of the medieval cathedrals. The great and prolonged effort which was put into these permanent messages in stone can surely not be accounted for solely by the intellectual beliefs which their builders held. The real driving force must have been unconscious; for the cathedrals have a significance which cannot be expressed in language. They were not built to provide places of worship in the deliberate way in which a modern government might decide on a housing scheme. If one sits in a cathedral, especially if it is

[1] *Possible Worlds*, p. 219.

empty, and, so to speak, *feels* it, the conviction comes home to one that it is the crystallization of a message that could not be expressed in words. No formal doctrine or dogma is enshrined in it but a reality which enters from beyond our life in time. It is this which must have inspired the planners and builders to carry on their long and laborious work—although they could not have said as much if they had been asked.

That there are different degrees and kinds of knowing is frequently brought home to us by our experience of the difference between verbal admission on the one hand and true grasp on the other. We may have repeated some statement all our lives and have argued about it and have been fully convinced that we understood it. Then, suddenly in a flash, its full significance will come home to us for the first time. This is not because we have learnt more about it in the ordinary way, but because we have suddenly become more *aware*.

We are, in fact, constantly changing our degree of awareness from that of *Homo faber*, when we are intensely absorbed in action, to that of the contemplative when we see into the heart of things: but we are apt to change our level so rapidly that we are scarcely conscious of doing so. To some extent we can however change our standpoint at will. Let us now make the experiment of looking at two typical human beings from two different levels of awareness. First let us assume the practical level which we normally occupy during our social or business activities. From this standpoint, let us assess a man of the world, who himself lives his life, or most of it, on this same level. We see before us a sane, balanced person, eminently sensible, sound in judgment, well versed in humanity, a good judge of character, possessed of tact and common sense, free from eccentricities or crankiness, a good mixer, shrewd in business—just the man to be entrusted with a responsible position. He appears to be typical of what a human being should be. Still retaining our point of view, let us then turn our attention to a different type. Let us look at a person who frequently vacates the practical level of awareness and rises to a different plane. He may be a poet, an artist or even a God-possessed mystic. What a different kind of man! How unpractical, how lacking in common sense and sound judgment, how given to idle fancies, how devoid of balance and all sense of proportion. He seems to be always falling foul of society and ignoring its conventions: he has no idea of business-values and is seemingly dead to the things of real importance in life. Trying to hitch his wagon to a star, he becomes an eccentric and a misfit.

Now let us change our level of awareness and look at these two human specimens again from a freer standpoint. As we rise, they appear to us to be different. The man of the world now seems to be a creature who lives in a groove and is unable to see over the sides of it. Within this groove, he is admirably adapted to conditions: but his qualities fit him to deal only with things which are immediate. Where anything larger is concerned, he is, as we can now see clearly, a childish and incomplete personality. His sense of values is canalized: he is absorbed to a ridiculous extent in trifles: he throws immense energy into things which, we now see, do not greatly matter, while he has no energy at all for things of real importance. He is blind to them: he fails to realize their existence, plodding along like a horse in blinkers. For him, trifles loom larger than eternal life and material values vastly outweigh spiritual values. In fact, we now see him as a being who is only half-conscious. Like a sleep-walker, he is unaware of the things of real importance with which he is surrounded. He throws his energy into a small abstraction of the things that matter least. As we see him now, he brings to mind a scathing remark made by Aldous Huxley: "Because a large part of our personality is naturally imbecile, because we like this imbecility and have a habit of it, we have built ourselves a largely imbecile world to live in."[1] But we also see that he is like this because adaptation is a prime necessity.

If we turn our attention to the unworldly individual, we also see him differently. He is one of the fortunate people, as we see him now, whose eyes are not entirely hooded with blinkers. He has looked beyond the illusions of the man of the world: he has looked over the sides of the groove and has seen something of what lies beyond. He is distressed and ill at ease just where the man of the world is most comfortable: he is at home when he realizes things of which the latter is ignorant. While the man of the world is congratulating himself on his "realism", the mystic sees that this so-called realism is shot through with illusion. In his elated moments, the unworldly dreamer experiences bursts of insight in which he becomes vividly aware of truths that cannot be expressed in words. Then, common-sense men of the world appear to him, in their self-confident satisfaction, like gaping goldfish in a bowl.

Moving thus from one level of awareness to another, we see that the ordinary world looks like Bedlam only when we see it from above. While we are in it, it appears perfectly sensible and sane. The difference between the two points of view is due to the adaptation of our mind and the partial escape from it.

The attempt to rise towards spiritual enlightenment tears the being away from the conditions of adaptation: yet the adapted characteristics follow and influence and hamper the higher characteristics. "The good that I would I do not", said St. Paul, "but the evil that I would not, that I

[1] *The Perennial Philosophy*, pp. 58-9.

do. . . . O wretched man that I am!" Obviously this state of internal conflict is inseparable from life in this world unless human beings descend to the fully adapted condition of an ant-community. Once the human being is seen from the standpoint we are adopting, free from the mental conventions of the specialist, the falsity of the view that he is an atom of consciousness thrown off by the body is apparent. There is nothing atomic about man except his body. His mind is more like a band on a continuous spectrum, nowhere coming to a definite end. His essence or self is incomprehensible and indefinable. It is because man is such an extraordinary synthesis, partly tied by adaptation and partly free, that his internal conflicts are perennial. And the state of conflict in the individual is reflected in society. The ideal of a social Utopia, blessed by permanent stability, peace and contentment, is an illusion based on a total misconception of the nature of man. His eternal restlessness and conflict is in itself a proof that he is not a creature belonging to this world only. The common-sense view of the human being, and of human problems, arises from illusions which Nature endeavours to force upon us. But it is inevitable that those who are most under the influence of the adapted mind should accept the common-sense view as final. The fundamental task of religion has always been to let in light which shows the common-sense view to be erroneous. The majority go on trying to evolve perfection in this world out of material which is innately and permanently imperfect and imperfectable.

Our survey of human behaviour in ordinary life has shown the adapted mind at work on every hand. It is not something which shows only here and there: it is everywhere and it is hidden by its very ubiquity. No technique of the specialist can reveal it because the adapted mind has been unconsciously assimilated into that technique and guides it towards a prearranged end. We cannot recognize adaptation and see what it is doing until we rise above the deflecting power of instinct. The deeper meaning of human life comes from beyond the range of the adapted mind, and the latter is incapable of seeing it. Until this is realized, the human picture remains one of baffling confusion and apparent senselessness. Only a vision of the deeper pattern can show that there is meaning behind this superficial and perplexing pattern.

In a review of a biography of H. A. L. Fisher, the following passage occurs: "Fisher had come to realize when he wrote it [A History of Europe] that the long record of European civilization reveals, not the workings of Providence nor the continuity of Progress, but a continual ebb and flow by which the summits of human achievements are alternatively revealed or obscured. He believed that events are shaped, not in accordance with any set of principles, but by contrast of circumstance with the dynamic, even daemonic, force of human personality. Confronted with a problem which has baffled greater men, he took refuge in a paradox, the paradox of the irrationality of *Homo sapiens*."[1]

But *Homo sapiens* is irrational because he is being dogged and hampered by *Homo faber*. Human rationality is not complete but is partial and problematical, shot through and through by instinct, struggling to rise to freedom amid violent oscillations, successes and relapses. Indeed, human life cannot be understood at all if it is assumed that the human being is the self-contained monad which it appears on the surface to be. Meaning flashes out only in proportion as intuition shows us something of the larger whole. History is puzzling and baffling. But, if human history be regarded as no more than a surface-pattern continuous with something beneath it, it begins to take on perspective. Dr. Fisher himself wrote: "The fact of progress is written plain and large on the page of history; but progress is not a law of nature. The ground gained by one generation may be lost by the next. The thoughts of men may flow into the channels which lead to disaster and barbarism."[2] But history gives a partial picture, not the whole: for human beings transcend the stage on which history is played.

Our sense of values is largely determined by adaptation, which places the things that matter for bodily well-being in the foreground; and our conception of the nature of things similarly rests on faculties constructed to serve a utilitarian purpose. We can rise above both these view-points by ascending the scale of awareness and seeing these things from above. Any considerable change thus effected would so thoroughly alter our perspective as to move us, in a larger sense, from a Ptolemaic to a Copernican outlook. The material universe would appear no longer as the centre but only as a fragment, while we ourselves would cease to be the atomic units we appear to be, in touch with reality only through our senses. *For the attainment of truth, everything depends on the level of awareness which has been reached by the individual.* This is the conclusion indicated by adaptation in ordinary life. We must now look for evidence of mental adaptation in other directions. We shall begin with the science of physics.

[1] David Ogg, *Herbert Fisher,* 1865–1940, reviewed by Edward Arnold in *The Times Literary Supplement,* August 16th, 1947.
[2] *A History of Europe,* p. v.

CHAPTER X

THE ADAPTED MIND IN PHYSICS

D OES the science of physics show traces of the adapted mind? The subject is, of course, almost entirely specialist and technical and it might seem at first sight as if there were no room for a non-specialist inquiry. But closer examination shows that there are principles in physics which can be appreciated without special knowledge of the subject. Also the assumption on which most of the sciences have proceeded, namely that their subject-matter is so thoroughly objective that very little account need be taken of the observer or experimenter, does not seem to be so necessarily unquestionable now that we have seen the extent to which adaptation of the mind influences ordinary life. While works on mathematical physics are meat for the specialist only, certain other books have been written which present physics to the layman in peptonized form. But even here the general reader is obliged, for the most part, to accept what is given by the specialist without criticism or comment. But there is one book which differs in this respect from most, namely Sir Arthur Eddington's work, entitled *The Philosophy of Physical Science*.[1] In this work, the author approaches his subject in the double role of specialist and non-specialist and thus invites the ordinary reader to reflect and even to comment upon what he says. That his approach is partly non-specialist is made clear by the following quotations from his book: "I am not among those who think that in the search for truth all aspects of human experience are to be ignored save those which are followed up in physical science. But I find no disharmony between a philosophy which embraces the wider significance of human experience and the specialized philosophy of physical science, even though the latter relates to a system of thought of recent growth whose stability is yet to be tested."[2] "The compartments into which human thought is divided are not so water-tight that fundamental progress in one is a matter of indifference to the rest."[3] "Generally I have abstained from mathematical formulae; this, however, is not wholly out of consideration for the general reader, but because those, whose minds are too much immersed in mathematical formulae, are likely to miss what we are here seeking."[4] "But in physics everything depends on the insight with which the ideas

---

[1] Tarner Lectures, 1938, Cambridge University Press, 1939.
[2] *P.P.S.*, p. ix.　　　　　[3] *P.P.S.*, p. 8.　　　　　[4] *P.P.S.*, p. viii.

are handled before they reach the mathematical stage."[1] "If I sometimes employ pure mathematics, it is only as a drudge; my devotion is fixed on the physical thought which lies behind the mathematics."[2] "It cannot be too strongly urged that neither relativity theory nor quantum theory are summed up in fool-proof formulae for use on all occasions."[3] Thus general, integrative thinking is to precede mathematical analysis; and the following sentence makes the non-specialist approach additionally clear: "When we put off the blinkers of the specialist, and view the two elements together in proper perspective, we shall find that they form a universe not unacceptable as an answer to the elementary questions which arise out of familiar experience, as well as to the more recondite scientific questions."[4]

Eddington's primary claim is startling: "I believe that the whole system of fundamental hypotheses can be replaced by epistemological principles. Or, to put it equivalently, all the laws of nature that are usually classed as fundamental can be foreseen wholly from epistemological considerations. They correspond to *a priori* knowledge, and are therefore *wholly subjective*.[5] He goes even further: "My conclusion is that not only the laws of nature but the constants of nature can be deduced from epistemological considerations, so that we can have *a priori* knowledge of them."[6] "Meanwhile I think that progress of the epistemological method has assured us that the constants of nature (apart from our arbitrary units) are numbers introduced by our subjective outlook, whose values can be calculated *a priori* and stand for all time."[7] "This means that the fundamental laws and constants of physics are wholly subjective, being the mark of the observer's sensory and intellectual equipment on the knowledge obtained through such equipment; for we could not have this kind of *a priori* knowledge of laws governing an objective universe."[8]

We might, perhaps, at this point, call to mind a remark made by Einstein: "How can it be that mathematics, being after all a product of human thought which is independent of experience, is so admirably appropriate to the objects of reality? Is human reason, then, without experience, merely by taking thought, able to fathom the properties of real things. In my opinion, the answer to this question is, briefly, this: As far as the laws of mathematics refer to reality, they are not certain and as far as they are certain, they do not refer to reality."[9]

One of Eddington's arguments is that the subjectivity of the physicist's findings are due to selection. The latter does not turn from his subject-

[1] *P.P.S.*, p. 55.   [2] *P.P.S.*, p. 74.   [3] *P.P.S.*, p. 56.   [4] *P.P.S.*, p. 16.
[5] *P.P.S.*, p. 57.   [6] *P.P.S.*, p. 58.   [7] *P.P.S.*, p. 78.   [8] *P.P.S.*, p. 104.
[9] *Sidelights on Relativity*, p. 28.

matter to examine himself and so is unaware of the selection which results from his limited senses and specialized mind. The principle of simple selection is illustrated by the metaphor of a fisherman who casts his net into the sea and proceeds to generalize about the nature of sea-creatures from an examination of his catch. He draws two conclusions, (a) that no sea-creature is less than two inches long and (b) that all sea-creatures have gills. He forgets the selective effect of his net, which would allow fish less than two inches long to escape through its meshes and would not be able to catch creatures without gills. The catch stands for the knowledge which constitutes the material of physical science; and the net stands for the sensory and intellectual equipment of the physicist.

From the quotations in which Eddington states the subjective character of physical laws and constants, one might imagine that he was saying that the net could create the catch. Indeed, the phrase "wholly subjective" is difficult to swallow and suggests that, taken literally, it is an exaggeration. He clearly does not intend to go as far as this however; for several passages in the book make it abundantly clear that he accepts the universe, as the physicist knows it, as being partly objective. For example: "I accept an objective element in physical knowledge on, I think, reasonably strong grounds, but not with the same assurance as the subjective element which is easily demonstrable. Selective subjectivism, which is the modern scientific philosophy, has little affinity with Berkeleian subjectivism, which, if I understand rightly, denies all objectivity to the external world. In our view the physical universe is neither wholly subjective nor wholly objective—nor a simple mixture of subjective and objective entities or attributes."[1] "We must therefore remember that not all our knowledge of the physical universe is comprised in knowledge of the laws of nature. The warning is not so superfluous as it seems. I have often found an impression that to explain away the laws of nature as wholly subjective is the same thing as to explain away the physical universe as wholly subjective. Such a view is altogether unfounded."[2] "I have referred also to an objective universe which cannot be identified with the universe of which the above-mentioned body of knowledge forms a description. The latter universe is, as we have seen, partially subjective and partially objective."[3] "It is not suggested that the physical universe is wholly subjective."[4] "Certainly an objective peg is necessary, but we need not suppose that it has disguised itself to resemble the cloaks."[5] ". . . as I have pointed out, the objective element bulks largely in the unsystematized part of our knowledge which also forms part of the description of the physical

[1] *P.P.S.*, p. 27.   [2] *P.P.S.*, p. 15.   [3] *P.P.S.*, p. 158.
[4] *P.P.S.*, p. 104.   [5] *P.P.S.*, p. 59.

universe."[1] There is something, then, in the physical universe which is not subjective in the sense in which the laws of physics are subjective. Eddington's critics have sometimes accused him of supporting a theory of extreme philosophical idealism; but this he explicitly denies when he says that selective subjectivism has little affinity with Berkleian subjectivism.

The main point in Eddington's argument, so far as a non-specialist can gather it, is that in physics the mind of the experimentalist and observer has a greater effect on the acquisition of knowledge than it is generally assumed to have, and that the progress of physics itself has brought this to light. It is not a question of whether Berkeley or the realists are right, but simply a question of the extent to which our minds act like tinted glasses. This recognition of the mind as a factor in natural science that cannot be neglected moves physics towards philosophy; so Eddington begins his book by saying: "Between physics and philosophy there lies a debatable territory which I shall call *scientific epistemology*."[2] "Theoretical physicists, through the inescapable demands of their own subject, have been forced to become epistemologists."[3] The mind—indeed the whole make-up of the observer, senses and mind together—inevitably act selectively on their material and thus bring in the observer as an essential factor in the situation. "The selection is subjective, because it depends on the sensory and intellectual equipment which is our means of acquiring observational knowledge."[4] "It is only with the recent development of epistemological methods in physics that we have come to realize the far-reaching effects of this subjective selection of its subject-matter."[5]

That is the real point at issue between Eddington and his criticis. How far does this subjectivity go? Eddington states significantly that physicists dislike the admission of epistemology into physics. "My impression is that general attitude might be described as *grudging acceptance*."[6] And again: "But there is an unaccountable reluctance to develop scientific epistemology systematically."[7] Why should this be so if the subject demands it? Surely it points to an unconscious factor in the background, which is endeavouring to make the reasoning mind resist it. Our reflections in Chapter VII have given us the clue to this, for, on the practical level, the human mind has been so indoctrinated as to accept the physical world as wholly objective. If this indoctrination be admitted, it would not be surprising to find that it crops up as a factor in physics. "Whatever we have to apprehend must be apprehended in a way for which our intellectual equipment has made provision."[8] It is hard to see how this statement can

[1] *P.P.S.*, p. 161.   [2] *P.P.S.*, p. 1.   [3] *P.P.S.*, p. 6.
[4] *P.P.S.*, p. 17.   [5] *P.P.S.*, p. 17.   [6] *P.P.S.*, p. 53.
[7] *P.P.S.*, p. 53.   [8] *P.P.S.*, p. 115.

be denied. Why, then, is it not frankly faced from the outset as an integral part of physical science? Why does it not enter into every branch of science as a matter of course? The only question is how important is this factor of our intellectual equipment? But, at the level of *Homo faber*, there is an innate resistance to admit that the observer is a radically important factor in any perceptual or observational situation. Is not this innate resistance showing itself by resisting the introduction of epistemology into physics?

Eddington refers to the intellectual equipment as a "form of thought" and asserts that physicists force physical knowledge into it after the manner of Procrustes, who stretched his visitors, or lopped them down, until they all fitted one bed. The question which this raises for the non-specialist is whether this Procrustean procedure goes on in physics unobserved because it is introduced unconsciously by an instinctive factor in the mind.

The specialist would have us believe that all the problems raised in modern physics depend for their solution on highly technical mathematics and he usually plunges into mathematics at once without any preliminary survey of the field. This is just where Eddington, in the book we are discussing, differs from the ordinary specialist. He is himself a highly competent specialist in the subject; but he sees that the non-specialist approach is essential as well. "Everything depends on the insight with which the ideas are handled before they reach the mathematical stage."

The frame of thought is represented as exerting itself in different ways. Eddington points to two methods of arriving at conclusions in physics, the *a priori* way and the *a postiori* way. Again he gives a simple illustration. If the articles in a house are examined and it is found that no article is worth more than sixpence, this information has been acquired by the *a postiori* method. If, on the other hand, the inquirer knew beforehand that the owner of the house had bought everything in Woolworth's, he would not need to examine the articles at all. He could say at once that nothing would be found in the house worth more than sixpence:[1] his knowledge would have been gained by the *a priori* method. "We may foresee *a priori* certain characteristics which any knowledge contained in the frame will have, simply because it is contained in the frame. These characteristics will be discovered *a postiori* by physicists who employ that frame of thought, when they come to examine the knowledge they have forced into it. Procrustes again! These foreseeable characteristics are not by any means trivial; they are laws or numerical constants which physicists have been at great pains to determine by observation and experiment."[2]

[1] Prices are not uniform at sixpence now.   [2] *P.P.S.*, p. 116.

Eddington gives examples of the way in which a physical law can be discovered either in *a postiori* or in a *a priori* fashion. "As an example we may take the law of increase of mass with velocity, which has been the subject of many famous experiments. It is now realized that this law automatically results from the engrained form of thought which separates the four-fold order of events into a three-fold order of space and an order of time. When knowledge is formulated in a frame which compels us to separate a time-dimension from the four-fold order to which it belongs, a component called the mass is correspondingly separated from the four-fold vector to which it belongs; and it requires no very profound study of the conditions of separation to see how the separated component is related to the rest of the vector which prescribes the velocity. It is this relation which is rediscovered when we determine experimentally the change of mass with velocity."[1] This illustrates what Eddington means in his summarizing statement on p. 104: "The subjective laws are a consequence of the conceptual frame of thought into which our observational knowledge is forced by our method of formulating it, and can be discovered *a priori* by scrutinizing the frame of thought as well as *a postiori* by examining the actual knowledge which has been forced into it."[2] We can see from this passage the sense in which Eddington uses the term "subjective". If you knew that the house had been furnished from Woolworth's, you might, in a sense, say that your knowledge about the value of the articles in it was "subjective". That would not prevent you from going into the house and checking this knowledge objectively by examining the articles afterwards. Perhaps we might introduce a little illustration of our own at this point. If someone who knew nothing about balances were placed in front of a balance, the mechanism of which was screened so that only the pans were visible, he would have to discover by experiment that when one pan ascends, the other descends in like proportion. This would be *a postiori* knowledge. But if he could see the mechanism and understood how it worked, he could predict the motion of the pans without making any experiment at all. This would be *a priori* knowledge. The law of the balance could thus be discovered either by the *a postiori* or by the *a priori* method. Knowledge and comprehension of the balance-mechanism would be the "frame of thought" which rendered the *a priori* prediction possible; and because it depends on this frame of thought, we could call the method, and even the knowledge, "subjective". We might call the law of the balance a "subjective law", although it could be verified empirically as well. Mental grasp of a new principle may render a law subjective because it makes it possible to attain

[1] *P.P.S.*, p. 116.   [2] *P.P.S.*, p. 104.

it by the *a priori* instead of by the *a postiori* method. But this is not to say that there are no objective facts behind the subjective law: it merely states that the state of mind or frame of thought decides in which way the law can be discovered. Besides laws there are special facts; and "the special facts," says Eddington, "are partly subjective and partly objective, depending partly on our procedure in obtaining observational knowledge and partly on what there is to observe."[1]

Another example is given of the influence of the frame of thought on the acquisition of physical knowledge. Subjectivity here turns upon the distinguishability of particles. This example takes us further on to specialist ground. As far as the non-specialist can gather, a certain co-ordinate was introduced into the study of particle-mechanics on the assumption that particles could be distinguished observationally from one another. The assumption of observational distinguishability is part of the furniture of the mind instilled into it by the experience of ordinary life; for molar bodies *are* observationally distinguishable. The study of particle-mechanics was apparently led astray because the mind unconsciously thrust this assumption into the field. It may seem incredible, Eddington says, that particles can be supposed to modify their behaviour according to whether we are able to distinguish them or not. "The objective particles are unconcerned with our inability to distinguish them; but they are equally unconcerned with the behaviour which we attribute to them partly as a consequence of our failure to distinguish them. It is this observable behaviour, and not the objective behaviour, that *we* are concerned with."[2] Here it seems that the frame of thought is unconsciously trying to make the facts fit in with its presuppositions.

A third case cited has to do with the cosmical number, N. Eddington says that he chose it because "the number of elementary particles had seemed least likely to be tainted with subjectivity." "But to the observer of observers, the exact value of the cosmical number is implicit in his first glimpse of an experimental physicist."[3] This example is, however, too technical for the non-specialist to tamper with.

The greater part of modern physics is admittedly the preserve of experts; yet there is one more principle which Eddington brings forward which can be appreciated without special knowledge. This is the method of analysis, or, as he calls it, the Concept of Analysis. The process of analysing, Eddington points out, is subjective in the sense that it forms a portion of the mental framework of the analyst; for the type of conclusion to which analysis leads is implicit in the method. The subject-matter before the analyst presents differences, and the aim of analysing is

[1] *P.P.S.*, p. 66.   [2] *P.P.S.*, p. 37.   [3] *P.P.S.*, p. 179.

H

to find an underlying cause for these differences. If an explanation is found for the differences, it must be in some common principle which lies behind them; and when this common principle is reached, the disparity has been resolved into a unity. So the "discovery" of underlying unity is *inherent in the method employed*: that is to say, analysis leads towards a foregone conclusion which is innate in the method, but does not necessarily reveal the truth about that which is analysed. *Selection* leads to the conclusions which the analytical method demands. If light from other sources were allowed to impinge, in convergent fashion, upon the matter analysed, the conclusion reached would be different. Science turns to the analytical method because the constitution of the human mind prompts it to do so. "I would not like to say that the concept of analysis is a necessity of thought, though it appears to be a necessity of any form of scientific thought. But, whether it is a necessary form or not, it has dominated the development of present-day physics, and we have to follow up its influence on the scheme of description of phenomena which has resulted."[1] In physics, it would appear that the particular system of analysis used has itself been selected; and this selective system Eddington calls the atomic concept, "or for greater precision, the *concept of identical, structural units*." This selective principle has resulted in the discovery that the physical world consists of a small number of fundamental particles: it is pursuing its course towards the ultimate "discovery" that a single entity underlies them. "I want to show, therefore, that the concept of identical, structural units expresses a very elementary and instinctive habit of thought, which has unconsciously directed the course of scientific development. Briefly, it is the habit of thought which regards variety always as a challenge to further analysis; so that the *ultimate* end-product of analysis can only be sameness. We keep on modifying our system of analysis until it is such as to yield the sameness which we insist on, rejecting earlier attempts (earlier physical theories) as insufficiently profound. The sameness of the ultimate entities of the physical universe is a foreseeable consequence of forcing our knowledge into this form of thought."[2] Again we read: "No sooner do we discover a difference between protons and electrons than we begin to wonder what makes them different. When this question arises, we always fall back on structure. We try to explain the difference as a difference of structure, the structure of the proton being presumably the more complicated. But if protons and electrons possess structure, they cannot be the ultimate units of which structure is built. Therefore the present variety of the end-products of physical analysis is an indication that we have not yet touched bottom;

[1] *P.P.S.*, p. 121.   [2] *P.P.S.*, pp. 123-4.

and we must push our investigations farther, till we reach identical units which will not challenge us to farther analysis."[1]

The fundamental question here raised is this. Is physics making progress towards an understanding of the objective nature of the physical world; or is it filtering out most of the character of that world and concentrating on the features which show through its own specially selected method of research? It is on this that one would like to hear the verdict of responsible critics. It is surely not necessary to go deeply into mathematical physics in order to understand whether the subjective factor which Eddington alleges to be behind the analytical method is there or not; or to arrive at a conclusion as to whether Eddington is right when he says that "we keep on modifying our system of analysis until it is such as to yield the sameness which we insist on." Do we? Cannot the expert in physics tell us that without delving into mathematics?

In still another way, Eddington shows how the conclusions arrived at in physics depend on the nature of the human mind and not wholly on that of the objective material it observes. When white sunlight is passed through a prism or made to impinge on a diffraction-grating, it is turned into a spectrum of colours. Have the coloured rays been *produced* by the prism, or were they in the white light all the time and were merely separated out by the prism? He quotes a passage from Preston's *Theory of Light*, which was formerly a standard text-book on the subject, in which it is stated that "Newton made the important discovery of the actual existence of colours of all kinds in the solar light."[2] But, as Eddington shows, this is an example of the frame of thought passing off its own assumption as an objective discovery. Whether the prism is conceived as *producing* the coloured rays or as *separating* out coloured rays which were there all along, amounts to no more than a double way of looking at one phenomenon. The one description is as true as the other. This shows how easy it is to project our mental processes into the external world; and the non-specialist cannot help wondering how far this kind of thing has insinuated itself into physics in general and, indeed, into science as a whole. When Eddington keeps on pointing to the influence of the mind on the conclusions of physicists, it is very hard to believe the entire question stands or falls with the validity of certain work in higher mathematics. But our previous survey of human behaviour is sufficient to show clearly that if Eddington is right, there would be a general tendency to escape from his conclusions, because the instinctive structure of the mind would be such as to resist them. "In introducing subjective selection, I attributed it to 'the sensory and intellectual equipment' used in obtaining observational knowledge. The inclusion of *intellectual* equipment may have seemed surprising. It is easy to see that our sensory equipment has a selective effect—that the nature and extent of our knowledge of the external world must be largely conditioned by its lines of communication with consciousness provided by our sense-organs. It is not so obvious that within the mind there is any further selection at work on the material thrust upon it by the sense-organs."[1] Exactly: the latter is automatically hidden.

Eddington does not himself state that the frame of thought is due to instinct. He leaves this an open question. "We might well leave open the question whether the forms of thought which dominate our outlook are *acquired* or *innate*. But I am inclined to believe that the ultimate root is definitely mental—a predisposition inseparable from consciousness."[2]

This passage comes rather near to suggesting that the influence which shows itself in physics is due to the biological adaptation of the mind. In speaking of errors of identification of observables, he quotes a physicist as saying: "*Observable* is a very elusive conception, and if we pursue the criticism to the end, we shall have to doubt a lot of things we do not in the least want to doubt."[3] The set, which instinct gives to the mind, reveals itself in candid admissions of this kind. There is no doubt that unconscious bias is at work. The question is: For how much is it responsible? "Even now," says Eddington, "we often find authors who are by no means ignorant of the reasons for the change of thought, propounding theories for which they claim the advantage that they involve only Newtonian conceptions. As though it could be an advantage to incorporate a fallacious view of the nature of observational knowledge!"[4] The mind always tends to cling to Nature's version of the world; and Newton's is closer to it than more recent versions.

The question at issue is whether innate tendencies in the observer's mind constitute a major or a minor factor in physics; and the important point to remember is that, whoever tries to decide this, is *himself* under the influence of these same innate tendencies. He will unconsciously try to make out that they are a minor factor. Can we, therefore, be quite happy about expert criticism of Eddington's views?

Ten years have elapsed since *The Philosophy of Physical Science* was first published; and no book has yet, to my knowledge, appeared in which the views put forward in it have been thoroughly and expertly examined. Yet few things could be more important than the issues which Eddington has raised. Two able reviews of the book have appeared, one

---

[1] *P.P.S.*, p. 114.   [2] *P.P.S.*, p. 132.   [3] *P.P.S.*, p. 54.
[4] *P.P.S.*, p. 55.

by Professor C. D. Broad in *Philosophy* for July, 1940: the other by Dr. R. B. Braithwaite in *Mind* for October, 1940. Professor Broad's clear summary of the book is, of course, given from the point of view of the professional philosopher and not of the physicist. The following paragraph from it, in particular, bears on the matter as we see it from our non-specialist point of view, "No one would wish to deny the possibility that some of the laws of nature, which appear to be merely inductive generalizations, are really consequences of certain facts about the sensory and intellectual equipment of human observers and the nature of experimental research and verification. But the question whether this possibility is realized, and, if so, to what extent, can be decided only by having the actual argument presented to one in each case in which it is alleged that a law can be epistemologically derived. The proofs of all such puddings are in the eating. Now the 'eating' can be done only by those who are able to chew and digest the extremely tough meat of Eddington's technical mathematical writings. A peptonized form of this is presented in his previous semi-popular book, *New Pathways in Science*: but, although the rather more detailed account of the Group Theory given in that does help one to *understand* much that is obscure from sheer sketchiness in the present work, it does not and could not put one in a position to estimate the validity of the arguments. Now in many cases this would not much matter. As philosophers we might reasonably be expected to accept as valid the technical deductions of so eminent an authority as Eddington, even though we could not follow the detailed reasoning ourselves. But, unfortunately, the situation is not so comfortable here. When I ask my expert colleagues whether I can safely accept Eddington's conclusions in these matters, they always answer in the negative. But this does not satisfy me. For I am quite convinced that their unfavourable answer is not based on a first-hand study of the arguments. It is quite plain that their attitude may be summed up in the sentence: 'This kind of thing *must* be wrong somewhere; but I can't be expected to waste my valuable time in finding out precisely where the mistake lies.' "[1]

We must certainly await the verdict of expert physicists upon the soundness of Eddington's mathematical physics: but the last sentence gives one an uncomfortable feeling. What is the origin of the assumption that "this kind of thing *must* be wrong somewhere"? Is not this *a priori* attitude likely to influence the conclusions that the specialist reaches afterwards? As non-specialists, we have the advantage of being able to consider one subject in the light of another, and we cannot forget that a mathematical demonstration of extra-sensory perception in psychical

[1] *Philosophy*, July, 1940, pp. 311-12.

research did not prevent many people from finding ways of setting the demonstration aside. May not this be prompted by an unconscious urge to defend the complete objectivity of the external world, which Nature subtly insinuates into the mind by instinct?

In his article in *Mind*, Dr. R. B. Braithwaite issues a warning: "The reader should be warned that not only is Eddington's main thesis unacceptable to most people whose judgment is of value, but a good deal of detailed work in mathematical physics upon which he bases his thesis is highly heterodox and does not form part of the agreed physics of to-day. The present reviewer is not in a position to judge whether Eddington's heresies will not be the corner-stone of the physics of the future; but he is bound to caution the unsuspecting reader." We must accept such caution from experts; yet it would be valuable if we could have a little more light on precisely what it is that renders Eddington's main thesis unacceptable to his colleagues.

A considerable part of Dr. Braithwaite's review is devoted to an examination of the structural concept of existence, which is highly technical and also appears to lie somewhat aside from the main issue which we are considering. Dr. Braithwaite, however, returning to this main issue, asks: "How can knowledge of laws which are not based on empirical facts be derived from observation of empirical facts?" This suggests to an observer, who is trying to take a bird's-eye view of the case, that Dr. Braithwaite has misunderstood Eddington from the start; for the latter states in at least half a dozen passages that there *are* objective elements in the physical universe, which can be empirically observed. The phrase "wholly subjective", which Eddington uses, is, however, admittedly confusing and suggests an overstatement of the case.

Commenting generally on Eddington's work, Dr. Braithwaite writes: "The effect produced upon me by the study of Eddington's three last books, *The Philosophy of Physical Science, Relativity Theory of Protons and Electrons, The Nature of the Physical World*, is similar to that produced by reading reasonable defences of theism by philosophers of repute (namely, many series of Gifford Lectures). It is impossible to deny that some weight should properly be attached to the various theistic arguments (namely, the cosmological argument or the argument from design); but the degree of this weight depends very largely upon one's previous attitude to the theistic hypothesis. Eddington's arguments are such that, if one was nearly converted beforehand to his thesis, the conversion might be completed: his evidence is all of the nature of circumstantial evidence, which supports an already strong case, but is otherwise capable of being explained away."

Surely this supports Eddington's general contention that the subjective element is a major factor in physics and is becoming more and more apparent. When physics began, the world it set out to elucidate was accepted without a single *arrière pensée*, as being completely objective. No one thought of suggesting that the discoveries made by early physicists could be rendered more or less acceptable according to the critic's initial state of mind. The work was being carried out in *Homo faber's* world of apparently complete objectivity. But as physics advanced, the mind of the investigator came more and more into the picture, the reason for this being that *Homo faber's* conception of the world was partly an illusion, and the illusion began to show through. The question that has forced itself to the fore in modern physics is this: What degree of influence are *we* exerting on what we discover? The philosophy of naïve realism, and science based on common sense, will no longer do when the problems to be investigated lie beyond the boundary of our world. If it is true, as Dr. Braithwaite says, that the cogency of Eddington's arguments depend upon our previous attitude of mind, this is surely an admission that modern physics has become impregnated with subjectivism.

Another critic of Sir Arthur Eddington's work is Professor L. S. Stebbing. Unfortunately her book, *Philosophy and the Physicists,* in which this criticism is principally contained, was published before *The Philosophy of Physical Science* appeared. But Professor Stebbing has a good deal to say about Eddington's previous works. Her criticism is to some extent confused by her attempt to deal with the work of Sir Arthur Eddington and Sir James Jeans together. "Both these writers," she says, "approach their task through an emotional fog; they present their views with an amount of personification and metaphor which reduces them to the level of revivalist preachers."[1] She is infuriated by the use of metaphor, which, she maintains, leads both author and reader to confusion. "Eddington, in his desire to be entertaining, befools the reader into a state of serious mental confusion." She complains that he does not show himself to be aware that exact thought cannot be conveyed in inexact language.

It is of course true that in technical science and in philosophy the exact use of words is essential. It is necessary when the matter dealt with can be completely conveyed in abstract language. But metaphor may help to clarify ideas which can be only partly grasped by the mind and cannot be fully or properly expressed by words with a defined, public meaning. Metaphor may also have a portmanteau use. For example it is much more convenient to use the word "nature" than to keep on repeating a long and exact definition of the conception which the word "nature" is meant to

[1] *P.P.,* p. 6.

convey. The use of metaphor is very old and was always accepted in pre-scientific times. If we were now to reject it as mere obscurantism we must reject with it the wisdom of many who lived before the scientific epoch began. Besides metaphor is innate in our language. We speak of a broad-minded man and no one asks for the breadth of his mind in inches.

Professor Stebbing does not appear to realize that Eddington approaches the subject of physics in the double role of specialist and non-specialist. One sometimes suspects that he may have produced metaphors with his tongue in his cheek. "He indulges in a specious personification of Nature", says Professor Stebbing, "ascribing to 'her' emotions, designs, frustrations and successes."[1] By doing this, she thinks he has confused himself as well as his readers. One imagines that if a booking-clerk had said to her: "This ticket will take you through to London," she would have upbraided him for using such a confusing metaphor and would have pointed out that the train and not the ticket would take her to London!

It seems strange, if one takes a wide survey of things, that anyone should believe that real progress in thought can be made by confining ourselves to the strict and publicly accepted meanings of words. How, by forcing exploratory ideas into the framework of rigid meanings that already exist, can we expect to enlarge our conception of reality? We may render our ideas apparently clear by doing this; but it is an artificial clarity, the clarity that results from forcing the unfamiliar into the familiar. By attempting to make progress wholly within the scope of existing words, we pile up "more and more about the less and less".

The subjective factors to which Eddington points do not appear only sporadically: they are pervasive and universal and it is only by dealing with general principles that they can be adequately discussed. Any critic who ignores the non-specialist aspect of Eddington's approach to his work and plunges into mathematical technicalities without thinking freely about the subject before applying the technical machine is likely to miss the point and to fail to see the wood for the trees.

Despite Professor Stebbing's vigorous protest against the use of metaphor, the attempt to draw ideas into the field of abstract language when these ideas, in their essence, transcend it, is itself a process which results in the unconscious creation of metaphor—and metaphor of a very confusing kind. For the idea which the mind attempts to understand is being represented by a ready-made idea—a metaphor which is inadequate to it. Also, synthesis is essential for the acquisition of truth. Eddington remarks: "The compartments into which human thought is divided

[1] *P.P.*, p. 15.

are not so water-tight that fundamental progress in one is a matter of indifference to the rest."[1] In other words, you must employ the method of synthesis if you wish your ideas to correspond with reality. But Eddington has made abundantly clear the operation of the adapted mind in physics. It will now be instructive to look at the subject of physics from a slightly different angle.

[1] *P.P.S.*, p. 8.

CHAPTER XI

PUTTING NATURE TO THE QUESTION

BACON announced the fundamental principle of science when he said that it consists in putting Nature to the question. He emphasized, in other words, the importance of learning from experiment instead of trusting to argument. In order to learn from experiment, the investigator endeavours to control the conditions relevant to the matter in hand, to vary them one at a time, and to note carefully the result. After many such experiments have been carried out by various individuals, the results are pooled and submitted to the process of induction; that is to say, some general law or principle is drawn from them. Sometimes, as in astronomical or geological science, it is not possible to make experiments: in that case the scientist has to rely on observation; otherwise the same process is followed.

In physics, observation and experiment have been employed for many years in an attempt to discover more about the nature of matter and of the physical universe in general. It will be interesting to take a rapid survey of the successive hypotheses about the nature of matter which have been put forward in the course of the development of physics. These hypotheses have been summarized in an admirably clear and succinct manner by Sir Edmund Whittaker in his Riddell Memorial Lectures for 1942, which were afterwards published in the form of a book entitled *The Beginning and End of the World*. It is from this book that the following quotations are made.

The first recorded attempt to look more deeply into the material world was made long before the age of modern science. It occurred to Lucippus and Democritus in the fifth century B.C. that matter might, in reality, be very different from what it appears to be. "They taught that matter consists of an infinite number of hard particles, the atoms, too small to be seen separately and moving about freely in otherwise empty space. The atoms are indivisible, unalterable, indestructible, and without beginning; they are all constituted of the same fundamental substance, but they exist in an infinite number of different sizes and shapes."

The Greek philosophers characteristically enlarged what would have been regarded to-day as a methodological postulate into a philosophy. They speculated as to whether the atoms were eternal and whether the universe which contained them was infinite. Matter, composed of eternal

and invariant atoms, became for them the basis of a materialistic philosophy. A similar tendency is, indeed, present with us to-day; but it
was more pronounced in the philosophical Greek mind than in our's,
which rests more on empirical science. The genius of ancient Greece
was not, however, canalized in one channel, but blossomed out in
many directions, so that a counterblast to the materialistic philosophy of
Democritus was provided by the philosophy of Plato.

This brilliant physical speculation remained for centuries a monument
to a period in which the human mind had risen to a height of speculative
freedom that enabled it to ask questions on every conceivable matter. It
was not until the nineteenth century A.D., however, that the next step in
the theory of matter was taken. "Dalton in 1808 taught that every
chemical element, such as oxygen and hydrogen, exists in the form of
atoms, the atoms of any one element being all exactly alike. When two
or more elements combine to form a chemical compound, the smallest
particles of the compound, called molecules, are constituted by the atoms
of the elements in some definite proportions: thus water is a compound of
hydrogen and oxygen, and a molecule of water consists of two atoms of
hydrogen and one of oxygen." Dalton's view of the atom was that it was
indestructible, ultimate and everlasting.

It is worth while to notice that the attempt to understand more about
the world presented by the senses did not lead to a simplification of what
was presented. "The simple, indivisible atom of Democritus has become a
fantastic and vastly complex whirl of entities or events, the description of
which undergoes changes every few years."[1] Once the stable simplicity
of Nature's sense-version of the world was broken through, the latter
became an ever-shifting complex. But the attempt to find out more
proceeded. In the science of physics, attention had been turned towards
the nature of light by Newton's classical experiments made towards the
end of the seventeenth century; and light, to the modern mind, came to
be regarded as physically objective, whereas in the time of Democritus
it was regarded as subjective.

The observed fact that light can be emitted by atoms at one place and
absorbed by atoms at another gave rise to two rival theories as to how this
came about. One was that small particles—corpuscles—were projected
by the emitting atom and absorbed by the receiving atom. The other was
that light was transmitted in the form of a disturbance in an invisible
medium in which all the atoms existed, something like a group of waves.
These two views, known as the corpuscular and the undulatory theories of
light, were maintained and discussed by their respective supporters from

[1] *M.M.,* p. 7.

the seventeenth to the nineteenth century. During the first half of the nineteenth century, it came to be realized that certain of the properties of light—diffraction and interference—could be accounted for satisfactorily only on the undulatory theory, so the latter came to be accepted as correct.

In 1867, William Thomson (afterwards Lord Kelvin) put forward the theory that the atom is a structure in the æther (the medium which the undulatory theory made necessary) of the nature of a vortex ring. It was observed that vortices might continue indefinitely in a frictionless medium; also that they actually rebounded on approaching each other, as atoms do. The mutual interactions of atoms could be illustrated by the behaviour of smoke-rings: the combination of two atoms to form a molecule would correspond to the union or pairing of two rings, which is also observed: and the phenomena of light could be represented by the disturbances set up by a vibrating vortex in the surrounding medium. The atom was thus no longer a tiny piece of material substance: it was a structure in a universal medium. Space was no longer a vacuum but a plenum. Science had taken one of its forward strides: but again the modern scientist had been forestalled by the ancient Greek. "The first æther-theory was indeed older than the atomism of Democritus, for it was put forward in the first half of the sixth century before Christ by an Ionian Greek, Anaximander of Miletus, who described it thus: 'The first principle and elementary constituent of all things is an infinite medium which is one and capable of motion: this medium is the source from which everything in nature is generated and into which everything returns.' "

The universal medium now became the centre of interest, and the attention of physicists was occupied by æther-theories. What properties must the æther possess in order to account for the physical facts? Attention was paid to a mathematical theory of solid bodies having various types of elasticity, the results of such studies being compared with the actual properties of light as revealed by experiment. Light seemed to have the character of the quiverings of a jelly when it is shaken. This did not agree with the vortex-theory of the atom, since that required that the medium in which it existed should be a perfectly elastic and frictionless fluid. What, then, was the physical character of this medium, the æther? It was found that, for the undulatory theory of light, it would need to have an enormously high density and rigidity, its density being a billion times that of water. This seemed a tall order. Could we all be walking about in a medium compared with which water would be the thinnest of vaporous clouds? The æther also had to be endowed with fresh properties in order to make it account for the phenomena of electricity and magnet-ism. Sir William Thomson devised another mechanical model with which, by the aid of the æther, to account for magnetism. But this gave no account of electricity; nor did the medium required by the model give any account of the properties of light; for the vortex-atom demanded that the medium should have the properties of a liquid and these would not support electro-magnetic radiation. So an attempt was made to account for electricity and magnetism in terms of the solid æther demanded by the latter. "This was achieved a few years later by another young Cam-bridge man, James Clark Maxwell. The model contrived by Maxwell, and published by him, in 1861-2, was a rather complicated mechanical affair of cells, vortices, and rolling particles, which was discarded when it had served its purpose; but it solved the problem he had set himself, namely to show that an æther, devised to represent electric and magnetic fields, would also propagate vibrations like those of light."[1] "Only the atoms of chemistry, with their chemical and gravitational properties, remained to be brought into the picture."

The word "atom" means "indivisible"; and the basis of the original atomic theory was that the atom was an *ultimate* particle. Since Dalton's time, however, it had meant the smallest portion of a chemical element which could have the chemical properties of the element. There was, on this view, no reason why such a particle should not be divisible into smaller particles, though such particles would not be particles of the element in question.

The nineteenth century, which had seen the invention of the steam-engine and the rise of the industrial revolution, was pre-eminently a century of mechanics; and so the physical theories put forward took the form of structures composed of "elastic strings, pulleys, gyrostats, ball-bearings, jellies, spheres immersed in liquid, vortices and so forth." The theories were built up of ideas which filled the minds of the physicists of the period. But Sir Edmund Whittaker adds: "The persistent endeavour of Thomson and his contemporaries to invent mechanical models of natural phenomena is a striking feature of the history of science in the nineteenth century: the explanation is to be found in their ultimate aim, which was the unification of the forces of nature."[2] So it was not only that nineteenth-century minds were preoccupied with mechanics. There was something else at work in them—the *urge to unify*: in other words to convert the divergent problem they had come across into a neatly con-vergent problem, ending in final simplicity, like those encountered by the mechanic and the engineer.

[1] *B.E.W.*, pp. 12-13. [2] *B.E.W.*, p. 12.

In 1897, J. J. Thomson showed, by experiments in the conduction of electricity through rarefied gasses, that the atom was not indivisible. He discovered particles much smaller than atoms, which were in fact torn out of them. These were called "electrons". A second type of particle was also found called a "proton". These particles, carrying opposite electric charges, constituted the atom. The atom was therefore definitely known to be not an ultimate particle.

The model now accounted for optical, electric and magnetic phenomena; but it did not account for gravitation. Newton, who had enunciated his law of universal gravitation in 1687, was opposed to the view of action at a distance: but between the time of Newton and Faraday, the action-at-a-distance school dominated philosophical thought. Here was an anomaly which needed to be brought into line with the phenomena already accounted for. This was accomplished by a scheme brought out by Lord Kelvin and G. F. Fitzgerald. They conceived a universal medium, having the properties needed to account for light, but full of "infinitely long, thin, straight vortex filaments running in every direction". This medium would transmit light, while electric and magnetic fields could be explained as the result of waves travelling along the filaments. The protons and electrons would be closed vortex-rings, "and the gravitational action between them would be due to the fact that each vortex-ring is associated with a motion extending throughout all space."[1] Thus all the entities of physics, then known, "were represented as vibrations, or stresses or structures in the æther".[2]

This æther, filled with vortex-filaments, was an ingenious model by means of which the physical phenomena known at the time when it was developed, could be explained. It did not prove that such a vortex-filled æther existed. This is an important point which should be carefully noted. What was actually known at the time was that the mathematical equations which applied to this particular kind of æther applied also to the observations which had been made on light, electricity, magnetism, chemical atoms and gravitation. But the same set of mathematical equations can apply to quite different physical phenomena. For example, a differential equation known as Mathieu's equation applies to the vibrations of a membrane which has the shape of an ellipse; but also applies to "the dynamics of a circus-performer, who holds an assistant balanced on a pole while he himself stands on a spherical ball rolling on the ground."[3] And there is the classical case of the equations of light which can be given a corpuscular or an undulatory interpretation. All that can be said, therefore, is that things happened *as if* this particular æther-theory were correct.

[1] *B.E.W.*, p. 16.   [2] *B.E.W.*, p. 16.   [3] *B.E.W.*, p. 17.

But in proportion as physical knowledge advanced, these mechanical models were superseded. There seemed to be overwhelming proof, however, of the existence of an æther, and its existence was firmly believed in by most nineteenth-century physicists. It was, in fact, the centre-piece of the physical universe for a long time; and Nature seemed to come forward to endorse its existence by offering a convincing proof. This proof was the observed fact that the velocity of light depends on there being a medium which transmits it. If we drop a stone into the water, it does not matter whether it is travelling obliquely. The ripples will spread just the same from the point at which it enters the water. It is the *water* which is responsible for them and for the rate at which they travel. "Suppose, for simplicity, that a double star consists of two components, one much larger than the other, so that the small one can be regarded as revolving round the larger. Then the velocity of the smaller star in our line of sight is sometimes greater and sometimes less than that of its more massive companion: if, therefore, the velocity of propagation of light depended on the velocity of the star emitting it, the velocity of light from the smaller component would be sometimes greater and sometimes less than the velocity of light from the larger component." But it is not; and the differences in velocity would be quite enough to be observed: so the reasonable conclusion is that there *is* an æther. Otherwise, how does light come to adopt a velocity which takes no heed of the velocity of the body which emits it? The fundamental principle of science had been applied—that of putting Nature to the question; and Nature had replied in perfectly clear terms, by endorsing the existence of the æther.

The æther, thus experimentally verified, was seen to be a medium filling all space and all matter. Such a medium must surely offer a criterion for the definition of absolute rest and absolute motion. If a body is absolutely at rest, this means that it is at rest with regard to the æther. The earth, then, cannot be at rest with regard to the æther for it is in continuous motion. It turns on its axis; it revolves round the sun; and the sun itself is in motion with regard to the other stars. If a particular point on the surface of the earth did happen to be at rest with relation to the æther at one particular moment, it could not continue to be so. Obviously the experiment to make next was to determine the velocity of the earth in relation to the æther.

Experiments were made—the famous Michelson-Morley experiment was made. The result was astounding. "To the surprise and confusion of the physicists, the result invariably obtained was that at all times and in all places, this velocity relative to the æther, of the laboratory in which the experiment took place, was zero. This seems impossible."[1] "When the explanation of the paradox was discovered, it was found to require the recasting of ideas that had always been held regarding space, time and velocity. In particular, it had always been supposed that if three bodies A, B, and C are moving in the same straight line in the same direction, and if the velocity of B relative to A is (say) 10 cm. a second, and the velocity of C relative to B is also 10 cm. a second, then the velocity of C relative to A is obtained by adding these numbers, that is, it is 20 cm. a second. It was now shown that this was wrong: the velocity of C relative to A is not 20 cm. a second, but differs from 20 cm. a second by about one part in 10^{19}."[2] This shows the danger of taking for granted more than bare observation shows. An assumption based on observation that seems quite unquestionable may turn out to be questionable after all.

The velocity of light relatively to A is the same as the velocity of light relatively to B, although A and B are moving relatively to one another. This experimental discovery destroyed the inference, seemingly so plain and inescapable, which had been drawn from the fact that the velocity of light is independent of the velocity of its source. The apparent proof of the existence of the æther fell to pieces. "Thus the universal medium out of which all things were supposed to be made, and which had played such a large part in natural philosophy since the days of Anaximander, was finally proved to be a theoretical impossibility."[3]

Perhaps we cannot say, in popular language, that the æther has been "debunked": but the kind of æther that can exist, if there is one at all, must be very different from the æther which was previously believed in. Einstein remarks: "We may say that according to the general theory of relativity space is endowed with physical qualities; in this sense, therefore, there exists an æther. According to the general theory of relativity space without æther is unthinkable; for in such space there not only would be no propagation of light, but also no possibility of existence for standards of space and time (measuring-rods and clocks,) nor therefore any space-time intervals in the physical sense. But this æther may not be thought of as endowed with the quality characteristic of ponderable media, as consisting of parts which may be tracked through time. The idea of motion may not be applied to it."[4] So that, at any rate, the æther of nineteenth-century physics has gone by the board. Experiment has rejected what experiment previously endorsed.

But the scientific method returns to the attack. Einstein says: "Now

---

[1] *B.E.W.*, p. 21.   [2] *B.E.W.*, p. 21.
[3] *B.E.W.*, p. 22.   [4] *Sidelights on Relativity*, pp. 23-4.

that science has failed to find any direct action of this æther on our senses, it has dropped the æther out of its stock of concepts, and finds that in doing so it can reduce the phenomena in question to complete order and consistency."[1] But how long will this order and consistency last?

Our attention is now called in another direction to the phenomenon called the "photo-electric effect", which resulted from the discovery of X-rays. It was found that X-rays cause electrons to be ejected from atoms, and in this process "the X-ray does not spread like a wave, but remains in a compact bundle like a particle." "This is only one among many phenomena discovered since the beginning of the century in which the behaviour of light seems to be corpuscular rather than undulatory."[2] These phenomena suggested that a return to the corpuscular theory of light, which was the one originally held, might be necessary. Yet, on the other hand, the interference effects still seemed to demand the undulatory theory. Light, as Eddington put it, seemed to be a wave on Mondays, Wednesdays and Fridays and a particle on Tuesdays, Thursdays and Saturdays. But in 1927 it was discovered that electrons, until then supposed to be genuine particles, could also produce interference and diffraction-effects precisely like those produced by light. "No one had doubted the status of the electron during the first thirty years after its discovery in 1897: it was believed to be a particle in the ordinary sense: that is to say a very small object having a definite position in space, and also a definite velocity. In 1927, however, it was discovered that streams of electrons could yield diffraction and interference effects, precisely similar to those which are so well known in connection with light, and which have always been regarded as the strongest proofs of its undulatory nature. Thus it appeared that the electron, like light, has a dual character: it is not simply a particle, but has two aspects, particle and wave. It was now recognized that this duality was something fundamental in physics: that the ultimate constituents of the universe are neither pure particles nor pure waves, but have properties which are associated with both these conceptions."[3] The name "corporundal" was suggested for an entity having this dual character.

There is some resemblance between this modern view and the early view of Democritus, who thought that matter consisted of different kinds of ultimate particles which were indestructible, indivisible and eternal. Science to-day recognizes different kinds of particles—photons, electrons, positrons, neutrons, mesons, and neutrinos; but these differ from the

---

[1] *The Mathematical Aspect of the Universe*, p. 12.   [2] *B.E.W.*, p. 22.
[3] *B.E.W.*, p. 23.

particles of Democritus in two respects. It seems probable that they can all be created or destroyed; and they are not tiny bits of matter: they have not a definite position in space which is correlated with a definite velocity, as bits of matter have: form and location in this sense do not apply to them. They cannot be pictured by the mind but have to be represented by mathematical expressions. All that comes to light about the world in this ultra-microscopic region is a statement of quantitative relationships, true no doubt, but true in what sense? We cannot help recalling what was said about Mathieu's equation. Supposing we know that it applies to *something* in the world which is not presented to us by our senses in any form, what is the objective reality to which it applies? There is, after all, a considerable difference between an elliptical membrane and a variety artist! The monadic type of idea, with which Democritus started, was a mental concept established in the human mind by its experience of ordinary matter; and physicists all through the nineteenth century formed hypotheses of a mechanical kind, because their minds naturally turned to mechanics. They submitted them to experiment for verification and *they were verified*, until further knowledge suggested a different hypothesis and a differnt kind of experiment. Then the new hypothesis was verified too, although it contradicted the old one. So the progress of physical science has gone on. Our conception of the physical world, which was quite simple and definite as Nature presented it, has become perpetually more elusive and more and more difficult to grasp. Also it has been reduced to a quantitative skeleton. "Modern mathematical physics, then asserts that, in the last analysis, the external world is constituted of entities (the corporundals) which have no permanent existence, no shape, and no location, and which cannot be pictured in intuition or described otherwise than by mathematical formulæ."

And what are we to gather from these quantitative relations? Are they the foundation of the independent world? Or is their apparently central importance due to the fact that we have *selected* them? Sir James Jeans took the view that the foundation of the physical world is mathematical and that its creator is a super-mathematician. Sir Arthur Eddington took the contrary view that the mathematics were not present in physics until *we* put them there. In this connection a remark of Bergson is significant: "All the operations of the intellect tend to geometry, as to the goal where they find their perfect fulfilment."[1] It suggests that the human mind selects from the real world those aspects that appeal to it.

The history of physics shows that the more the knowledge of the subject grew, the more the ordinary conceptions with which the human

[1] *C.E.*, p. 222.

mind was furnished, failed to explain the facts. "Now the notion which has always been at the root of attempts to find physical reality, *in esse* *secundum rem,* is that Nature is a mechanism, like a gigantic and complicated clock: and the object of the physical investigator was, so to speak, to take the clock to pieces, to identify the permanent and elementary parts of which it is constituted, and to understand their mode of interaction. This was the motive behind the incessant model-making of the nineteenth century. . . ." "All the effects known before 1900 were such as could be copied by models in this way. But a quantum or corpuscular cannot be imitated by a model formed from ordinary gross matter: it is, so to speak, a ghost of a particle, sometimes appearing as a wave."[1] The discoveries in physics that took place during the twentieth century proved that the construction of a model to represent physical phenomena was "not merely hard and perplexing but actually impossible".[2]

Mechanical ideas seemed to succeed at first and were endorsed by experiment: but as knowledge increased they were found to be inadequate. They were subjective importations of the human mind, and further experiment rejected them.

Another conception had been growing up in physics and was destined to become of great importance. This was the conception of Energy. A moving body possesses energy, which is measured by half the product of its mass and the square of its velocity. This is called its kinetic energy. But bodies which are not moving also possess energy in potential form. For instance, a weight suspended by a string possesses potential energy; and if the string is cut the body will fall and the potential energy will be converted into kinetic energy. In the bob of a swinging pendulum, kinetic and potential energy are continually being converted into one another. At the mid-point of its swing, all the energy of the bob is kinetic. At either end of the swing, all the energy is potential. But throughout the entire period of swing the sum of the two kinds of energy is constant; whatever is lost in one kind is gained in the other. This principle was found to apply to all dynamical systems.

In 1823, Fresnel had experimented on the refraction and reflection of light, which he regarded as consisting of vibrations of the æther, and as therefore containing energy of motion, the amount of which per unit volume could be calculated. Energy thus came to be regarded more as a quality belonging to substances than as a mere mathematical expression. Soon after 1840, Joule demonstrated the connection between energy and heat. He showed that when mechanical energy is spent in churning up

[1] *B.E.W.,* p. 24. [2] *B.E.W.,* p. 20.

water, it becomes converted into energy in the form of heat. The water becomes warmer and the relation between the two types of energy is exact. A mass weighing 776 pounds descending through a space of *one* foot will raise the temperature of a pound of water by 1 degree Fahrenheit. Heat therefore came to be regarded as a form of energy.

Finally, energy in all its various forms—potential and kinetic, heat, chemical and electrical—were united by Helmholtz in 1847 in the general theory of the *Conservation of Energy*. That is to say, all the different kinds of energy were regarded as being interchangeable: and in any system, which receives no energy from without and gives no energy away, the amount of energy remains constant. "This theorem was proved by deductive reasoning from the axiom that perpetual motion is impossible: and so irresistible did the argument seem that in the latter half of the nineteenth century, energy was elevated to a place side by side with matter as a constituent of reality. . . ."[1] Thus matter and energy became the twin causes of physical phenomena.

Now, physicists have always been dissatisfied with duality or plurality in the ultimate data of physical reality and have sought for a single underlying unity. This is the challenge provoked by the analytical method. Must matter and energy remain for ever divided? In 1881, J. J. Thomson began to study the motion of a material body which carried an electric charge. The moving body possesses kinetic energy; but the field associated with a moving electric charge also possesses energy. Thomson found that the effort required to set the charged body in motion with a definite velocity was greater than that required when the body was uncharged. The charge had, in effect, increased the mass of the body.

Many years later, it was shown that energy of any kind, if associated with a body, increases its effective mass. The kinetic energy which a body has when it is in motion, increases its effective mass, so that its effective mass is greater when it is in motion than when it is at rest. This was verified experimentally, and in the end it was shown that mass and energy are mutually convertible, $9 \cdot 10^{20}$ ergs of energy being equivalent to a mass of one gramme. Hence the duality between matter and energy had been overcome and their essential unity established and confirmed by experiment. The universe, it seemed, was being *simplified* by science. Energy was now the central factor in it and conservation of energy the central law. It now became usual to look at a physical problem from the point of view of energy.

This gain in knowledge concerning energy suggested a further experi-

[1] *B.E.W.*, p. 28.

ment. Since ordinary masses have gravitational properties, it seemed likely that energy, now known to be the equivalent of mass, would have them too. Light is a form of energy: would not a ray of light passing near the sun be deflected by the sun's gravitational field? The experiment was tried during the eclipses of 1919-22 and this was found to be the case.

But meanwhile, with the disappearance of a locatable æther, the theory of relativity had appeared as a fundamental conception in physics. And, because of the theory of relativity, the apparent simplification brought about by the unification of mass and energy fell to pieces. The kinetic energy of a moving body depends on its velocity. But what *is* its velocity? Had there been a stationary æther composed of particles definitely located in space, absolute velocity would have been definable. But the relativity theory had banished the æther in this sense. What is the velocity of a moving body? How is it to be measured? We can measure it relatively to a point on the earth's surface: but the earth is in motion: the sun and the heavenly bodies are all in motion, and there is no criterion of absolute velocity or rest. Kinetic energy no longer has any clear meaning.

Again, in the nineteenth century, energy was supposed to be definitely located in space. So much energy was supposed to be contained in such and such a volume of space. "But actually in the curved space of general relativity it is not necessarily true: the energies in the sub-regions may be different in kind, like components of velocities in different directions, and so may be incapable of arithmetical addition. In fact, 'The total amount of energy in a finite region' is a phrase that no longer has a meaning in general relativity."[1]

What had seemed to make energy such a clear and definite thing in the objective world was, after all, knowledge of a group of mathematical relations. It is the same situation that arose in connection with the Mathieu equations. Physicists had been hypostatizing this knowledge, attributing substantiality to energy and seeking to trace its adventures in space and time. *The mind's subjective contribution had been at work, unrecognized and unsuspected.* Energy is no longer the master key to the philosophy of the universe. "It may be asked, then, what becomes of the great doctrine of the Conservation of Energy? In its nineteenth-century form it is no longer valid: its place is, indeed, taken by a theorem which is interesting and beautiful but which can be stated only in rather technical mathematical language: *the divergence of the energy-tensor is null.*"[2]

Looking back over this brief glimpse of the history of physical theory,

[1] *B.E.W.*, p. 31.   [2] *B.E.W.*, p. 31.

we cannot fail to be struck by two outstanding facts. (i) The first is that
Nature was put to the question by careful and prolonged experiment, and
again and again she replied by reflecting the thought of the experimenters.
(ii) The second is that physicists have sought by research to arrive at a
better understanding of the physical world. They have found out a great
deal about it: but still the only intelligible, comprehensive and consistent picture of that world which anyone has so far attained, is the
picture with which they started. Both these facts throw a vivid light
on the nature of science in discovery and both show what it is that
marks it off from science in action. That strange dichotomy which we
vaguely glimpsed at the beginning of Chapter III now begins to take
shape.

(i) With regard to the first of these remarkable facts, we may ask:
Why did Nature, when put to the question, seem to play the part of
Echo? When physicists thought in terms of mechanics, experiment
endorsed the theory of the mechanical atom. When they thought in
terms of an æther located in space, experiment vindicated the existence of
the kind of æther they imagined up to the hilt. When they started to look
at physical problems in terms of energy, experiment showed energy to be
the central factor in physics and the Law of Conservation of Energy to be
the central law. Had physical investigations stopped at any of these points,
it would have been accepted as unquestionable that the method of putting
Nature to the question had provided a final answer to the problem
presented. When we look into it, we find that there is nothing after all
that is mysterious about this. Nature was not playing the part of a malign-
ant spirit, trying to mislead humanity. It was simply that physicists formulated their hypotheses in terms of ideas which filled their minds. They
could do no otherwise. They were in reality attempting to solve problems
which lay outside the subjective boundary of the familiar world. But they
did not realize this: nor did it occur to them that, outside this boundary,
the ideas that filled their minds were not likely to correspond with reality.
They submitted their hypotheses to the test of experiment and experiment confirmed them one by one. Because each experiment had been
devised in the light of limited knowledge, it was also interpreted in the
light of that same limited knowledge. Kelvin's theory of the vortex-atom
showed that atoms behave like vortices in the æther and have the properties
of vortices. One objection brought against the vortex-theory at the time
was that the inertia of a vortex-ring increases as its energy increases, so that,
in this respect, the vortex seemed to differ from the atom. It was then
believed that the inertia of an atom was bound to be constant under all
circumstances. Had it been known in those days that the mass of a body

increases with its energy, this would have been a remarkable additional proof that the vortex-atom theory was true!

If physical research had stopped at this point, or at any subsequent point, men of science would have been firmly convinced that the latest theory which experiment had endorsed was true beyond doubt and true in a final sense. We see, therefore, that throughout the history of physics, a subjective factor has played a major role in experimental technique. The experiment that is planned, and the conclusion drawn from it, both depend on the mental constitution of the experimenter. But if he goes on experimenting, fresh items of knowledge, or fresh ideas, come into view and these suggest new experiments, which lead to different conclusions, often at variance with the previous ones. Thus, the belief that any experiment will, under any circumstances, provide an absolute and unequivocal piece of true knowledge is false. So long as exploration is of a geographical kind, it is carried on within the world to which man's body and mind have been previously adapted. Then the principle of putting Nature to the question succeeds; for the conclusions to which experiment leads *are* final and intelligible (so far as they penetrate) because they lie within the region whose *apparent* finality and intelligibility have been prearranged by Nature. But when the principle of putting Nature to the question is carried beyond the area of pre-adaptation, its chief result is to reflect back the ideas of the investigator; for he interprets his experimental results according to the way in which his mind is constituted. This has happened all through the history of science. But new ideas arise as individual minds reach upwards to higher grades of awareness, and these suggest new experiments which enlarge the area of scientific knowledge —pressing outwards the subjective boundary of the world, as we should say from our point of view—but they do not convert far-reaching, divergent problems into convergent ones. The continual attempts of scientists to make them converge by the use of selection and analysis are disrupted and rendered divergent again by fresh discoveries. The scientist is very slow to realize the difference between geographical and nongeographical exploration, between the areas of adaptation and nonadaptation and between the convergent and the divergent. He assumes that he possesses a universal and infallible method of research.

This was very interestingly illustrated by some radio-talks on astronomy given by Mr. F. Hoyle, astronomer and lecturer in mathematics at St. John's College, Cambridge. In the last of these talks, in which the author sums up and glances forward into the future of astronomical theory, we find the following passage: "Is it likely that any astonishing new developments are lying in wait for us? Is it possible that the cosmology of five hundred years hence will extend as far beyond our present beliefs as our cosmology goes beyond that of Newton? It may surprise you to hear that I doubt whether this will be so. I am prepared to believe that there will be many advances in the detailed understanding of matters that still baffle us. Of the larger issues I expect a considerable improvement in the theory of the expanding universe. Already it is fairly clear that the theory of relativity is not an ideal tool for dealing with this problem. Continuous creation I expect to play an important role in the theories of the future. Indeed, I expect that much will be learned about continuous creation, especially in its connection with atomic physics. But, by and large, I think that our present picture will turn out to bear an appreciable resemblance to the cosmologies of the future."[1]

Now, exploration of the universe by the most recent telescopes and other instruments is *geographical* exploration. There is no more reason why discoveries of this kind should change, except for the emergence of further details, than there is that the shape of the Antarctic continent should change after it has been surveyed and mapped by geographers. But Mr. Hoyle is exploring extra-geographically as well. He suggests the creation or sudden appearance, as if from nowhere, of atoms of hydrogen throughout space. If a complete explanation of the appearance of these atoms from a source we can perceive and by methods we can fully understand were discovered, then this factor would be of a geographical nature too. "Creation" would then cease to be an applicable word. But if the cause of the appearance of the hydrogen lies beyond our ken and depends on principles we do not understand, and which our minds are not constituted to grasp, then the problem is not of the nature of geographical exploration. It goes beyond our world and is divergent. Theories and experiments would probably be continued and very likely each theory put forward would be endorsed by experiment. But they would continue indefinitely, cancelling previously endorsed theories, till the human mind reached the end of its tether.

The divergent character of the search for the origin of the physical world is further brought out by one sentence in the above quoted passage. "Already it is fairly clear that the theory of relativity is not an ideal tool for dealing with this problem." Just at the time when Professor Einstein is endeavouring to make all physical phenomena converge under the relativity theory, Hoyle brings forward a new theory which seems to disrupt this attempt. So it has been all through the history of physics. It was the theory of relativity which, ironically, disrupted the convergence that seemed to arise from the unification of energy and mass. The factor

---

[1] *The Listener,* March 9th, 1950, p. 422.

of paramount importance in every far-flung theory is the adapted character of the human being. Mr. Hoyle, in his summing up, turns to the question of what light the latest discoveries in astronomy throw on the nature of man and the human situation. His approach is entirely characteristic of the scientific outlook. It assumes that we must deduce from what we know or surmise about the physical world information about ourselves, instead of criticizing our views of the physical world in the light of our own peculiar constitution. "Here we are in this wholly fantastic universe with scarcely a clue as to whether our existence has any real significance."[1] This topsy-turvy method of procedure arises from the urge of our adapted instincts, which project us into the world of the senses that science has swallowed whole without reflection or criticism.

(ii) The second fact which our inquiry brought to light is that all the attempts of physicists to arrive at a better understanding of the physical world have resulted in making it far less intelligible than it was (or appeared to be) before they started. As Max Planck has put it: "The ideal aim before the mind of the physicist is to understand the external world of reality." Or, again: "To bring the approach closer and closer to truth is the aim and effort of all science."[2] This ideal can surely be regarded as lying within the range of possibility only by those who have not begun to see the universe in true perspective. It assumes, either that the human mind is capable of grasping the ultimate; or else that the universe is so simple and limited that a puny intelligence can grasp it all. Both views are so childish that we can only attribute them to instinctive adaptation. Nature's perspectiveless view, which telescopes everything on to one plane, is essential for practical purposes; and the belief that physics is working towards a final goal of complete understanding shows as clearly as anything could that the adapted mind has the physicist firmly in its grip.

The passage from convergence to divergence is indeed difficult for our minds to realize. Geographical exploration on the near side of the boundary, where the mind *can* arrive at final conclusions, passes without giving any signal into exploration on the further side of the boundary, where it *cannot* reach finality, and where its conclusions keep on changing as it pursues its Will-o'-the-Wisp. Success in the former area inspires the mind with great confidence, so that it will not listen to the warnings which tell it that to ask questions about fundamentals is to pass across the Rubicon. The scientist who has no wide background will no doubt deny that there is any Rubicon to cross.

Our brief survey of physics has shown from two points of view that the adapted mind powerfully influences it. There has indeed been progress in

[1] *Ibid.*, p. 423.   [2] *Where is Science Going?*

physics; but it is progress of the kind exemplified by the process of throwing out cantilevers from the cliffs. Had the restrictions imposed by the adapted constitution of man been realized from the start, it would have been known that science can only take a few limited steps into the infinite —as far as the cantilever construction will support it. But *Homo faber* has too strong a hold on *Homo sapiens* to allow this fundamental truth to be generally realized.

CHAPTER XII

THE ADAPTED MIND IN BIOLOGY

IN approaching biology from the non-specialist angle, we are not concerned with the technical details of the subject, with which the majority of scientific text-books are filled. We are concerned with the views which biologists hold about the nature of Life. That biologists are not agreed on this matter is evident from the outset; and it is obvious that the facts so far discovered have not provided a definite answer. It is, indeed, doubtful whether bare facts alone could provide an answer; for the results of experiments have to be interpreted, and it is in the interpretation that the crux of the matter lies. In biology, as in other branches of science, it is better to turn to books of a more general type, in which the scientist has something to say about the significance of his subject. There is a small book, entitled *Man a Machine*,[1] in which the well-known biologist, Dr. Joseph Needham, gives the kind of appraisement of biology that the non-specialist needs. It is to this book that we shall first turn.

That a materialistic or mechanistic interpretation of life makes a special appeal to the scientific mind is not surprising.

The idea of mechanism as an explanation and materialism as a philosophical doctrine, are, as William McDougall has pointed out, closely connected: "Modern materialism is the assumption that such mechanistic science can in principle achieve a complete and satisfactory account of the world and of man, his nature, origin and destiny."[2] Nevertheless, opinions differ radically as to the competence of the mechanistic theory to give a satisfactory explanation of life. For example, Bertrand Russell says: "There are some who maintain that physiology can never be reduced to physics, but their arguments are not very convincing and it seems prudent to suppose that they are mistaken."[3] At the same time, J. S. Haldane says: "The mechanistic theory of heredity is not merely unproven, it is impossible."[4]

Man a Machine was written, at any rate partly, as a reply to a book entitled *Man not a Machine, a Study of the Finalistic Aspects of Life*, published by Signor Eugenio Rignano in 1926. It is possible that Dr. Needham might not now find himself in complete agreement with all that he

---

[1] Kegan Paul, 1927.
[2] *M.M.*, p. 12.
[3] *W.I.B.*, pp. 11-12.
[4] *Mechanism, Life and Personality*, p. 58.

said in 1927; but, at any rate, *Man a Machine* is typical of a widely disseminated conception of the nature of life as drawn from the science of
biology.

Dr. Needham defines himself as a "neo-mechanist" and, at any rate in
the role of biologist in this book, he enthusiastically defends the mechanistic interpretation of life. The standpoint of neo-mechanism he has
described elsewhere as follows: "Neo-mechanism is the mechanistic
theory of life . . . freed from all the illusions it gained from its deplorable
friendship with scientific naturalism. It realizes itself for what it is, the
backbone of scientific thought in biology, and lays no claim to validity of a
philosophical kind. It knows itself to be universal in applicability and
restricted in essence. If biology is to be a science, in biology it must reign.
I profess myself a Neo-Mechanist."[1] *Man a Machine* is a satisfactory book,
for in it we find a scientist expressing himself on the general issues with
which his science is concerned; and this is a phenomenon all too rare. The
essential character of science is described as follows: "Science is the study
of the quantitative relationships between the phenomena of the world we
live in. Anything that can be measured, anything that can be weighed,
anything that can be numbered, anything that can be expressed mathe-
matically, 'the pointer-reading, the scale and the clock', all these can be
laid up in the bursary and the treasure-house of science."[2] On the other
hand: "The work of the great classificators in biology does not merit
the name of science, except in a preparatory and undeveloped sense."[3]
We see, on this view of science, how the principle of selection, to which
Eddington points, creeps into the subject. Mechanism and quantity
appeal to the adapted mind, because it is constructed to deal with inanimate matter. We are reminded of Bergson's remark: "That is why the
intellect always behaves as if it were fascinated by the contemplation of
inert matter."

From the non-specialist standpoint, an interesting light appears on
scientific theory at the outset. We can see from that point of view that
biological methodology took its shape from the special limitations and
characteristics of the scientist's body and mind; yet the scientist shows no
sign of being alive to this fact and its consequences. From the bird's-eye
view-point, the biological investigator looks like a traveller in difficult
country, who asks a guide to show him the best path to his destination.
The guide points out the path on which it is easiest for him to travel,
omitting to take into account the destination to which the path leads.

Dr. Needham emphasizes the success which has resulted from following

[1] *The Hibbert Journal,* Vol. XXV, p. 284.   [2] *M. a M.,* pp. 87-8.
[3] *M. a M.,* p. 88.

the quantitative path to knowledge: "Arthur Thomson, E. S. Russell, W. McBride and many other hormists, refuse to admit that a description of biological happenings could be given without the introduction of psychical—and therefore unquantitative—terminology. The answer to all these objections takes a solid form, namely, the entire range of journals from the *Archiv f. Entwick Lungsmechanik* and the *Journal of General Physiology* to the *Biochemische Zeit-schrift* and *Protoplasma,* in which there appear each year some thousands of papers all adding to our knowledge of the way the living machine works, and all dependent for their very existence on the method of the exact sciences."[1] Of course there is bound to be a great deal of mechanism in any material organism, and quantitative experiments may indeed be the best way of exploring this mechanism. But mechanism need not be the whole story; and we should be forewarned by the fact that this method is the path towards which the adapted mind naturally turns: "All we shall ever know of them scientifically will be mechanistic, expressed in the language of determinism, and related as closely as possible to physico-chemical facts obtained from observations on cerebral metabolisms. The experimental psychology is the only scientific psychology."[2] All we shall ever know—but what conclusions will this knowledge justify? Dr. Needham appears to assume that the incompleteness of our knowledge, actual and possible, need not be taken into account, in coming to a final conclusion.

Dr. J. Gray, in a Presidential Address to the British Association in 1933 remarked: "Not a few biologists have, in fact, maintained that living matter 'owes its origin to causes similar in character to those which have been instrumental in producing all other forms of matter in the universe' (Schafer, 1911). This was the view of Ray Lankester, who elaborated a series of intermediate steps whereby the first type of living organism was evolved from inanimate matter. I imagine that not a few modern zoologists would tolerate, if not actually accept, a similar view. From this it is often, but not always, implied that there is a fundamental continuity in the properties of all matter and that the only properties which a living organism can possess are those which can be defined in physico-chemical terms." We see the instinctive effort of the mind to confine the problem of life to the region with which it can deal. Inanimate matter, because it forms the foundation of our world, *must* be capable of explaining everything; and argument is subtly deflected so that this becomes a foregone conclusion. "Although we are still in the earliest stages of any real theory of living organization, we can yet see that biological order, like crystal order, but on a much more complicated plane, is a natural consequence of the

[1] *M. a M.,* p. 37.   [2] *M. a M.,* p. 71.

properties of matter, and one characteristic mode of their manifestation."[1]

It is this instinct in the mind which, as Eddington so clearly points out, leads to the method of Procrustes, by drawing intractable problems into the familiar world and the forcing upon them solutions framed in terms which we can understand. This process, however, leads to dual conclusions, scientific methodology pointing one way and individual insight another. The following passage shows how the dual point of view arises: "Morphologists, turning over the pages of the present book, will probably be inclined to remark that the author finds only 'a mass of substances' in the living and developing organism. Yet that is precisely what the organism is, containing in itself innumerable molecules of small size some of which are indeed the morphogenic inductors, as well as the giant protein molecules, which, by responding by new orientations, form the basis of the cellular and organic architecture. Nevertheless the biochemist approaching morphological problems does not forget that all these molecules are ordered and organized in a totally different way to anything which occurs, outside living organisms. His difficulties arise rather from the vagueness and lack of quantitative precision common to so much morphological work and perhaps inseparable from it. But everything that can be done to move this vagueness is being done and after all we have already a great many extremely well-defined histological and morphological factors, which can be correlated with bio-chemical ones. Some may feel that terminology of inductors, competences, etc., is too 'cut and dried', but the history of science abundantly shows that in every age, whether of the 'word-rectification' school in ancient China, the Arabs, Albertus Magnus, the early Royal Society, or the time of Haller and Boerhaave, the invertion and clarification of terms is one of the greatest limiting factors in scientific advance. A clear formulation, even though partial, is better than a vague one; and we must not, in avoiding rigidity, fall into obscurantism."[2]

There the difficulty of problems outside the boundary of the visible world comes into view. A "mass of substances" is precisely what the organism is—that is what the senses and the mind insist on. Yet, to draw the mystery of life into scientific terminology seems too "cut and dried". The mind, when it rises to anything like freedom, can see the absurdity of Procrustean treatment, yet the mind, influenced by its adapting instinct, insists on formulating everything in clear, abstract language in order to avoid vagueness and obscurantism and in so doing falls into illusion. Then a peep from the higher level shows that Procrustean clarity is "one of the greatest limiting factors in scientific advance."

[1] *B.M.*, p. 679.   [2] *B.M.*, p. xiv.

All this is an indication that the biologist is trying to deal with something which lies outside his scope. The problem of life is essentially divergent. But science has grown up from the soil, and on account of its successes in the practical field, where problems are convergent, it assumes that *all* problems must be convergent. Science has the effect of destroying our sense of perspective. So the dilemma grows. "It seems astonishing to us to-day that Driesch should have had recourse so soon in his analysis to a conception so obscure in all its particulars, so out of harmony with the natural products of the scientific method, so certain to close the door to further experimentation, so resembling the Galenic δύναμις or 'faculty'. We cannot see to-day why it is necessary to place the intense manifoldness of the egg outside the physical world, in view of the tremendous complexity which the colloidal constitution of protoplasm must involve."[1] The hope of tying life down to the material plane lies, then, in material complexity. But the principal point in this quotation is that the scientific *method* is taken as the standard by which to judge conceptions of the nature of life. Driesch's view of Entelechy may be open to objections on other grounds: to this we shall return later. But Dr. Needham's objection to it is that it is out of harmony with the natural products of scientific *method*. Yet the scientific method is dictated by human characteristics and limitations: its adoption is a matter either of necessity or convenience. Are hypotheses to be judged by whether or not they are consistent with the arbitrary circumstances which Nature has imposed upon us?

Perusal of this interesting and revealing little book makes it more and more evident that the author's mind is torn in two directions. Freedom of thought, regarded as a state of higher awareness, pulls one way: the scientific method, controlled by the adapted mind, pulls another. "Many biologists, though they may not be at all convinced of the ultimate validity of the mechanistic hypothesis, yet find it convenient, even indispensable in practice, and it determines and restricts the nature of their research."[2] The divergent views led to by a convenient method of research on the one hand and independent insight on the other is plain. No one who looks at life from a standpoint of relative freedom can fail to see its innate purposefulness, or its goal-seeking or teleological character —there is no really adequate word to express the character of life.

Scientific research, which is on the public level of thought, and below the level of individual insight, cannot deal with the essential character of life; therefore it must somehow contrive to blind itself to the real character and get it out of the way. "In this first instance too much attention is

[1] *M. a M.*, p. 120.　　　　　　　　　　[2] *M. a M.*, p. 2.

paid to the meagre purposiveness of the process, far too little to the mechanical. Those in daily contact with the facts find that when living matter is approached in the scientific method, it demonstrates at every turn its obedience to physico-chemical laws. Its teleology appears then as a faint thread; not indeed inconvenient, for it cannot affect their procedures; because they cannot altogether divest themselves of the common and vulgar ways of thought."[1] These are the procedures of scientific men, who have not quite learnt to rid themselves of the "common and vulgar" habit of noticing facts with which their methods cannot deal. Again: "This subject of the way in which teleology and mechanism intertwine is worth pursuing for a little. The former is only present on the mind of the scientific worker, because he is still, to some extent, an ordinary man."[2] And yet again: "In the last section I spoke more than once of a thread of teleology, running through one's ideas about the living cell not supported by experiment, and presenting itself indeed, in the guise of an illusion. What degree of realness is there about this trace of teleology? Scientifically speaking, none. It cannot be dealt with under any of the headings of number, measure, weight, intensity or capacity. It appears to the scientific worker only because he is not completely divested of the mental habits of common sense."[3] The capacity of scientific method is evidently the supreme test of truth. A perfectly trained scientist is one who has learnt to blind himself to all facts or suggestions which cannot be dealt with by his methods. This is stated with remarkable candour: "Science, with the determinism and mechanism, which form so unalterable a part of its existence, cannot be expected to take into account notions incompatible with its peculiar mental twists."[4] Again, the reason for the scientific rejection of teleology is very clearly stated: "Whatever we may think of teleology, we cannot have anything to do with it in the laboratory."[5]

Scientific methodology depends on the adapted character of man's mind and body; consequently: "Mechanism and materialism lie at the foundation of scientific thought."[6] Dr. Needham, however, is a man as well as biologist, and so he employs the higher and freer outlook of the individual as well as the communal outlook of science. It is therefore inevitable that he should fall into the dualism which science produces when it endeavours to deal with problems which lie outside the area of the world to which our minds are adapted. "Materialism, as Frederick Lange showed long ago, is the only philosophy upon which science can get to work; methodologically it is essential. And if I do not believe in it for a

[1] M. a M., pp. 42-3.

[2] M. a M., p. 45.

[3] M. a M., p. 73.

[4] M. a M., p. 92.

[5] M. a M., p. 93.

[6] M. a M., p. 96.

moment as a man, I recognize its fundamental importance as an experimentalist."[1]

If this dualism be frankly recognized, the question of what science is really doing, when it essays to investigate life, becomes acute. It is evidently not dealing with the problem as a whole but only with that part of the problem which is amenable to its methods. The conclusion we are bound to draw is that science would be perfectly justified in bringing to light the mechanistic aspect of the living organism if it admitted that this is only one aspect of the problem of life, namely the aspect with which it is competent to deal, and that no general theory of the nature of life could be based on this partial knowledge. But scientists do not as a rule take this view. They claim that science is capable of dealing with the *whole* problem of life. If we ask why they claim this in face of the manifest limits inherent in their methods, we can see that the answer is that the instinct of the adapted human mind refuses to allow that any problem can be divergent.

The antagonism between the view of the scientist and the view of the man compels us to label the mechanistic theory of life "for laboratory use only". It is a guide to experiment and not an explanation in any true sense of the word. Others besides Dr. Needham have felt the dual pull. Some have sided more with the man and some more with the scientist. Dr. William Brown says: "The total reaction of the body—not only of the human body, but the bodies of animals right down to the protozoa themselves—shows certain characteristics that cannot, in my opinion and in that of a large body of scientific observers, be fitted into a mechanical scheme."[2] Dr. J. S. Haldane has said: "Not by the wildest stretch of imagination can we conceive of structural machinery which goes on reproducing itself indefinitely; and the more structure and chemical complication we actually discover or assume in our organism the more hopeless does the problem of its reproduction and maintenance become from the mechanistic standpoint."[3]

A really important point, however, is that the limitations which are inherent in ourselves result in *selection* of evidence. It is true that we cannot help our limitations: we cannot help the way in which our bodies and our minds have been constructed and adapted for practical life. But, *if we realized the situation,* we could make allowances for it. The astronomer cannot help making his observations from the planet Earth; but he allows for the position and motion and all the peculiarities of his enforced

---

[1] *M. a M.*, pp. 71-2.   [2] *Mind and Personality*, p. 18.

[3] *Religion and the Sciences of Life*, p. 58.

observation-post. Otherwise, of what value would his observation be? "Innumerable reasons lead to the adoption of the mechanistic theory of life by the biochemist and some of them I have already outlined in other essays. The difficult question as to whether physico-chemical biology is the only possible sort of biology will perhaps solve itself as we go towards the end of this one. At any rate it is clear that if one could see one's way to being a scientific naturalist, all the biological difficulties would disappear. If all things in heaven and earth could really be thought of as capable of being fully and finally revealed to man by the scientific method; if physics was not only the most fundamental of philosophies; if, indeed, there could exist no metaphysic but science, then of course the world would be safe for mechanistic biology and a fit place for biochemists to live in. Unfortunately this is an impossible dream. Ruins are ruins, and to make the scientic method, with its dependence on inductive process, its constant employment of statistics, its suppression of the individual, its inevitable tendency to analyse, its rejection of all entities which cannot be numerically expressed and, in a word, its formidable subjectivity, into what- might be called God's Own Method, is now more than ever a hopeless task."[1]

The truth which emerges in this passage is that sole reliance on the scientific method introduces into the scientist's conclusions an element of *subjectivity*. The object of employing quantitative methods and mathemathics is to render scientific research *objective*: but what is the use of this if previous selection of a subjective kind has been introduced? E. S. Russell points this out: "With the natural bias towards a mechanistic explanation there goes an inability to see any alternative mode of approach, save that of dualistic vitalism, which is rightly rejected."[2]

The inadequacy of the mechanistic concept to explain life is emphasized also from another point of view. Mechanical ideas have faded out of physics: why should they be regarded as adequate in biology? Sir James Jeans has pointed out that the mechanical concept "left off bringing law and order into the phenomena of nature, and brought contradictions and nonsense instead."

It would seem that biologists cling to the mechanistic theory mainly because it suits their methods and appeals to the type of thought which comes naturally to the human mind. Two more sentences of Dr. Needham support this: "In contradistinction to neo-vitalism and neo-finalism, it [neo-mechanism] recognizes the supreme jurisdiction of the mechanis-

[1] J. Needham, *The Hibbert Journal*, January, 1927.
[2] *D.O.A.*, p. 3.

tic theory of life, but admits it at the same time to be a methodological fiction."[1] "But the state of exact science where Man is a Machine is no mean city, even though it be the city of a dream."[2]

The conflict between the level of thought at which there is insight and the level which is dogged by *Homo faber* is almost pathetic; but it throws an extremely interesting light on the nature of science. In order to keep to the scientific level, intractible facts have to be thrust aside, or else they must be forced into existing categories. Some biologists are, however, too much impressed by these awkward facts to be able to ignore them. They look at the subject more from the intuitional level; "In the exclusive light of existing physical and chemical conceptions, reproduction appears as nothing less than miraculous."[3] "When we consider how definite in almost endless detail the structure of an adult organism is shown to be, and how definite also are its characteristic reactions with environment, as shown in its life history, we can see at once that the mechanistic theory of life implies amazing complications in, at any rate, a germ. But the germ not only gives rise to the adult organism, but also to the indefinitely large succession of further germs so that each germ must contain the necessary mechanism for making an indefinite number of further similar mechanisms. We are thus involved in the assumption of absolutely endless and totally incredible physical and chemical complications."[4] Evidently the mind does not cling to the mechanistic hypothesis because it is simple or because it is explanatory, but because it is congenial to its own nature. Another biologist sees this clearly: "I suggest simply that, instead of making continual and vain efforts to squeeze biological facts within the materialistic frame, and attempting analysis without end, we accept them *as biological*, that we deal with the problems of development, maintenance and reproduction in terms of the observable activities of the organic agencies concerned, without making the gratuitous hypothesis that these activities are mechanistic. Only in this way can we hope to establish the laws of organic activity."[5] The author of this passage sees clearly the Procrustean tendency of the mind's predilection for analysis. It is precisely the tendency that Eddington points to in physics. What could be simpler or more natural than E. S. Russell's proposal? To the poet, unversed in scientific analysis, it is obvious:

> For of the soul the body doth form take,
> For soul is form and doth the body make.[6]

[1] *M. a M.*, p. 100. [2] *M. a M.*, pp. 110-11. [3] *P.B.*, pp. 36-7.
[4] *P.B.*, p. 35. [5] *D.O.A.*, p. 192. [6] Spenser.

"The more clearly we realize what is implied in the physically interpreted processes of diffusion, filtration, osmosis, and chemical affinity,
the more clear does the co-ordination which is present in living metabolic
activity become, and the more inadequate the attempts to interpret this
activity physically and chemically."[1] "The real basis of biology as a
science is the conception of life, and apart from this conception biology
would only be a chaotic collection of imperfectly defined physical and
chemical observations—imperfectly defined because they do not express
the co-ordinated maintenance."[2] That is to say, J. S. Haldane realizes that
"the conception of life"—something we can watch at work in every
organism but cannot clearly grasp or define—is indispensable if we are to
attempt to envisage life as it is, and that it is hopeless to try to force upon
it purely physical and chemical interpretations, although the latter
agree with our natural mental functioning. So we can see from what
biologists themselves say that the mind is at work on two levels and this
involves two kinds of interpretation. The operation of the adapted mind
fills biology. E. S. Russell gives some quotations from Sir Charles
Sherrington, which further show these two levels at work—the instinctive
level which dominates science and the one which is comparatively free.
"The wonder of development is celebrated in a most vivid, even lyrical
fashion, by Sir Charles Sherrington, and his testimony is the more
remarkable because he is, in the matter of physiological method, an
avowed mechanist. In the human child at birth, he tells us, there are some
twenty-six million million cells: 'They have arranged themselves into a
complex, which is a human child. Each cell in all that more than million-
fold population has taken up its right position. Each has assumed its
required form and size in the right place. The whole is not merely specific
but is a particular individual within the limits of the specific. In that
individual, that "persona", each cell has taken on the shape which will
suit its particular business in the cell-community of which it is a member,
whether its skill is to lie in mechanical pulling, chemical manufacture,
gas-transport, radiation-absorption, or what not. More still, it has done so
as though it "knew" the minute local conditions of the particular spot in
which its lot is cast. We remember it is blind; senses it has none. It knows
not "up" from "down"; it works in the dark. Yet the nerve-cell, for
instance, "finds" even to the finger-tips the nerve-cell with which it
should touch fingers. It is as if an immanent principle inspired each cell
with knowledge for the carrying out of a design. And this picture, which
the microscope supplies to us, supplies us after all, because it is but a
picture, with only the static form. That is but the outward and visible

[1] P.B., p. 92. [2] P.B., p. 49.

sign of a dynamic activity, which is a harmony in time as well as space' (*Man on His Nature*, p. 106)."[1]

This is the kind of thing which makes it perfectly plain to the freer level of consciousness that "the conception of life" is behind it all—not a conception that can be fully grasped and specifically expressed in words in the way that a philosopher would demand, but a principle which transcends the intellectual categories, yet can be partially assimilated by the higher or intuitive level of consciousness, which reaches out towards it. Yet the mechanistic interpretation returns and re-establishes itself in the mind of the author of this passage. In a second quotation, E. S. Russell says: "Most of the theoretical difficulties of biology arise from a blind acceptance of the Cartesian dichotomy of matter and mind. This works admirably in the physical sciences, where life and mind do not come into the story. Applied to living things it leads inevitably to the conclusion that they are nothing but energy-systems, that, as Sherrington puts it, the difference between the living system and the inorganic system 'is one not of ultimate nature but of scheme and degree of complexity' (*Man on His Nature*, p. 85). The rock, and the dragon-fly that circles above it, as pure energy-systems, fall into one category, and all the faculties or functions of the cell are processes 'which examination resolves wholly into chemistry and physics' (*Man on His Nature*, p. 86)."[2]

According to our present outlook, the "Cartesian dichotomy" arises fundamentally from the evolutionary pattern woven into the human mind at birth. It is an illustration of the way in which an intellectual principle can arise out of an unconscious, instinctive urge. But the present point is that Sir Charles Sherrington, after pointing to the uncomprehended life-principle at work in the human child, reverts again to a mechanistic interpretation of it all. "Sherrington himself brings out the orderliness and directiveness of the physico-chemical processes underlying the life of the cell. 'Our conceptions of it', he writes, 'fail if not dynamic. It is a scene of energy-cycles, suites of oxidation and reduction, concatenated ferment-actions. It is like a magic hive the walls of whose chambered sponge-work are shifting veils of ordered molecules and rend and renew as operations rise and cease. A world of surfaces and streams. We seem to watch battalions of specific catalysts, like Maxwell's "demons", lined up, each waiting, stop-watch in hand, for its moment to play the part assigned to it, a step in one or other great thousand-linked chain process. Yet each and every step is understandable chemistry' (p. 78)."[3] The adapted instinct of the mind here appears to win in the end.

The perusal of Dr. Needham's book, *Man a Machine*, shows very clearly

[1] *D.O.A.*, p. 150. [2] *D.O.A.*, p. 181. [3] *D.O.A.*, p. 182.

that the fundamental condition which shapes scientific investigation in biology is the constitution of the human being. Methodology is shaped and limited by the nature of the human body and its senses. Interpretation of experiment is shaped by the constitution of the human mind. Of course the independent facts are there; but they are seen through tinted glasses. One almost feels sorry for the primitive instinct at work in the mind, which so desperately tries to read its own interpretation into the phenomena of life. Is there not some more cogent piece of evidence which could give support to the mechanistic theory? Might there not be hope in the view that the living organism consists of a system of complicated, mechanical, reflexes? There certainly are reflexes which are automatic in their action and which take place without the aid of consciousness; and there is an argument which supports this reflex theory: it runs as follows. The nervous structure involved in actions, which are apparently *voluntary*, is of the same kind as that involved in involuntary automatic reflexes. The only difference is one of complexity. Why, then, introduce the unnecessary complication of mind when mechanism will serve the purpose? To quote Dr. Needham: "From this we may trace a direct line to modern researches such as those of C. F. Sherrington, from which it appears that all our actions may be some day described as reflex. The afferent fibres coming into the central nervous system from the sense-organs at the periphery of the body interlace everywhere there with the efferent fibres going out and conveying the impulses to the muscles and other effector organs. There is no gap; their is no physiological evidence for a seat of the soul."[1] This view has been examined by Professor Broad in his book, *The Mind and its Place in Nature*, the following passage from which clarifies this reflex-theory: "It is admitted that the mind has nothing to do with the causation of purely reflex actions. But the nervous structure and the nervous processes involved in deliberate action do not differ in kind from those involved in reflex action; they differ only in degree of complexity. The variability which characterizes deliberate action is fully explained by the variety of alternative paths and the variable resistances of the synapses. So it is unreasonable to suppose that the mind has any more to do with causing deliberate actions than it has to do with causing reflex actions. I think that this argument is invalid. In the first place I am pretty sure that the persons who use it have before their imagination a kind of picture of how mind and body must interact if they interact at all. They find that the facts do not answer to this picture, and so they conclude that there is no interaction. The picture is of the following kind. They think of the mind as sitting somewhere in a hole in the brain surrounded by telephones. And they think of

[1] *M. a M.*, pp. 25-6.

the afferent disturbance as coming to an end at one of these telephones and there affecting the mind. The mind is then supposed to respond by sending an efferent impulse down another of these telephones. As no such hole, with afferent nerves stopping at its walls and efferent nerves starting from them, can be found, they conclude that the mind can play no part in the transaction. But another alternative is that this picture of how the mind must act if it acts at all is wrong. To put it shortly, the mistake is to confuse a gap in an explanation with a spatio-temporal gap, and to argue from the absence of the latter to the absence to the former."[1] If we look back at Dr. Needham's argument, we see that this is precisely what he has done. Let us consider this idea. The spatio-temporal gap is assumed to be necessary because it is taken for granted that the mind is obliged to act on the brain in a spatial context if it acts upon it at all. The mind is hazily supposed to be somewhere in space; or, if not thought of quite as crudely as that, it is supposed that it must be an entity identifiable in the spatio-temporal world acting *in* space upon another identifiable entity in that world—the brain. If no telephone-exchange can be discovered in the brain in which the mind, so conceived, could operate, then the mind cannot be independent of the brain in any sense; it can be no more than a throw-off or epiphenomenon of the organic matter of the brain and so is incapable of operating on it. But these ideas are *our* ways of thinking, based on the instinctive conviction that the spatio-temporal world includes within itself the whole of reality and that nothing can exist which transcends it or has a totally different nature. The ideas arise, not because they explain that which has to be explained, but because they are the kind of ideas that our minds naturally harbour. Mental adaptation is again at the bottom of the reflex theory.

There is also a further argument against the view that the organism is a bundle of mechanical reflexes. Deliberate action differs from reflex-action. "The really important difference is that, in deliberate action, the response is varied *appropriately* to meet the special circumstances, which are supposed to exist at the time or are expected to arise later; whilst reflex-action is not varied in this way, but is blind and almost mechanical. The complexity of the nervous system explains the *possibility* of variation; it does not in the least explain why the alternative which actually takes place should, as a rule, be appropriate and not merely haphazard."[2] So the reflex theory is not an explanation of the living organism after all but merely a reflection of the thought of those who put it forward.

Dr. Needham refers to "words like 'entelechy', which are incapable

[1] *M.P.N.*, pp. 110-11.   [2] *M.P.N.*, p. 112.

of formally correct definition and hence can only occur in meaningless statements."[1] Dr. E. S. Russell, on the other hand, says: "We really require new terms to characterize the goal-directing and biologically purposive activities of living organisms, of which only some reach the level of conscious purposiveness."[2] One would have thought that E. S. Russell's way of approach is the obvious one to adopt. How can the explorer expect to make progress unless he breaks new ground? Are we to have new words for new ideas? Or must all our ideas be forced into the compass of old words? But when once we have grasped the fact that the human mind has been adapted in the way outlined in Chapter VII we see why Dr. Needham's way of looking at the problem wins general approval while E. S. Russell's way does not. To admit that the problem of life goes beyond our grasp and has its origin in an uncomprehended region beyond the boundary of the visible world, implies the overcoming of an instinct that refuses to admit the existence of the boundary. According to *Homo faber's* instinct, everything must lie within our ken. The adapted mind is thus very clearly at work in biology, deflecting reason in accordance with the promptings of Nature.

Let us pay a little further attention to the relation between mind and body and ask whether mind acts on body or body acts on mind, or whether each acts on the other. The theory of one-sided action of the body on the mind is called "epiphenomenalism". Psychologists incline to a hyphenated mind-body theory of man, in which consciousness is regarded as one aspect of the organism while bodily process is another. But this theory, in effect, appears to differ little from epiphenomenalism.

One argument which has been brought against the theory of interaction between mind and body rests on the law of Conservation of Energy. With regard to this, Professor Broad says: "I imagine that the argument, when fully stated, would run somewhat as follows: 'I will to move my arm, and it moves. If the volition has anything to do with causing the movement, we might expect energy to flow from my mind to my body. Thus the energy of my body ought to receive a measurable increase, not accounted for by the food that I eat and the oxygen that I breathe. But no such physically unaccountable increases of bodily energy are found. Again, I tread on a tin-tack, and a painful sensation arises in my mind. If treading on the tack has anything to do with causing the sensation we might expect energy to flow from my body to my mind. Such energy would cease to be measurable. Thus there ought to be a noticeable decrease in my bodily energy, not balanced by increases anywhere in the physical system. But such unbalanced decreases of bodily

[1] *B.M.,* p. 123.   [2] *D.O.A.,* p. 192.

energy are not found.' So it is concluded that the volition has nothing to do with causing my arm to move, and that treading on the tack has nothing to do with causing the painful sensation. Is this argument valid? In the first place it is important to notice that the conclusion does not follow from the Conservation of Energy and the experimental facts alone. The real premise is a tacitly assumed proposition about causation; namely that, if a change in A has anything to do with causing a change in B, energy must leave A and flow into B. This is neither asserted nor entailed by the Conservation of Energy. What *it* says is that, *if* energy leaves A, it must appear in something else, say B; so that A and B together form a conservative system. Since the Conservation of Energy is not itself the premise for the argument against Interaction, and since it does not entail that premise, the evidence for the Conservation of Energy is not evidence against Interaction."[1]

Even in purely physical systems, A can cause a change in B without there being any interchange of energy between A and B. Of this an example is given: "Take the case of a weight swinging at the end of a string hung from a fixed point. The total energy of the weight is the same at all positions in its course. It is thus a conservative system. But at every moment the direction and velocity of the weight's motion are different, and the proportion between its kinetic and its potential energy is constantly changing. These changes are caused by the pull of the string, which acts in a different direction at each different moment. The string makes no difference to the total energy of the weight; but it makes all the difference in the world to the particular way in which the weight moves and the particular way in which the energy is distributed between the potential and the kinetic forms."[2]

Further, with regard to the general question of two-sided interaction, Professor Broad continues: "I conclude that, at the level of enlightened common sense at which the ordinary discussion of Interaction moves, no good reason has been produced for doubting that mind acts on the body in volition, and that the body acts on the mind in sensation. The philosophic arguments are quite inconclusive; and the scientific arguments when properly understood, are quite compatible with Two-sided Interaction. At most they suggest certain conclusions as to the form which interaction probably takes if it happens at all."[3] And he adds, when finally summing up the mind-body problem, that "no argument has been produced which should make any reasonable person doubt that mind acts on body in volition and that body acts on mind in sensation".[4]

[1] *M.P.N.*, pp. 106-7.   [2] *M.P.N.*, pp. 107-8.
[3] *M.P.N.*, p. 113.   [4] *M.P.N.*, p. 132.

The arguments usually brought against interaction between mind and body are not, in reality, cogent. But the matter of great importance, which all these arguments bring out, is that the course which they tend to take, if not criticized from a high and free level of thought, tends to accord with the innate tendencies of thought of those who produce them rather than with the demands of the subject-matter.

CHAPTER XIII

MECHANISM, VITALISM AND EMERGENCE

PROBABLY the word "teleology" does not express the essential character of life at all adequately. Living organisms have the capacity for making for a goal instead of being pushed like inanimate matter, hither and thither by external forces; but the faculty differs from human purpose. E. S. Russell describes the goal-directed activity as follows: "(1) When the goal is reached, action ceases; the goal is normally a terminus of action. (2) If the goal is not reached, action usually persists. (3) Such action may be varied: (a) if a goal is not reached by one method, other methods may be employed; (b) where the goal is normally reached by a combination of methods, deficiency of one method may be compensated for by increased use of other methods. (4) The same goal may be reached by different ways, and from different beginnings; the end-state is more constant than the method of reaching it. (6) Goal-directed activity is limited by conditions, but is not determined by them."[1]

The principal ends of these activities are maintenance, development and reproduction; for the goal-directed activity has been adapted so as to seek the goals which are of the greatest practical importance. It was the recognition of this goal-seeking activity that gave rise to the theory of Vitalism. "Until about the middle of the nineteenth century, Vitalism continued to represent the usual belief among scientific men, including physicists and chemists who had given special attention to the phenomena of life." "Soon after the middle of the last century, it thus became a general belief among most biologists and numerous popular writers that life must ultimately be regarded as no more than a complicated physico-chemical process. In the writings of Huxley, for instance, we find this belief very clearly formulated." "The publication of Darwin's *Origin of Species* in 1859 further strengthened the revolt against Vitalism."[2]

It is often assumed that the choice lies between mechanism and vitalism of one particular kind. Professor Broad has however shown that there are two distinct kinds of vitalism—Substantial Vitalism and Emergent Vitalism. The first point to be cleared up is, however, the question of whether Teleological systems exist. If we find a system composed of such parts arranged in such ways as might have been expected *if* it had been

[1] D.O.A., p. 110. [2] P.B., pp. 39, 45.

constructed by an intelligent being to fulfil a certain purpose: and if, further, investigating it more carefully, we find hitherto unnoticed parts or relations which accord with this hypothesis, then the system may be called teleological.

Unquestionably, on this definition, there are teleological systems. Machines are such. Professor Broad says on this point: "Now it seems to me equally clear that living organisms are teleological systems in the sense defined."[1] Machines are designed by human minds; and if we use the words "mind and design" in regard to organisms, Professor Broad argues that we must use them in a sense comparable to that in which we use them in regard to machines; or else we must cease speaking of "minds" and "design" and admit that we are going beyond that which is clearly intelligible.

If a mind, in the sense in which we understand the word, did design organisms, it must have possessed superhuman knowledge and skill, and may fairly be called a "god". It might of course be said that organisms are purely mechanical systems not constructed by minds but constructed by one another; just as it is possible for a humanly designed machine to be so constructed that it will make another machine. But this merely postpones the difficulty of design; for the first machine of any series must have been designed by a mind. The first organism which created a chain of self-reproducing organisms must similarly have been designed by a mind, and a mind far exceeding in capacity that of any human being. "Thus the proper complement to a completely mechanistic theory about organisms is some form of the doctrine of Deism; a result which accords very well with that simple piety which is so characteristic of Biological Mechanists."[2] Biological mechanists, on this reasoning, are therefore logically committed to a belief in God, although they do not always seem to be aware of the fact.

With regard to the theories of Substantial and Emergent Vitalism, the former assumes that the characteristic behaviour of living things is due to the presence in them of a component which does not occur in inorganic matter. This component is often called an "Entelechy". Some analogy to an entelechy might be sought in chemistry where certain carbon-hydrogen groups play an essential part in determining the characteristic behaviour of certain compounds; yet these groups cannot exist in isolation. There is however a difference between such groups and an entelechy; for no entelechy, or anything like it, has ever been isolated; whereas chemical groups similar in general character to the unisolable groups have been isolated. It is known what kind of things these unisolable groups are;

[1] *M.P.N.*, p. 83. [2] *M.P.N.*, p. 90.

whereas an entelechy is a complete mystery. Substantial Vitalism as put forward, for example, by Driesch, is therefore regarded by Professor Broad, and probably by the majority of biologists, as an unsatisfactory theory. The unacceptable character of Substantial Vitalism is due to the fact that the theory postulates something which is unapproachable and indefinable; and yet is supposed to exist *within* the sensible world.

The rejection of Substantial Vitalism does not, however, involve the rejection of Emergent Vitalism. The latter is based on the observed fact that, with the passage of time, systems manifest new characteristics which could not have been foretold from a knowledge of their previous characteristics. These new characteristics are spoken of as "Emergents". It may sometimes seem that emergent properties can be foretold; but Professor Broad points out that this is due to a factor in the situation which has escaped our attention. There is a suppressed premise. Chemical compounds afford examples of this. A compound possesses properties which could not have been predicted from a knowledge, however complete, of the properties of its components. "The suppressed premise is the fact that we have examined other complexes in the past and have noted their behaviour; and that we have found a general law connecting the behaviour of these wholes with that which their constituents would show in isolation; and that we are assuming that the law of composition will hold also of the particular complex whole at present under consideration. For purely dynamical transactions this assumption is pretty well justified, because we have found a simple law of composition and have verified it very fully for wholes of very different composition, complexity, and internal structure. It is therefore not particularly rash to expect to predict the dynamical behaviour of any material complex under the action of any set of forces, however much it may differ in the details of its structure and parts from those complexes for which the assumed law of composition has actually been verified. The example of chemical compounds shows us that we have no right to expect that the same simple law of composition will hold for chemical as for dynamical transactions. And it shows us something further. It shows us that, if we want to know the chemical (and many of the physical) properties of a chemical compound, such as silver chloride, it is absolutely necessary to study samples of *that particular compound*."[1]

In the same way it could be said that the properties peculiar to a living organism, even if they were admitted to be completely determined by the character and relations of its chemical constituents, could

[1] *M.P.N.*, pp. 63-4.

not have been inferred from any amount of knowledge of these constituents. This is briefly the principle of Emergent Vitalism. It differs from Substantial Vitalism and does not appear to be open to the same objections.

Having clearly realized this distinction, it is worth while to reflect on the meaning of "Emergence". C. Lloyd Morgan, one of the foremost protagonists of Emergence, describes it as the Evolutionary unfolding of what is implicit. How this unfolding comes about he does not attempt to explain: he leaves it as something to be accepted "with natural piety". "For what is evolution", he asks. "As the word, properly understood, implies, it is the unfolding of that which is enfolded; the rendering explicit of that which is hitherto implicit. The evolution of mind in the history of events is the progressive coming to its own, in the fullness of time, of the intelligence or reason inherent always in the very nature of the world. In the beginning the end was enfolded. . . ."[1] Again: "Emergence, in the sense intended, is, I believe, an oft-recurrent feature in the Inherent constructiveness that obtains throughout nature. It is that which introduces, again and again, something new in the course of evolutionary process. What seems to happen is on this wise. We find certain components, say this, that and the other, which enter into 'fellowship' to give some product. We may know much about each of them severally before they become partners in constituting the product. And one might suppose that this suffices to enable us to know just as much about the product. We have, one might say, only to add up what we know about this, that and the other, severally as components, to know all there is to be known about the product as the sum of the components taken collectively. But seemingly that is not so. There is somewhat new in the character of the product as a whole. And this somewhat new is disclosed only when the product comes into existence and could not be foretold before it came into existence. To that which is new and unpredictable the word 'emergent' is by some of us applied. It comes when some new mode of relatedness comes. And it matters not whether the new mode of relatedness is physical or mental; something new and unforeseen and unpredictable, and in that sense emergent, may suddenly appear under the inherent constructiveness of nature. Why we know not; we loyally accept what we find."[2]

We learn that the atom, the molecule, the crystal, the organism, the person are all ascending steps in the emergent process, which passes from the inorganic to the organic realm without a break. "Liquidity, solidity, life and mind are, one and all, names that we give to a specific kind of

[1] *E.E.*, p. 111.
[2] C. Lloyd Morgan, *Science and Drama*, p. 22.

relatedness."[1] Liquidity and solidity are thus emergent properties according to Lloyd Morgan. The liquid is more highly evolved than the gas; the solid more highly evolved than the liquid, the crystal more highly evolved than the amorphous solid; for evolution is the "process of developing from a rudimentary to a complete stage".

It is not easy to see why mere spatial rearrangements of atoms and molecules should be regarded as steps in evolution from a lower to a higher grade, or as stages in Emergence. The idea of *value* appears to be subtly wrapped up in the word "emergence". Yet in these cases it is difficult to see that anything is happening beyond change. But the essential characteristic of emergence is stated to be its inherent unpredictability.

Lloyd Morgan distinguishes between two types of evolutionary products, "Resultants" and "Emergents". The difference between them is that a resultant can be predicted while an emergent cannot. Both are illustrated by the formation of a chemical compound. For example, if the vapour of sulphur be passed over heated carbon, a compound known as carbon-bisulphide is formed, whose properties differ entirely from those of sulphur and of carbon. Carbon-bisulphide is very volatile and inflammable and has an unpleasant smell. These are "emergent" properties, for they could not have been predicted from a knowledge, however complete, of the properties of carbon and sulphur. On the other hand, the weight of any portion of carbon-bisulphide is equal to the sum of the weights of the sulphur and carbon which went to form it. This latter is not an emergent property, for it could have been predicted simply from a knowledge of the weights of the carbon and sulphur used. It is a "resultant" property.

The question which here arises is whether the distinction between a resultant and an emergent is *intrinsic* to the system under consideration, or whether it is subjective in the sense that it depends on the limits of human knowledge? Is our knowledge of the weights of the carbon and the sulphur *alone* sufficient to tell us what the weight of the carbon-bisulphide will be? Surely not. We have to discover the law of Conservation of Mass before this knowledge enables us to make any prediction about the weight of the carbon-bisulphide. We assume that this law will hold in this particular case solely because past experience tells us that it has held in countless similar cases before. Unless it be maintained that we possess innate knowledge about mass and its conservation, we must discover the law from experience. That bodies retain their mass or weight as an invariable property seems so obvious to us that we do not realize that it has to be learnt by experience. The science of chemistry is

[1] *E.E.*, p. III.

founded on this law; and yet the law is not universally true as atomic research has clearly shown. The fact is that *all* the knowledge we possess is the result of experience whether or not it is so familiar that we accept it as a truism. The only way we have of making predictions is by the memory of past experiences of a more or less similar kind and the assumption that the kind of thing which happened before will happen in this particular case. How else could a valid prediction be made? There are, indeed, two other ways in which predictions can be made. One is to state what we intend to do and then to fulfil the prediction by doing it. The other is to make a prediction of a paranormal kind without conscious knowledge of any kind, such as we find examples of in psychical research. Apart from these two modes of foretelling, the only way of making a prediction is by reasoning on the analogy of past experience. It is by doing this that we can predict what Lloyd Morgan calls "resultants"; and we could do it in no other way. What, then, is it in the character of "emergents" that prevents us from predicting them also?

It is perfectly true that if no one had ever seen a sample of carbon-bisulphide before, or anything like it, its properties could not be inferred from even the most minute knowledge of the properties of carbon and sulphur. But this principle is true of everything else as well. Our power of predicting how a machine will work is dependent on the analogy of this particular machine with numerous other machines. We may be inclined to think that the generality of mechanical laws places machines in a different class from chemical compounds, which show far greater individual differences. But this is only because most machines are based on narrow and universally familiar principles. If we were to encounter a machine which incorporated an electronic gadget, we should have to acquire special knowledge of this type of gadget before we could predict the machine's behaviour.

Now, it is quite possible to make predictions about "emergents" by using the same principle by which we can make predictions about "resultants" or anything else. To make predictions of any sort, we must reason on the analogy of similar cases. A number of predictions of "emergent" properties have, in fact, been made in this way. "The clearest proof of the value of the periodic classification has been the prediction of 'new' elements, and accurate knowledge of their properties. Thus, when Mendeleef first described the system, the element germanium, discovered by Winkler in 1886, was unknown; but from the properties of the elements surrounding a gap in the system, the Russian chemist was able to predict its properties with almost incredible exactness, as the following table shows:

Atomic weight	72·0	72·3
Specific gravity	5·5	5·469
Atomic volume	13·0	13·2
Formula of oxide	GeO_2	GeO_2
Specific gravity of oxide	4·7	4·703
Formula of chloride	$GeCl_4$	$GeCl_4$
Boiling point of chloride	Less than 100°	86°
Specific gravity of chloride	1·9	1·9
Formula of flouride	$GeFl_4$	$GeFl_4$
Formula of ethyl compound	$Ge(C_2H_5)_4$	$Ge(C_2H_5)_4$
Specific gravity of ethyl compound	0·96	Lower than water[1]

These are "Emergent" properties predicted on the strength of analogy with similar cases, just as "Resultant" properties are predicted. Our experience of the constancy of weight is immense, while our experience of elements analogous to germanium is small: that is the only difference. Thus it appears that the predictability of so-called "emergents" does not depend on any unique properties of the emergents *themselves* but only on the extent of our knowledge. It is therefore a *subjective* and not an *intrinsic* difference. There is nothing inherent in "emergent" events or properties which distinguish them from "non-emergent" events or properties. Apart from the two other modes of prediction we have mentioned, everything that happens is unpredictable unless we have past experience that enables us to reason by analogy. Lloyd Morgan says that "something new and unforeseen or unpredictable and in that sense emergent, may suddenly appear under the inherent constructiveness of nature. Why we know not; we loyally accept what we find." The word "new" is used in two senses. In one sense, everything that comes to pass is new; that is novelty in the sense of becoming. Every event is unique, for it will never occur again. Other events like it may occur; but *that* event cannot recur. So that, in this sense, change, and even endurance, continually give rise to the new. Whether or not we can predict the new depends on our past experience and on whether the particular event in question is similar to other events in the past.

But the word "new" is used in another sense as well. It is used to indicate what is unfamiliar to *us*. If a stone is thrown into the air it falls to the ground. We do not call this a "new" phenomenon because we have witnessed this kind of thing thousands of times before. We recognize it as exemplifying the law of gravitation, which is universal to matter. But events do occur in the material universe which are called "new" in the

[1] *F.E.*, pp. 12-13.

sense of being markedly dissimilar from anything which, as far as we know, has preceded them. A nebula condenses and forms stars. These compact, glowing spheres differ from the diffuse matter that preceded them and are therefore entitled to be called novelties. The matter of a cooling planet forms itself into various crystalline bodies; and these are new in the same sense. Later, little pieces of matter manifest the properties of life; and still later some pieces of living matter manifest consciousness. All these are novelties in the sense of being different from that which preceded them. They are what C. Lloyd Morgan calls "emergents". We cannot, however, accept the existence of "emergents" as a separate category without criticism. Every event that occurs in time is "new" in one sense, for novelty is an inherent factor in becoming. Whether an event can be predicted or not depends on our own knowledge.

It depends on whether we have sufficient past experience of events of a similar kind. If an event has never happened before—such as the appearance of the first living cell—we feel inclined to call it "new" in a sense which belongs exclusively to *it* and has nothing to do with ourselves. But we have this inclination because the event is *spectacularly* new. For every event which has not been preceded by another event which is exactly like it in every respect has in it novelty of the same kind as the novelty of the first living cell. But we feel less inclined to call these events "new" because they have been preceded by other events which bear some resemblance to them.

The conclusion we have to come to is therefore that *intrinsic* novelty is the property of every event that "becomes" in time. On the other hand, novelty which is not intrinsic—novelty in the sense that the event in question is new *to us*—depends on the extent of our past experience.

The important question raised by emergence is this. What is the cause of the novelty in the "emergent" which renders it markedly different from previous events? For example: what caused protoplasm to manifest the properties of life when no other matter on the earth had done so before? Similarly, what caused certain higher organisms to manifest consciousness? Lloyd Morgan attributes this to a "new relatedness" which he admits to be a mystery: "The evolution of kind, then," he says, "means to us the coming into being of a kind of relatedness which at preceding stages of evolutionary progress has, as such, no being at all."[1] What kind of relatedness was it? And what were the relata? Here lies the crux of "emergence". It is here that the idea it stands for passes into vagueness. That the novelty of the "emergent" is not due to the entry of anything extraneous into the material world is a point on which Lloyd Morgan is

[1] *E.E.*, p. 113.

emphatic. It is the already existing material world which supplies the relata for the new relatedness. "No mind without life; and no life without a physical basis."[1] And again, speaking of the material world, he says: "Life and mind in no sense act into it."[2] Also: "The advent of novelty of any kind is loyally accepted wherever it is found, without invoking any extra-natural Power (Force, Entelechy, Elan, or God)."[3] It is taken as axiomatic that the material world is a closed system, which cannot be affected by anything from without. Here again the adapted mind is at work, urging the assumption that the visible world is all-inclusive. This is not merely the personal conviction of C. Lloyd Morgan; it is part and parcel of the scientific outlook.

When matter assumes a crystalline form, has not something new arisen *in* the world on account of a new relatedness of the molecules? This new relatedness can explain it; there is no need to invoke any external cause. Why, then, when matter manifests the properties of life, should an external cause be invoked? Have we not here two examples of "emergent" properties? When matter assumes a crystalline form, what is happening in it more than change in known relationships? Will this kind of new relatedness account for life? Crystallization is accounted for by a new relatedness of a comprehensible kind and we cannot trace the new relatedness which would account for the appearance of life. What do we do, then? We postulate an unknown relatedness which we locate in the known world and say that it brings into being something quite unprecedented. What is this but a device, under the name of "emergence", to help the adapted mind? "Emergence" avoids the introduction of any entity *ab extra*, such as Driesch's Entelechy or Bergson's *Élan Vital*. These are postulated as being unknown, yet potentially identifiable entities or modes of relationship. Yet they cannot be discovered in the familiar world. So their existence is turned down and "emergence" is postulated instead. The "emergent" performs a skilful feat of tight-rope balancing. It avoids having to produce itself *in* this world by taking refuge in the mystery of novelty. Yet it avoids being classed as an incomprehensible by passing itself off as a "new relatedness" appearing in matter. It thus balanced with consummate skill on the border-line between the comprehensible and the incomprehensible. Why should we not frankly admit that life and mind are in their essence incomprehensible and that they enter the familiar world out of the blue? If it were once admitted that our world has a subjective boundary and that reality stretches away from us continuously like the ocean, our horizon being a limit depending on ourselves, then there would be no need to deny that we can grasp the causes

[1] *E.E.*, p. 15.   [2] *E.E.*, pp. 13-14.   [3] *E.E.*, p. 2.

of some things but not of others. But acknowledgement of the boundary is taboo. The struggle to modify facts in order to appease the adapted mind permeates the whole field of theoretical science. "Not so long ago, expectation was entertained by many that mind would with the growth of knowledge prove to be energy in some form as yet perhaps not delimited. . . . This expectation has not been fulfilled. Further knowledge has not brought them together. It has more definitely parted them."[1] How strongly the mind fights against the idea of divergent problems.

Time is the real mystery behind the idea of "emergence": "It is true that nothing ever arises out of absolutely nothing. There is always something out of which it grows. But that does not explain it wholly. It does not account for the *new* in it. It is only in so far as it is still the old, or the old over again, that it is accounted for by what it grew out of. In so far as it is new, it remains unaccountable, unpredictable, uncontrolled, undetermined, free. *That* factor in it, therefore, *has* arisen out of nothing and Novelty as such means Creation out of nothing!"[2]

We must now go back to an idea which was broached earlier.

---

[1] Sir Charles Sherrington, *Man on his Nature.*
[2] F. C. S. Schiller, *Must Philosophers Disagree?*, p. 231.

CHAPTER XIV

THE PATTERN BEHIND THE PATTERN

I N Chapter VII, when we were considering the ways in which man has been adapted to his world, it was pointed out that Nature (as we metaphorically used the word) was confronted with a double problem in rendering that adaptation complete. In the first place, man's physical environment had to be such that it would meekly respond to all his dealings with it. It could not be rebellious, for man had to grow up in it without loss of confidence. In the second place, it had to be made to appear much simpler than it really is and also without bound or confine.

It is the first of these considerations to which we shall now return. If the nature of the physical world had been different, surprising and even terrifying things might have happened when pre-scientific man began to act upon it by lighting fires, quarrying stone, smelting metals and so forth. If the unexpected had happened during these operations, man might have lost confidence in his world. But the material world is so constituted that alarming things did not happen. Most people would take it for granted that they should not, and would not regard this as fortunate but rather as an inevitable state of affairs. But if we look more closely into the nature of the physical world, we find that it has been adapted to be the home of life with far greater thoroughness than these introductory thoughts suggest. A simple remark of E. S. Russell sets the ball rolling: "The first living things were no doubt very simple in organization, but they must have been integrally adapted to their environment, otherwise they could not have existed. . . ."[1] If it is the general rule that living creatures survive in their environment solely because, in the course of their evolution, *they* have become adapted to *it,* how did the earliest creatures manage to survive before this kind of adaptation had had time to establish itself? He goes on to state the difficulty more fully: "Evolutionary diversification obviously cannot proceed unless the essential conditions for living and reproducing are present from the beginning. Of these conditions adaptation to environment is one, and it cannot have arisen in the course of organic evolution, for evolution presupposes it."[2] If adaptation on Darwinian lines is an essential prerequisite for the survival of living forms, how did life ever get started? Must there not have been conditions which

[1] *D.O.A.,* p. 188.　　　　　　　　　　[2] *D.O.A.,* pp. 189-90.

were favourable to life from the start? This question is dealt with in a remarkably interesting book by Professor L. J. Henderson, entitled *The Fitness of the Environment*. The author, at one time, professor of biological chemistry in the University of Harvard, speaks with the authority of a specialist. He points out that those elements of the physical universe which are directly concerned with the evolution of life possess a remarkable combination of characteristics. If it had not been for these qualities in inanimate matter, it is difficult to see how life could have appeared in the physical universe at all.

Water has qualities almost, if not quite, peculiar to itself. In the first place, it has a remarkably high specific heat. In respect of this quality it is rivalled only by hydrogen and ammonia. The effect of this high specific heat is to make the temperatures of the oceans relatively constant; and that is a matter of the greatest importance for the development of living things. The high specific heat of water is also of great service to life in another way, for water forms a large constituent of the living organism, and because its specific heat is so high, a great deal of heat can be absorbed by the organism without causing a great rise in temperature. Thus the high specific heat of water renders organisms resistant to changes of temperature. "It is therefore incontestable that the unusually high specific heat of water tends automatically and in the most marked degree to regulate the temperature of the whole environment, of both air and water, land and sea, and that of the living organism itself." [1]

Again, the heat of evaporation of water is high and this also helps to keep temperatures uniform; for a great deal of the sun's heat is absorbed in causing evaporation to occur from the surface of a piece of water and so this heat is not available for raising the temperature of the body of water as a whole. This property of water is also important in other ways. For example, it helps to regulate the meteorological cycle of evaporation in one locality and the fall of rain at another. Evaporation at one part of the earth's surface and condensation at another causes a large amount of heat to be transferred from the tropics to colder regions and so assists in equalizing the earth's temperature in respect of latitude. "To sum up, this property appears to possess a three-fold importance. First it operates powerfully to equalize and to moderate the temperature of the earth; secondly it makes possible very effective regulation of the temperature of the living organism; and thirdly it favours the meteorological cycle. All of these effects are true maxima, for no other substance can in this respect compare with water." [2]

Transparency is another important property of water, for it causes

[1] *F.E.*, p. 91.   [2] *F.E.*, p. 105.

radiant heat to pass down from the surface into the body of the water and to warm the lower levels, thus preventing an extreme contrast between the temperature of the surface-layer and the rest.

Another property of water is quite extraordinary. The general rule is for liquids to become denser as their temperature descends until it reaches the freezing point, where the density is a maximum. Water becomes denser as its temperature is lowered until it reaches 4° C, after which the density decreases until the temperature reaches 0° C, when the water freezes. This unique property of water is of the highest importance for the maintenance of life, for if water were to follow the general rule, life would be frozen out of existence in the colder regions: "The coldest water would continually sink to the bottom and there freeze. The ice, once formed, could not be melted, because the warmer water would stay at the surface. Year after year the ice would increase in winter and persist through summer, until eventually all, or much, of the body of water, according to the locality, would be turned to ice."[1]

Again, water is a remarkably efficient solvent: "For no other chemically inert solvent can compare with water in the number of things which it can dissolve, nor in the amounts of them which it can hold in solution.[2] "It cannot be doubted that if the vehicle of the blood were other than water, the dissolved substances would be greatly restricted."[3]

Water, in addition, has a high surface-tension: "Of all common liquids, except mercury, water has the greatest surface-tension."[4] This is very important for life because it is the surface-tension which causes water to rise in the interstices of the soil by capillary action. Capillary action also plays an important role in the physiology of plant circulation, and, indeed, in all living organisms.

Other characteristics of water which are peculiar to it and very favourable to life are the high value of the heat of combustion of hydrogen, the latent heat of ice which is very high, the freezing point of water which is high compared with that of many other substances. Water is, in fact, the only substance which possesses *all* the properties necessary for the evolution of life.

Carbon dioxide also plays an important role in the constitution of plants and of the atmosphere; and it, too, has properties which exactly fit it for this role. Its special properties co-operate with those of water in making the ocean a fit place for life to arise in. "Thus the fitness of the ocean appears as an embodiment of the physical fitness of water and carbonic acid, resulting directly and inevitably from these and other

[1] F.E., p. 109. [2] F.E., p. 115.
[3] F.E., p. 116. [4] F.E., p. 126.

natural phenomena, and providing a lodgement for life and a medium for its earlier development upon the earth. No philosopher's or poet's fancy, no myth of a primitive people, has ever exaggerated the importance, the usefulness and above all the marvellous beneficence of the ocean for the community of living things."[1]

The chemical as well as the physical properties of matter are uniquely adapted for the development of life; for the organized matter of which living creatures are composed depends for its suitability on the peculiar properties of the elements carbon, hydrogen and oxygen. It is because these three elements, unlike the rest of the chemical elements, link together in innumerable complex groupings that the unstable, complex and flexible molecules necessary for life are possible. "In the course of the wonderful development of organic chemistry, which must ever be counted as one of the greatest achievements of the nineteenth century, enormous numbers of new chemical substances were discovered. In 1883 the number of carbon compounds had reached 20,000, in 1899, 74,000, and in 1902 it exceeded 100,000."[2]

The material of which living organisms are composed thus depends on the unique properties of these three elements and perhaps particularly on the unique character of carbon.

Taking all these peculiarities together, we are faced with a view which, from our ordinary standpoint, is altogether surprising. The myriads of living things with which the earth is peopled attained each its own special adaptation to its surroundings by evolutionary change, as Darwin discovered. But the fitness of the physical universe to support life as a whole was pre-arranged or innate in the character of inanimate matter: "We have found that the properties of the environment, biologically considered, present the same fitness as the properties of life. In each case the fitness results, at least in part, from an evolutionary process."[3] Having tabulated these peculiar characteristics of matter, Professor Henderson adds: "All the properties or other phenomena noted in the above table . . . are in character or in magnitude either unique or nearly so and are in their effect favourable to the organism as defined in the fundamental postulates. Indeed, they constitute or bring about an extraordinary set of conditions favourable to life—ubiquity, abundance, variety, stability, mobility, constancy of composition and invariants of physico-chemical conditions in the environment; number, variety, complexity, adaptability, availability, activity and a richness in energy of the substances which take part in the metabolic process and in the chemical and physical formation of the organism; constancy of physico-chemical conditions, such as temperature,

[1] *F.E.*, p. 190.   [2] *F.E.*, p. 193.   [3] *F.E.*, p. 280.

alkalinity, colloidal disperseness, etc., within the organism; the efficiency of many physiological processes, the availability of electrical forces."[1]

The suitability for life of the conditions which actually exist can be seen to extend further if we take into account the peculiarities of our planet. The rate of rotation of the earth gives days and nights of suitable length: the angle at which the earth's axis is inclined to the ecliptic causes the seasons to be suitably spread over most of the area of the planet: the distance of the moon provides manageable and not destructive tides: the atmosphere is thick enough to protect us from a bombardment of small meteorites; at the same time it is so constituted that it screens us from the injurious rays contained in solar radiation: the force of gravity is such that a good deal of hydrogen escaped from the atmosphere, otherwise there would have been too much water; yet it was strong enough to prevent all the hydrogen from escaping, otherwise there would have been no water at all: the fortunate inertness of nitrogen exactly fitted it to be an atmospheric dilutant. L. J. Henderson arrives at the following conclusion: "In truth, Darwinian fitness is a perfectly reciprocal relationship. In the world of modern science a fit organism inhabits a fit environment."[2] This conclusion, sponsored by purely chemical and physical facts, is shocking to the adapted mind; for it opens the deepest of mysteries. It presents a problem which is insoluble in terms of the resources of the familiar world. We can understand, or at any rate we can persuade ourselves that we understand, how living organisms became adapted to their physical environment in the course of time; but we cannot conceive how the environment came to be adapted to life long before life came into existence. Surely every instinct within us must urge us to explain away this temporarily inverted type of adaptation. Physical and chemical constants are not easy things to deny; but there is always chance. Could we not argue that the properties of water, carbon-dioxide, oxygen, hydrogen and carbon happened to possess their peculiar properties by chance? Could we not say that, if they had happened to have different properties, there would have been no life—and that is all? There was no pre-adaptation: during illimitable stretches of time, might not any kind of atoms have been produced at last by purely chance associations of the constituent corpuscles? As for the fortunate characteristics that our earth possesses, may there not be millions of planets in the stellar universe which do not possess these properties and so remain without life? We are here solely because the earth happened to possess these fortunate properties by chance. This is the sort of way in which our minds tend to argue when Nature stands behind us and feeds us with instinctive premises. Chance, for the

[1] F.E., pp. 252-3.   [2] F.E., p. 132.

mind that is trying to escape by constructing tendentious reasons, is a
very present help in trouble. L. J. Henderson says: "There is in truth no
one chance in countless millions of millions that the many unique
properties of carbon, hydrogen and oxygen and especially of their stable
compounds, water and carbonic acid, which chiefly make up the atmosphere of a new planet, should simultaneously occur in the three elements
otherwise than through the operation of a natural law which somehow
connects them together."[1]

The only alternative to chance is something against which our innate
instinct rebels. L. J. Henderson puts it in this way: "In short, we appear to
be led to the assumption that the genetic or evolutionary processes, both
cosmic and biological, when considered in certain aspects, constitute a
single orderly development that yields results, not merely contingent, but
resembling those which, in human action, we recognize as purposeful."[2]
So the teleological bugbear arises again in a worse form than ever. How
can the cosmic and biological processes of Nature be united in a single
synthesis? Theologians would say that the preparedness of the physical
universe for life is an example of the purpose of God; but the scientific
mind always rebels against final causes. "But one thing is certain,"
Henderson continues, "no such discussion, be it ever so important to the
philosopher or the theologian, can directly contribute to scientific knowledge and comprehension of the underlying phenomena, which are the
sole positive and certain knowledge of the subject that we possess. For
these facts an explanation of a different sort would be necessary, something
logically resembling natural selection, a natural process acting automatically through the properties of matter and energy, and never overstepping
the limits of matter and energy, space and time; neither supernatural nor
metaphysical but purely mechanistic. Lacking any indication of what such
an explanation may be, or how it is to be sought, we shall do well to turn
to other considerations."[3] This again reminds us of the widespread
predilection to ignore the evidence of psychical research. When faced
with evidence that cannot be explained away, the only thing to do is to
look steadfastly in another direction.

In another volume, Professor Henderson, like Dr. Joseph Needham,
is brought face to face with the inevitable dualism of outlook which
scientific methodology produces. "We may progressively lay bare the
order of nature and define it with the aid of the exact sciences. Thus we
may recognize it for what it is and now at length we clearly see that it is
teleological. But we shall never find the explanation of the riddle, for it
concerns the origin of things. Upon this subject, clear ideas and close

[1] F.E., p. 276.   [2] F.E., p. 279.   [3] F.E., pp. 280-2.

reasoning are no longer possible, for thought has arrived at one of its natural frontiers. Nothing more remains but to admit that the riddle surpasses us and to conclude that the contrast of mechanism with teleology is the very foundation of the order of nature, which must ever be regarded from two complementary points of view, as a vast assemblage of changing systems, and as an harmonious unity of changeless laws and qualities working together in the process of evolution."[1] In other words, the problem oversteps the boundary of the world and becomes divergent. It has revealed something of a deeper pattern than that of causality—the pattern behind the pattern. It is the opening up of a perspective which reaches away from us and passes beyond our grasp, and that is what is so important. Theologians might attribute the pre-ordination of the physical universe for the reception of life to the direct action of God. But if God is conceived as a magnified man acting *within* the limited world which is open to our senses, in the way in which a human being acts, interfering with the causal pattern of events in the way in which we ourselves interfere with it, then the perspective which this deeper truth has opened to us is destroyed. If the theologian does this, he does what the scientist has been doing. He re-introduces the illusions of the adapted mind and distorts our conception of God by drawing God into the sensible world. It is difficult to see what religion can gain from the repudiation of the divergent perspective, in the light of which alone true religion can hope to exist. That there is a pattern behind the pattern is the first step towards the realization of greater things—not a separated pattern, but one which is integrated with the causal pattern—in fact, a glimpse of reality extending away from our specialized standpoint. It is not that the causal pattern is non-existent or that the empirical work of science, which is based on it, is invalid, but that the conclusions arrived at within that pattern are contingent and never final. Regarded in this light, scientific conclusions are "true". The causal pattern is valid: chance, the sceptic's friend in need, is valid also if its explanatory powers are not exaggerated: but it is interlocked with a deeper pattern, which we can only begin to comprehend in intuitive fashion. Chance appears to us to be a final explanation. In the ordinary world, where so many things are final in a practical sense, chance *is* a final explanation. But it is the finality of pre-arranged convergence. When applied to divergent problems, it is no longer a final explanation. It disintegrates, like all our practical ideas, when projected out of its field.

Let us say that the special features of our planet, which support each other so fortunately in favour of life, combined in this way by chance.

[1] *The Order of Nature*, pp. 208-9.

But for this chance we should not be here. So far the chance-argument works and *appears* to solve the problem. But the properties of oxygen, hydrogen and carbon, which create the field for life in so many different ways, are universal and not peculiar to our planet; an urge to include them in the chance-scheme arises in our minds. Why should their properties not be due to chance also? But the chance-explanation becomes "sicklied o'er": we have to bolster it up with tendentious reasoning. There is something behind it which we cannot understand and cannot honestly deny. The special peculiarities of our planet and the universal properties of the chemical elements are somehow intertwined; and the chance-explanation, which seems plausible at first, comes more and more to have a surface-plausibility only. Whether we admit this or resist it depends on the degree to which our minds insist on holding on to an explanation they can thoroughly understand. If we knew more, we should see the universe in quite a different light. The causal pattern which now appears to us to be self-sufficient and all-explanatory, on account of our limited knowledge, would be seen to be merely a glimpse of the fore-. ground.

Perhaps there is a sense in which life appeared on the earth by chance. But with deeper insight, we should see that there is a great deal more in the story. Our present need in dealing with these divergent problems is, not for further masses of detailed facts, but for a valid, general outlook. We need another and a greater Copernican revolution to cure us of our sense-bound cosmology. Pre-Copernicans thought that the planet Earth occupied the centre of the universe. We make a similar mistake on a larger scale by supposing that the material cosmos occupies the whole.

Hints of a deeper pattern come through to us also in ways which inevitably seem queer. Probably the core of what is called the "occult" consists of symbolical representations of glimpses of the deeper pattern. Superstition gathers round such symbolism and obscures it; and then we instinctively sweep away the whole as rubbish. But it may well be that a deeper pattern is showing through. We must remember that anything lying outside the world to which our minds have been adapted would seem queer to us, just as the habits of foreigners seemed queer and somewhat ridiculous to the untravelled Englishman of a century or two ago. Astrology probably affords an example of this. According to the scientific view of the present day, astrology is one of the superstitions of poor, ignorant, pre-scientific man. But when it is examined, it seems to present empirical evidence for some kind of correlation between the positions of heavenly bodies and human affairs. If it be granted that pre-scientific humanity did not consist wholly of fools, it seems unlikely that astrology

would have been practiced for forty centuries if it never produced anything but imaginary results. It would not be that the planets *causally*
influence human beings or *vice versa*. But what might be the underlying
principle of astrology would come as a great shock to our purely causal
habit of thinking. The principle would be that there is a non-causal
pattern running through the universe in which series of events run
parallel to one another and are correlated in a certain way without being
in direct causal relation. We think we know that such a pattern is impossible and that such non-causally related series of events cannot exist.
But on what grounds are we sure of this? Is it the structure of our own
minds which makes us so certain about it? The correlation between
heavenly bodies and human happenings would, on this view, be merely
one example of a pattern running through all things, which is part of the
cosmic structure and which was discovered because it was the easiest
example of such correlated series to discover by empirical means. There
may be all kinds of other series of correlated events for all we know
(perhaps the practice of divination arose out of something of the kind),
but in a scientific age we should never think of looking for them because
we feel assured that science has discovered all the principles on which the
universe is founded. When the deeper pattern shows itself, we instinctively turn away from it and try to explain the evidence for it away. This
is what is to be expected if the constitution of our own minds is the most
fundamental factor in determining the conclusions at which we arrive.
This little glimpse into the pre-adaptation of the physical universe for life
affords yet another example of the disparity between things as they are
and things as we insist on seeing them.

CHAPTER XV

THE ADAPTED MIND IN PSYCHOLOGY

PSYCHOLOGY is a science which presents an anomaly at the outset; for it is, at once, in difficulties about the subject-object relation. The difficulties arise, however, in the exploratory and not in the applied branch of the subject. The kind of difficulty that confronts psychology does not arise to anything like the same degree in sciences which deal with the external world. The question which presents itself in psychology is whether any genuine progress can be made towards understanding the mind by using the methods of natural science. The mind must be studied by means of the mind; yet the fundamental position from which psychology starts renders the central task of the psychologist an impossibility. This was realized centuries ago by the penetrating insight of ancient India. "You cannot see that which is the seer of sight, you cannot hear that which is the hearer of hearing, and you cannot think that which is the thinker of thought, you cannot know that which is the knower of knowledge."[1] This should surely be recognized to be the starting point of psychology by anyone who takes a preliminary survey of the field. That which *is*, yet can never be studied objectively, is the elusive quarry of the psychologist. One wonders whether Descartes should not have said: *Sum ergo cogito*, so fundamental is the unanalysable fact of selfhood.

R. G. Collingwood makes an interesting comment on the work of Lachelier: "His brief essay on *Psychology and Metaphysics Oeuvres*, Paris, 1933, Vol. I, pp. 169-219, is a masterly exposition of the thesis that psychology, as a naturalistic science, cannot grasp mind as it actually is; it can only study the immediate data of consciousness, our sensations and feelings; but the essence of mind is that it knows, that is, has as its objects not mere states of itself but a real world. What enables it to know is the fact that it thinks; and the activity of thought is a free or self-creative process, which depends on nothing else except itself in order to exist. If then we ask why thought exists, the only possible answer is that existence itself, whatever else it may be, is the activity of thinking. The centre of Lachelier's argument here is the idea that knowledge itself is a function of freedom; it is only because the activity of spirit is absolutely spontaneous that knowledge is possible. Hence

[1] *Brhadaranyaka Upanishad*, iii, 4-2, quoted by Sir S. Radhakrishnan.

natural science, instead of casting doubt on the reality of spirit by failing to discover it in nature, or vindicating it by discovering it there (which it can never do) vindicates it in quite a different way, by being itself a product of spiritual activity in the scientist."[1]

But the psychologist, like the scientist in general, approaches his subject without giving himself over to previous reflection: he takes over the method of natural science as if it were a machine and begins to operate without making any previous survey of the field; for he believes the scientific method to be a magic key which will open all doors. If his assumption be accepted, the most scientific school of psychology would appear to be Behaviourism. This school arose out of Pavlov's work on "Conditioned reflexes" and was carried further by others, notably by Professor J. B. Watson in America. Behaviourism relies on objective methods of research such as are used in biology and the physical sciences. J. B. Watson says of it: "Most of the younger psychologists realize that such formulation as behaviourism is the only road leading to science. Functional psychology cannot help. It died of its own half-heartedness before behaviourism was born. Freudianism cannot help. Where it is more than a technique it is emotional defence of a hero. It can never serve as a support for scientific formulation."[2] Again, he says: "Behaviourism is founded upon natural science; structural psychology is based upon crude dualism, the roots of which extend far back into theological mysticism."[3]

The initial action of the Behaviourists, as they set out to explore the realm of the mind, is indeed startling. "If behaviourism is ever to stand for anything (even a distinct method) it must make a clean break with the whole concept of consciousness."[4] This enthusiastic protagonist of the scientific method is so enamoured of objectivity in research that he proclaims it with a polemical ardour that reminds one of Voltaire upholding the cause of the Enlightenment. "Psychology," he says, "up to very recent times, has been held so rigidly under the dominance of both traditional religion and of philosophy—the two great bulwarks of medievalism—that it has never been able to free itself and become a natural science."[5] To deal only with that which is perceptible by the senses appears to be the ideal of the scientific psychologist. "States of consciousness, like the so-called phenomena of spiritualism, are not objectively verifiable and for that reason can never become data for science."[6] "The behaviourist finds no evidence for 'mental existence' or 'mental processes' of any kind." "According to the opinion of many scientific men to-day,

---

[1] *The Idea of History*, p. 186.
[2] *P.S.B.*, p. viii.
[3] *P.S.B.*, p. viii.
[4] *P.S.B.*, p. viii.
[5] *P.S.B.*, p. 1.
[6] *P.S.B.*, p. 1.

psychology, even to exist longer, not to speak of becoming a true natural science, must bury subjective subject-matter, introspective method and present terminology. Consciousness, with its structural units, the irreducible sensations (and their ghosts, the images and their affective tones, and its processes, attention, perception, conception) is but an indefinable phrase."[1] "Whatever scientific value there is in the colossal number of volumes written in terms of consciousness can be better defined and expressed when the psychological problems which gave rise to them are solved by genuine objective scientific methods."[2]

This passion for objectivity, in an inquiry whose business it is to deal with the subjective, accords significantly with the tendency of the adapted mind. Natural science took over the instincts of natural man, and in its early dealings with the external world found them extremely helpful: but it took them over unconsciously and so did not realize why they were so helpful at first and why they would fail to be helpful in researches not connected with the external world. Carried blindly forward, this instinct turns scientific research in Behaviourism into a comedy. Nothing could show mental adaptation in action more clearly than the conclusions of the Behaviourists. For them, thinking becomes "subvocal talking". Instinct is reduced to a type of bodily motion: "We should define instinct as an hereditary pattern reaction, the separate elements of which are movements principally of the striped muscles."[3] Behaviourism, in fact, by-passes the mind because mind is not amenable to its methods, and concentrates on biological observations and experiments. These are, no doubt, carried out in a perfectly scientific manner; and if Behaviourism presented itself as a collection of biological observations and experiments and not as a form of psychology, it would be open to no criticism. But, as the latter, its Procrusteanism carries it to heights of absurdity. "It seems to me", says Professor Broad, "that Reductive Materialism in general, and strict Behaviourism in particular, may be rejected. They are instances of the numerous class of theories which are so preposterously silly that only very learned men could have thought of them."[4] The irony of the situation arises from the fact that the Behaviourist unwittingly inserts subjectivity into his methods in the very act of trying to be objective. By refusing to face the situation which mind presents, and by turning away from mind to experiments with matter, he creates an artificial situation by imposing his own subjective habits upon the facts.

"It is a fallacy, but an exceedingly common fallacy, to imagine that by giving a psychological analysis to any 'mental event' we have done

[1] P.S.B., p. 3.
[3] P.S.B., p. 262.

[2] P.S.B., pp. 3-4.
[4] M.P.N., p. 623.

anything whatever towards either discrediting or commending it as an attempt at achieving truth, goodness, beauty, or the like. Its character as such an attempt is precisely what psychology ignores; and hence thinking, as such an attempt, is not even recognized by psychology to exist. In behaviourism, psychology becomes aware of this self-imposed rule, and asserts it explicitly. Hence it is idle to protest against the behaviouristic tendency to regard thought as a mechanism; we ought rather to be grateful to the behaviourists for revealing the true nature of psychology and pushing it to its logical conclusion. But this logical conclusion is nothing more or less than a *reductio ad absurdum*. If psychology is a correct account of thinking, it is a correct account of the thinking of psychologists; that is to say, psychology itself is only a kind of event which goes on in the minds of people called psychologists, a complex of mental idiosyncrasies innocent of any distinction between truth and falsehood. But no psychologist believes that his own psychological theories and enquiries can be described in this way. He tacitly excepts his own activity of scientific thinking from the analysis which he is giving of mind in general. . . ."[1]

The same *reductio ad absurdum* arises out of the philosophy of strict determinism. To insist that the subjective must be rendered objective to suit our convenience and that the "thinker of thoughts" must become amenable to the scientific method or else be dismissed as non-existent is to follow a path which leads inevitably to nonsense.

That the adapted mind is at work in Behaviourism is so blatantly obvious that there is no need to dwell upon it. We might go on to look for evidence of the adapted mind in less extreme schools of psychology. We should undoubtedly find it there: but it is not necessary to do so. It will be more interesting to turn to the therapeutic branch of psychology in order to see whether mental adaptation shows itself there. For this purpose we will glance briefly at some of the conclusions of Freud.

Medical psychology differs from other branches of the subject in that it has taken a very important step in crossing the boundary of normal consciousness and entering a new field, which it calls the "unconscious". Freud investigated factors in the human personality which lie beyond the conscious threshold. This field had been recognized before Freud produced his analytical technique. It had been recognized in France by such psychologists as Janet, while in England, Frederic Myers had, at an early date, enunciated the theory of the "Subliminal Self". Edmund Gurney, in the 1880s, had also investigated the phenomena of hypnotism, which have their seat beyond consciousness. But the medical branch of psychology as a whole, by devoting its attention to phenomena beyond normal

[1] *S.M.*, p. 275.

M

consciousness, had definitely crossed an important boundary and had attempted to carry discovery beyond the confines of the familiar world. One effect of this invasion of unknown territory was that the clarity belonging to scientific investigation was left behind. A vague, subjective, strange looking picture came into view instead. Mechanistic explanations could not afford the solace to the Freudian that they offered to the biologist, "The Freudian school, although it has much to say of 'mental mechanisms', and professes strict determinism, is thoroughly hormic—that is to say, it recognizes that all mental activity, conscious or unconscious, is sustained by impulsions towards goals."[1] Faced by this unfamiliar environment, the adapted mind did not feel at home. Freud and his followers showed signs of embarrassment at being engaged upon such a scientifically unrespectable inquiry and they endeavoured to make up for it by eulogizing science and clinging to the materialistic outlook as closely as possible. Freud did not appear to realize that he was dipping into the fringe of a vast and unknown extension of the real world; rather, he seemed to regard the "unconscious" as no more than a repository for thoughts and emotions repressed from consciousness. At the same time he inflated the potentiality of these unconscious factors of the mind until they formed, for him, a main explanation of the causes of human behaviour throughout history. It was a case of the frog that tried to swell itself into a bull. Dr. Kenneth Walker quotes Dalbiez as saying: "Psychoanalytical investigation does not explain the philosophical aspect of philosophy, the artistic aspect of art, the scientific aspect of science, the moral aspect of morality and the religious aspect of religion. The specific nature of the spiritual values eludes the instrument of investigation which Freud's genius has created. Psycho-analysis leaves the fundamental problems of the human soul where it found them."[2]

The psycho-analytical branch of psychology arose out of a practical technique; but the fact that it had strayed across the conscious boundary, away from the checks provided by the sensory controls of the external world, had the strange effect of turning it into a cult rather than a science. "With the new psychologies," wrote Dr. R. J. Dingle, "we find ourselves, not in the world of science where hypotheses are discussed, but in that of theology where heresies are dammed."[3]

But it is Freud's general outlook which throws most light upon the question of whether or not his conclusions have been influenced by the promptings of the adapted mind. For this, we may turn to his book, *The Future of an Illusion.* He appears to accept the view, which we discussed in

[1] *M.M.,* p. 217.   [2] *Meaning and Purpose,* p. 78.
[3] *The Nineteenth Century,* December, 1949.

Chapter VIII, that savage or primitive man had no conception of natural law, but regarded everything that happened around him as the work of invisible, animate beings. These imaginary beings, according to Freud, were projections of impulses or desires in the unconscious. "Similarly man makes the forces of nature not simply in the image of men with whom he can associate as equals—that would not do justice to the over-powering impression they make on him—but he gives them the character-istics of the father, makes them into gods, thereby following not only an infantile, but also as I have tried to show, a phylogenetic type."[1] No doubt unconscious causes do, and always have, played an important part in the life of man. We ourselves maintain that unconscious factors in the mind play a very important role indeed. The conscious mind, however, can be influenced not only from below; it can also be influenced from above. If we adopt the standpoint of the non-specialist, we can see *both* factors at work. Repressed desires and neuroses do, no doubt, account for something; but they do not account for everything. If it be granted that the mind of man is not a neatly rounded-off, monadic, mental atom, but is *graded* and without a defined boundary, then there is no reason why it should not extend both upwards and downwards beyond the arbitrary bounds of pragmatic consciousness. Intuitive knowledge, descending into it from above, may take symbolical form in consciousness just as the sexual impulse may do, rising from below and symbolizing itself in the form of a dream. Artistic inspiration, on the one hand, and the sexual dream on the other, need not proceed from the same source merely because both enter consciousness from without.

Early glimpses of the spiritual, entering consciousness from a higher level, may have taken the form of childish symbolism. Yet they may have been genuine forerunners of religion; they need not all have risen from below in the form of neurotic illusions. But Freud maintains that the belief in God or gods, is an illusion which arose in the human mind "from the necessity for defending itself against the crushing supremacy of nature". It was a device of escapism because man could not bear the harsh-ness of the world in which he found himself. "Thus religion would be the universal obsessional neurosis of humanity."[2] As religion developed, and in later times crystallized into dogmatic form, these dogmas were, according to Freud, still solely the result of subsconscious factors of the psycho-analytical type. "Religion consists of certain dogmas, assertions about facts and conditions of external (or internal) reality, which tell one something that one has not oneself discovered and which claim that one should give them credence."[3] "These which profess to be dogmas, are

[1] *F.I.*, p. 30.   [2] *F.I.*, p. 76.   [3] *F.I.*, p. 43.

not the residue of experience or the final result of reflection; they are illusions, fulfilments of the oldest, strongest and most insistent wishes of mankind; the secret of their strength is the strength of these wishes".[1] It is, incidentally, a strangely ignorant view of religion which supposes it to consist solely of intellectual propositions. But Freud's arguments are palpable examples of the working of the adapted mind. He attempts to force the dawning experience of religion, Procrustes-fashion, into the psychological framework he has constructed for it. Freud has a somewhat larger field to draw upon than has the natural scientist, for he has crossed the bourne of consciousness and has penetrated a little way into the world beyond it. Where, for example, an anthropologist and prehistorian, such as Professor V. Gordon Childe, attributes the belief of the ancient Egyptians in immortality to their discovery of the remarkable power of the local sand to preserve bodies buried in it, Freud attributes religious beliefs of this kind to the existence of neuroses in the human mind, which, before the dawn of the scientific era, he conceives to have been in a state of childhood. Professor Childe says: "The remarkable preservation of bodies buried in the dry, desert sand seems already to have suggested particularly lively speculations about the future life and started a quest for 'immortality'."[2] Whether the direct experience of the higher levels of consciousness are explained away by the preservative power of sand or by suppressed wishes, recently discovered by a medical technique, it is abundantly clear to anyone who takes a balanced view of things that both are due to the pattern of thought in the mind of the interpreter rather than in the facts to be interpreted. One can see here that instinct is modifying the reasoning process and trying to thrust away the experience which infiltrates from the larger world and to build up some kind of explanation which lies *within* the confines of the adapted mind. It is in reality a revolt against that which threatens to expose the boundary.

Freud's reasoning is based on the idea that the history of the human race is nothing but the history of the human individual writ large, and that, in the course of history and pre-history, the race has passed through the mental phases through which a child passes. With the coming of the scientific epoch, the human race is supposed suddenly to have grown up. "Man cannot remain a child for ever; he must venture at last into the hostile world. This may be called *'education to reality'*; need I tell you that it is the whole aim of my book to draw attention to the necessity for this advance?"[3] This is a convenient doctrine for a mind which is trying to force the facts into its own particular mould; but the picture of mankind presented by history does not in the least support it. Since history began,

[1] *F.I.*, p. 52.   [2] *What Happened in History*, p. 114.   [3] *F.I.*, p. 86.

there is nothing to show that human intelligence has grown as the intelligence of a child grows. Nor is there any evidence that human character has altered in any perceptible degree as individual character alters in adolescence. As Arnold Toynbee says: "There has been no perceptible variation in the average sample of human nature in the past; there is no ground in the evidence afforded by History, to expect any great variation in the future either for the better or the worse." The life-history of mankind has consisted of a series of ups and downs, of civilizations which have risen and declined, of a high peak of culture at one period followed by a regression at another. The only factor that has shown a more or less continuous upward trend is the accumulation of the knowledge on which the material side of civilization is founded. But the Freudian view that the human race has grown to adulthood with the advent of science is typical of the outlook of the present day. Every age has its illusions, and this is one of ours. "Science always believes that it has just discovered the ultimate truth and that all past ages have been sunk in a fog of ignorance and superstition."[1] Freud shows that he uncritically accepts this distorted view of history. "We say to ourselves: it would indeed be very nice if there were a God, who was both creator of the world and a benevolent providence, if there were a moral world order and a future life, but at the same time it is very odd that this is all just as we should wish it ourselves. And it would be still odder if our poor, ignorant, enslaved ancestors had succeeded in solving all these difficult riddles of the universe."[2] They were in a state of racial childhood, poor fools! But now that their descendants have suddenly grown up, flashed into adulthood by the impeccable light of science, they have acquired a tool by means of which they can solve every problem! Freud evidently takes the view that from science, and from science alone, enlightenment of every description must come; yet, oddly enough, the scientific character of his own psychology is far from being firmly established. "No, science is no illusion. But it would be an illusion to suppose that we could get anywhere else what it cannot give us."[3]

But the psychological situation, like every other, is by no means simple. The factors to which Freud points do exist in man. Doubtless they have played a part in the growth of religion as well as in much else. The claims of psycho-analytical psychology would be quite valid, as also would be the claims of the Behaviourists, if kept within their proper bounds. What ruins them is that they are inflated into a major source of all human experience. It is very instructive to examine and to compare the claims of Behaviourists and of Freudians; and it is the kind of thing that a

[1] S.M., p. 191. [2] F.I., p. 58. [3] F.I., p. 98.

non-specialist should do. One should probe into the causes which under-lie them. If we do this critically and with balance, and avoid being carried away by extravagant flights of pseudo-reasoning, we can see that psychology has done two things which are very necessary at the present time. It has turned our attention towards *ourselves*, and this, in the end, may have the effect of modifying our uncritical trust in the external world. Also, it has crossed the boundary of human consciousness and has taken a few steps into the limitless world which lies beyond. This is a move in the right direction; for in time we may begin to realize that in this direction, and not in that of the senses, the main avenue to reality lies. The adapted mind of *Homo faber* permeates psychology as it permeates the other sciences; in fact, it permeates all our intellectual activities just as it permeates our daily life. It is to the individuals, here and there, who are able to transcend its influence, that we must look for genuine enlighten-ment. C. G. Jung says in an interesting passage: "Just as the human body connects us with the mammals and displays numerous relics of earlier evolutionary stages going back even to the reptilian age, so the human psyche is likewise the product of evolution which, when followed up to its origins, shows countless archaic traits."[1] One wonders why he did not proceed from this frank recognition of the evolutionary adaptation of the human mind to develop the view set forth in the present volume.

[1] *M.M.S.S.*, p. 144.

CHAPTER XVI

THE LIGHTED FOREGROUND

WE have examined from our "aerial" point of view the three branches of science in which theory plays the most important part and have found that all are permeated by instincts which are innate in the mind of *Homo faber*. Science has been particularly open to the sway of these instincts because it grew up from the soil and, founding itself on common sense, took over all the factors which common sense comprises.

The root-principle of science was already in existence when man began to mould his physical surroundings to his own advantage. About the beginning of the seventeenth century, the age of modern science began; but it had behind it this foundation of utilitarian experience, stretching back beyond the dawn of history. Science is pre-eminently the product of "organized common sense" and it is not surprising, therefore, that it should have incorporated into its foundation the habits of thought of practical man.

One of the outstanding features of the practical mind is, we have seen, its instinctive acceptance of the external world as a primary datum which is prior to criticism. We have here pointed out that this datum includes, not only the bare deliveries of the senses (these have been analytically criticized by philosophers), but also certain data supplied by the mind, which are inseparable from these deliveries.

This acceptance of Nature's presentation of the external world as the fundamental starting point for all inquiry may be described as the central scientific dogma. The subtle quality of invisibility, with which Nature has invested this acceptance, causes it, however, to be held implicitly rather than explicitly. Passages such as the following from *The New Realism*,[1] by Professor W. T. Marvin and others, emphasize this dogma: "Once subjectivism and mysticism are discredited, the work of philosophy becomes continuous with that of all who have chosen to limit more narrowly the field of their labors."[2] "The disregard of epistemological considerations which is characteristic of special investigation is now justified."[3] "No light is thrown by the theory of knowledge upon the nature of the existent world or upon the fundamental postulates and generalizations of science, except in as far as the knowledge of one natural

[1] The Macmillan Company, New York, 1912.   [2] Pp. 41-2.   [3] P. 41.

event or object enables us sometimes to draw inferences regarding certain others."[1] "We have to start logically somewhere, but this 'somewhere' is not with a theory of knowing; and in so starting, we do indeed shut out all theories of knowing which contradict whatever constitutes the ultimate crucial tests of our theories. My own conviction is *perception is that ultimate crucial test,* and as such it does not presuppose its own possibility."[2] "As to our sensory and intellectual limitations, only the elaborate empirical and inductive studies of the psychologist can give us precise information; and psychology is one of the special sciences posterior to several others."[3] But the psychologist himself accepts this fundamental scientific dogma before he begins to investigate. He first goes out into the sensible world and then turns back to study the mind from there. "Thus our general conclusion, I believe, must stand: *The theory of knowledge is not logically fundamental to the sciences, and it cannot by any direct or a priori study of the knowing process ascertain the possible field or the limits of the sciences.*"

It is not for us to discuss the theory of knowledge from a specialist point of view, or to delve into Kant or into other philosophers. Our function is to take a bird's-eye and *pre*-specialist view. Seen thus, it becomes clear that Professor Marvin's statements are a crystallization of Nature's primeval instinct. The important point is, not the logical structure on which empirical science is founded, but the unconscious premises inserted by instinct into that structure. It is these that the scientist ignores with such fixity of persistence.

It might be objected that by "positive" science is meant no more than experiment as against argument. But the essence of this scientific dogma is not that it upholds empiricism against *a priori* reasoning, but that it plunges into experiment without pausing to consider what it has unreflectingly taken for granted. It is this omitted preliminary exploration of the field which makes all the difference; and it is this that Professor Marvin, voicing the attitude of "positive" science, so emphatically repudiates.

Philosophers have long ago shown the inadequacy of assumptions based on naïve realism and raw common sense; but innate instinct is the *creator* of common sense and it strenuously brushes criticism aside lest the mechanism of the adapted mind be revealed and the fictions which go to make our nursery-world should come to light. It is up in arms at once against any mode of thinking which would prevent it from accepting the external world as Nature presents it. The dogma upon which "positive" science is based is supplied by Nature's crystallized instinct. To be "positive" is to accept without reflection what Nature urges us to accept.

[1] P. 50.   [2] Pp. 66-7.   [3] P. 73.

In practical life, "positivism" of this kind is extremely successful: so it is in the field of applied science. But in science which essays to explore far afield it leads the mind fatally astray. *For we see everything through the glass of our mind*; and the glass has been constructed for success in practice. But, for the very reason that the dogma about "positive" science is based upon instinct, those who hold it uncritically will go on holding it, just as birds will go on building nests and rabbits will go on digging holes.

The efficiency of the human mind in practical affairs, compared with its fumbling inefficiency in far-flung exploration, brings home its pre-adapted character with startling force. Consider the wonderful rapidity with which aircraft have been perfected, or the superb triumph of thought and skill exemplified in the construction of the Mount Palomar telescope, or the ingenuity displayed in the "electronic brain". Compare these achievements with the shifts and devices used to reduce the phenomena of life to a form of mechanism, to get rid of the evidence for telepathy, or to explain away consciousness as an epiphenomenon of matter. The passage from being in gear with reality to being out of gear with it becomes as plain as a pikestaff once we manage to look at things from outside the specialists' groove.

Elementary science, though exploring geographically, as in Galileo's study of falling bodies, Torricelli's demonstration of atmospheric pressure with a primitive barometer, the isolation of chemical substances and so on, did make valid progress because it was exploring within the field of adaptation. It was only when exploration no longer explored the sense-given world that the mind's instinctive takings-for-granted led it away from truth instead of towards it.

Science has always been at work on the sensory foreground; and when it attempted to explore further afield, it tried to draw everything it came across into that foreground. Practical experience had convinced the scientific mind that every secret in the universe could, in principle at least, be unveiled by the scientific method. Therefore it pursued all problems, far and near alike, without any sense of perspective. The Cartesian philosophy presented two finalities, both within intellectual reach, material substance and mental substance, thus giving academic endorsement to the instinct of the adapted mind. The foreground-view of the universe waxed until it became predominant. Science, a growth from the soil, passed from strength to strength chiefly on account of its practical successes, but endowing at the same time its perspectiveless view of reality with the prestige gained from these achievements. The scientific outlook of to-day is the result of intense concentration on the special field of the foreground.

The following sentence, I believe, occurs in Descarte's *Discourse on Method*, stressing belief in the potential omnipotence of the human intellect: "There is nothing so far removed from us as to be beyond our reach, or so hidden that we cannot discover it, provided only we abstain from accepting the false for the true and always preserve in our thoughts the order necessary for the deduction of one truth from another." The idea is that the human intellect is paramount. The opposite view is more or less expressed in a sentence of Lord Haldane's: "We keep on with our pictorial representations of what cannot be pictorially represented under these narrow categories, at a level of conception too low to enable us to get any adequate comprehension of reality." The crux of the matter lies in the acceptances that fill our minds before we embark, either on experiment or argument.

The truth is that, throughout history, neither science nor the sense-bound mind of man have ever been in raw contact with reality. Mental and physical adaptation have always been there as a go-between. This is the fundamental fact which we must grasp if we are to have any hope of seeing things as they are. The sense of being in raw contact with the objective world is a device of Nature. The glass of the mind is always there; but it has been very cunningly shaped and polished so as to make it appear unquestionable that the ordinary world is exactly what it appears to be. Science took over this assumption and founded its methods upon it, never for a moment suspecting that the glass is there and that we are all looking through it. (Eddington may be classed as an exception.) Therefore it never dawns upon us that the glass can cease to behave as a lens and can act as a frosted window-pane when the subjective boundary of the world is crossed. No one realizes when the convergent becomes divergent. The practical successes of science have indeed made it very difficult for us to realize the situation.

We can now see plainly the dichotomy in science which was vaguely glimpsed in Chapter III; how success on the near side of the boundary turns into the pursuit of divergent problems on the far side. We can also see how important the dichotomy is. It has given us a more crabbed and distorted general outlook than that possessed by our "poor, ignorant" ancestors. The "sunrise of the scientific spirit" was indeed an adventure; it ushered in the "Enlightenment"; but the Enlightenment was, in a sense, a false dawn. Science has illuminated the foreground so brilliantly that, like the stage of a theatre, it attracts the gaze of all beholders. Meanwhile everything off the stage is plunged in shadow and largely ignored. Hosts of scientific specialists believe that a training in the technique of the laboratory places in their hands a key which will unlock every door.

This naïve conviction has given rise to a false conception of the universe and a false conception of the nature of man. We have so lost our sense of proportion that we cannot distinguish between a street-lamp and a star. All reality, in the modern outlook, lies on one flat plane; hence it appears to a mind which sees things thus in two dimensions that the control of ions in a vacuum tube and of human beings in society are problems of the same kind. Having succeeded in the control of inanimate matter, the scientist believes that, by the use of the same methods, he can control anything. "A man who has never reflected on the principles of his work has not achieved a grown up man's attitude towards it: a scientist who has never philosophized about his science can never be more than a second-hand, imitative, journeyman scientist."[1] But the impulse not to reflect is deeply rooted in the scientific mind. We should tie these journeymen scientists to their lasts and prevent them from taking part in the organization of society or pronouncing on the nature of the human individual. We should always remember their illusions about "positive" science, and the instinct which fosters them.

All that has been said above will probably be misrepresented as an attempt to decry reason and to exalt instinct in its place. Actually our theme leads to the exaltation of reason to a higher plane than that which it occupies in scientific philosophy. For in the latter it is fixed: in our own view it is limitless in the sense that awareness can potentially be indefinitely increased. But it will probably be said that it was reason and not instinct that lifted man to the heights of civilization. "What eternally fascinates us in Greece is, to say all in a word, the emergence there of mind, suddenly, like a figure shining in full armour, such as Spenser might have imagined from the Forest of Unreason. Veiled with exceeding art as ancient savagery is in Homer, behind him in that forest lurk the grim shades of the aboriginal horror, the superstitions, the sorceries, the human sacrifices, *the washing out of mud with mud*, in the phrase of Heraclitus—and for gods, beings more powerful than these, but not less cruel, lustful, jealous, vindictive than their worshippers. In Greece, on this primeval darkness, the dawn rises, in Greece and for the world. There, broad awake, the mind first examined the very base of things, the roots of being, justice, law, conscience, duty—not omitting the Olympians themselves from the account."[2] Has not reason been man's saviour and the conqueror of the dark shadows of the world of instinct?

This is fully granted; but the mistake is to believe that reason reigns alone in isolated grandeur. Reason was evolved and is permeated with

[1] R. G. Collingwood, *The Idea of Nature*, p. 2.
[2] W. Macneile Dixon, *Tragedy*, p. 49.

instinct from below but it is also reinforced by inspiration from above. Without the inspiration of heightened awareness, reason would be no more than a mechanical drudge hedged in by the laws of logic. Even the Greeks recognized other sources of illumination besides that of pure reason. Edwyn Bevan points out that "nobody has attached a higher value than Plato to the clear operations of the logical mind: his philosophy is pre-eminently intellectualist and rational. And yet Plato felt keenly that something divine might reveal itself in utterances which were not due to the logical reason but to an abnormal state of exaltation. He had, after all, the example of his master, Socrates, to keep him always in remembrance that men might receive intimations from *daimonion ti* side by side with the convictions they reached by following the argument (*logos*). He always speaks with respect of the Delphic oracle, the oracle which had declared Socrates the wisest of men."[1] The human mind is fed intuitionally from above while it is constrained by instinct from below. It is a mistake to regard it as something fixed and without context. To see ourselves as beings without context, neatly compact and self-complete and yet, mysteriously, having no perceptible limit to our grasp is just the view which Nature attempts to force upon us.

Our present view in no way belittles reason; it merely reveals the specialized character of the practical mind and the unspecialized reaches which lie beyond. The very feature which enabled reason to become "broad awake" in ancient Greece was its ability to rise higher in the mental spectrum into states of higher awareness. In proportion as it gained more freedom, the mind shook off the domination of instinct and began to see things as they are. Increasing awareness enabled the leading Greeks to ask searching questions. Increasing awareness, in fact, led to the development of science itself, as we saw in the example of Newton and the apple. But great flashes of insight are the attainments of relatively few, and much of the work of science has depended on the slow application of trial and error and the use of common sense. This enables scientists to accumulate immense masses of detailed knowledge and to spread out geographical exploration within the precincts of the familiar world, but it does not enable them finally to solve far-reaching problems. Instinct does, indeed, tend to deflect reason towards certain foregone conclusions; but this does not impair the validity of reason as a process any more than a man's reason is impaired when he is persuaded to accept a lie.

It has been pointed out that heightened awareness does not necessarily imply the direct prehension of infallible truth. But it raises another difficult question, that of the distinction between subject and object. This is a

[1] *S.S.*, pp. 140-1.

problem which trenches on specialist ground. It seems, also, to carry us very quickly out of our intellectual depth. Awareness, as a state of *being*, and awareness *of*, do not appear to be as rigidly separated in actual experience as they are in logical thought. It is possible that the subject-object relation in sense-perception, which we accept as normal, is in reality an extreme case. Even in sense-perception, if we include kinaesthetic sensations, the degree of objectivity appears to vary. It is a maximum in the senses of touch and vision and a minimum in the case of internal bodily sensations. Between these extremes, there appear to be a graded series or *degrees* of objectivity. We think that there must be a hard and fast line between awareness *of* and awareness in which we feel *somehow*; but experience seems to point to gradations between the two extremes. What is perhaps more important is that the higher the sense in which we are aware the more important subjective experiences seem to be. It is *we* who clothe the external world with the qualities which really matter. It is the character reflected from, or transmitted through, *ourselves* that makes our world what it is in respect of all that matters most. Without the indefinable, but all-important qualities that we ourselves provide, the world would be a dead skeleton. The qualities that matter most are not those that philosophers discuss—shape, size, colour and so on—but the qualities which poets recognize. We have only to think of Wordsworth, who went some way towards giving these qualities expression. Whether beauty is inherent in objects of sense, or is bequeathed to those objects by the percipient, is an old theme of discussion. Experience teaches us that there is not the clear distinction between observer and observed that the logical mind demands. The answer is beyond us intellectually; but we may realize more and more of the answer to it intuitively. Advance of this kind is personal and we look in vain for words with which to make it public. There is Art, the revealer. Does art reveal what is in consciousness or what exists independently and without? Intellectual analysis fails to keep pace with concrete experience; and the lesson we should learn is the limited scope of the former. Subjectivity and objectivity are inextricably intertwined: yet it is clear that the subjective factor is the one of principal importance. External objects are not important in themselves, but only as they affect us.

Another important question arises. Science has tried to create an all-inclusive picture of the universe based upon a study of the sense-given foreground. May it not be that that foreground has been endowed with a false character from the outset? In other words, is Matter the kind of thing we assume it to be? If it is not, the picture of the universe which science has painted may be based on a false assumption.

We all take it for granted that matter is an entity complete in itself:

but why should it be? Nature has a good practical reason for making us imbibe this assumption: but is Nature to be trusted? The more we reflect on the nature of matter, the more it looks as if we have been jockeyed into a false idea which we have used as a foundation upon which to build. Is matter really the kind of thing that we can, so to speak, walk all round and contemplate from all sides? We assume that it is, not only in everyday life, but all through science and philosophy as well. When, for example, the mind-body relation comes under discussion, it is assumed without criticism that matter possesses no properties behind the scenes which might take part in this relation. All arguments are based on the assumption that the properties of matter are exhausted by those potentially open to our senses. Yet, even within these limits, a hint is open to us that there is probably more behind. There are, for example, electro-magnetic vibrations which do not affect our eyes or our skin. There are vibrations of the air which do not affect our ears. Why should there not be a further category of properties which lie outside the field of the senses in principle? We decide on the general character of matter *before* launching a scientific attack in order to find out what its character is.

Perhaps we ought not to use the word "matter" at all, because it is bound up with this idea of self-completeness. How do we know that our senses are not revealing certain selected properties of something we might call X, which is not an isolated entity, but is continuous with an unperceived and possibly limitless background? We assume that matter is, metaphorically speaking, an island when it may be the tip of a peninsula, looking like an island because it is projecting out of the mist. If the latter were the case, all our discussions of the relation between life and matter, or between mind and matter, would be beside the point. X might have mind-like properties behind the scenes, and mind might be in relation with these in the background. Matter, *as we know it*, and mind, *as we know it*, need not be in direct relation at all; and the indirect relation might well be behind the scenes and inconceivable by us. Such a view of matter would account for the divergent character of all problems connected with the nature of life and mind. But the adapted mind fights vigorously against any such view and sets to work to drag such problems into the field which it understands. This revolt would probably be defended more or less as follows: That is all very well, but you are suggesting only a vague possibility. There is no positive evidence for this extravagant view of matter. Science relies on positive evidence only, which is verifiable by the senses: it does not build on speculative possibilities.

This brings us back to our old position once more. Science makes fallacious assumptions *before* it sets to work with its "positive" methods and taints its "positivism" with subjectivity from the start. Besides, the question is not to be settled only by appealing to the senses. Probability has to be taken into account as well. What are the probabilities that matter is an island as science assumes? Considerations about the evolution of the human mind, which we discussed in Chapter VII, are extremely relevant here. Unless we dismiss the view that the human mind was adapted to its world, as we know the human body was, as mystical moonshine, it is clear that the material world *had* to be made to appear complete in itself. Therefore matter *had* to be made to appear to be complete in itself. How probable is it that this self-completeness is an appearance rather than a fact? The history of physics is relevant here for it has shown that attempts to discover the ultimate nature of matter have diverged into an endless quest in spite of every effort on the part of physicists and mathematicians to make them converge to finality. Why should this be so if matter is the island-entity it is assumed to be? Scientific exploration itself points in the direction of the peninsula view. What likelihood is there that Nature, always with pragmatic ends in view, would have rendered visible to man all the properties that matter possesses? The obvious course would be to *suggest* the non-existence of the unnecessary properties by the use of instinct. When the scientist says that he needs positive evidence before he can be convinced that matter has unperceived properties, he is demanding evidence of a particular kind which can pass through the meshes of the net of sense-perception, where it has to run the gauntlet of the instinctive mental factor. He does not regard the situation synthetically. The probabilities are strongly in favour of the view that matter, as presented to *Homo faber* and pressed upon *Homo sapiens, has* been endowed with a specious appearance of self-completeness that it does not possess.

The main problem of biology—the discovery of the nature of life— would be rendered equally hopeless if the peninsula-view of matter were true. We must therefore expect this view to be strongly opposed by the non-philosophical scientific mind. The true explanation of any far-reaching problem is bound to lead the intellect out of its depth. This is what science all along resists.

There is one small piece of evidence for the peninsula-view of matter, which would probably be classed as "positive". It occurs in psychical research and will therefore be passed over by many. But it rests on careful observation and not on hear-say evidence. The evidence shows that there are persons who possess a kind of sensitivity by means of which they can give true information about a person unknown to them if they hold in their hand an object which has belonged to that person. The first hypothesis that suggests itself is that the owner's mental characteristics have been in some way stamped on the matter of the object and that the sensitive has the power of reading them off. But it has been found that, when once the object has played its role of linking the sensitive with the mind of the owner, it may be destroyed and still the sensitive can continue to make true statements about events happening to the owner, some of which have happened after the object was destroyed. Thus it would seem that the object establishes a kind of mental link between the sensitive and the owner of the object; but it is difficult to see how any of the known properties of matter could account for this. Material properties of a quite unknown kind are suggested.

Spinoza's parallelistic theory of the relation between mind and matter appears to have involved a conception of something which is neither mind nor matter, but which lies behind both. This might perhaps be regarded as a hint at the peninsula-view: but not much is heard of this theory to-day.

The effect of scientific concentration on the foreground has given rise to a widespread concept of Nature which has the delusive appearance of being founded on the firm rock of objectivity. We have challenged the soundness of this belief. We have challenged also the assumed objectiveness of all science which has strayed outside the area of the pre-adapted mind. The continued concentration of science on the foreground, without preliminary criticism or appraisal of its own situation, has led to the artificial philosophy of Logical Positivism.

Philosophy, during the last century, has been increasingly influenced by science; it, also, concentrates its attention on the foreground which science has so brightly lit. The idea that reality may fade gradually into the unknown instead of ending abruptly at the limit of the scientific search-light is altogether repulsive to this type of modern thought. A pertinent remark was made by J. D. Beresford: "It is so difficult for our feeble minds to grasp the simple truth that the incomprehensible cannot be comprehended."[1] Of course it is. Nature has seen to it that it should be.

[1] *What I Believe*, p. 140.

CHAPTER XVII

THE ADAPTED MIND IN PHILOSOPHY

P HILOSOPHY is more than ever to-day the business of professionals and it is only from the most general standpoint that a non-specialist can venture to survey the field. But two observations, needing no special knowledge, can be made by the outside observer. One is that never before has philosophy been so word-ridden. The other is that philosophy does not stand on an independent pedestal of its own: it is influenced by contemporary thought that arises outside its province. In medieval times it was drawn into the service of theology. To-day it has been drawn into the service of science.

The growth of Positivism in philosophy is partly the result of increased subservience to verbal forms and is partly due to the influence of the scientific method. Regarded from the non-specialist standpoint, the subservience of philosophy to semantics appears extraordinarily cramping. The fundamental difficulty which besets every attempt to make a real advance in thought is that every conception that is genuinely new to us can find no adequate expression in terms which we already possess. It is incapable of finding adequate expression in words. We have either to coin new words in order publicly to make use of the new conception, or else to speak of the new conception in terms which are inadequate to express it. We choose the latter course on the ground that otherwise we shall not know what we are talking about. The counter-argument to this is that if we use words which do not adequately express the idea that has formed in our mind, we are not talking about that idea but about something else. To force every idea into an existing framework is to use the method of Procrustes.

There is, of course, a large region of thought within which the words we possess do adequately express the ideas dealt with. Within this region, the philosopher's insistence on clear formulation is amply justified. But in philosophy as in science we unconsciously cross a boundary and, once beyond it, the precise use of language fails. Once across the boundary, words become pointers rather than containers of meaning. This is accepted neither in modern science nor in modern philosophy, again because the existence of the boundary is not recognized. It is asserted that anything which cannot be clearly stated in abstract language is meaningless.

But if we are not immersed in the specialist's groove, it is obvious at

N

once that this is not the case. It is clearly mental adaptation which prompts the mind to assume that it is; for within the area in which mind has been pre-adjusted to its environment, the statement is true. What happens outside the area of pre-adaptation is that an idea grows gradually, like a photograph in the developer. Words are pointers towards such growing ideas. In so far as they express them, they express them metaphorically. It is extraordinary that this takes place in concrete experience: yet common sense sweeps it aside as "mystical" nonsense. To recognize this experience would involve our seeing ourselves as we are—conscious beings whose consciousness shades off into uncomprehended regions instead of neat, self-contained monads, which Nature presents to our minds. There is no sudden jump from the intelligible to the unintelligible. But in practical life there must seem to be, because clear-cut boundaries are essential. The assumption that every idea can be precisely expressed in words arises from the assumption that every problem is convergent. This is where the adapted mind is seen to be at work in philosophy.

It is, of course, widely held that thought without words or images is impossible. Here again instinct lies at the root, pressing its insistence that the mind is a closed system. The idea that consciousness is like a spectrum would not fit the necessities of practical life. Experience shows it like this; but experience has to be resisted. Within the range of the *normal* consciousness, thought is no doubt dependent on words or images. But thought which purveys anything original does not take its rise *within* normal consciousness, but enters from further reaches of the spectrum-band. The latter is blacked out from normal vision. Universal experience shows that ideas enter the mind from without. They do not form themselves *in* the mind where their formation can be watched. This seems to be the point of Bertrand Russell's remark, quoted earlier, that "reason is a harmonizing, controlling force rather than a creative one". The boundary of consciousness is variable. It contracts when we are engaged in action and expands when we are engaged in reflection; and the deeper the reflection the further the boundary of consciousness retreats.

Examples of the way in which original thought enters from beyond this variable boundary, have been provided by the statements of many eminent men and women—poets, authors, artists, musical composers and even scientists. An interesting collection of these is to be found in Dr. Rosamond Harding's book, *An Anatomy of Inspiration*. "The thinker does not sit down", she says, "and say to himself: 'now I am going to think out the relations between so-and-so'. The process is not so much an active as a passive one."[1] If thought were inseparable from words, it

[1] P. 5.

would surely take its rise in verbal form where introspection is possible. Or it might enter the conscious mind ready clothed in words so that the recipient would have nothing to do but to write the words down. The latter does happen at times in cases of what is called "automatic writing"; but that is not the way in which work of creative or intuitional originality is done. Inspirational thought enters normal consciousness from an apparent extension of consciousness not clothed in words or images and consciousness has to struggle to provide adequate means of expression. Dr. Harding quotes some relevant statements of Sir Francis Galton on this matter. "Galton says: 'It is a serious drawback to me in writing, and still more in explaining myself, that I do not so easily think in words as otherwise. It often happens that after being hard at work, and having arrived at results that are perfectly clear and satisfactory to myself, when I try to express them in language I feel that I must begin by putting myself upon quite another intellectual plane. I have to translate my thoughts into a language that does not run very evenly with them. I therefore waste a vast deal of time in seeking for appropriate words and phrases, and am conscious, when required to speak on a sudden, of being often very obscure through mere verbal maladroitness, and not through want of clearness of perception. This is one of the small annoyances of my life. I may add that often while engaged in thinking out something I catch an accompaniment of nonsense-words just as the notes of a song might accompany thought. Also, that *after* I have made a mental step, the appropriate·word frequently follows as an echo; as a rule it does not accompany it. Lastly I frequently employ nonsense-words as temporary symbols, as the logical x and y of ordinary thought, which is a practice that, as may well be conceived, does not conduce to clearness of exposition'."[1] This shows the crossing of conscious fringe where pure thought turns itself into verbal thought.

It may be argued that Galton's was not pure thought existing apart from a mode of expression, but thought in terms of imagery of some kind which was afterwards converted into words. Indeed, when thinking about geometrical problems, Galton says that he did think in images. But the use of nonsense-words as temporary symbols, when he was thinking of non-geometrical things, suggests that no previous symbolism was there.

An important question is whether words are necessarily *containers* of thought, or whether they are sometimes *pointers* to thought. If words necessarily contain all the thought they stand for, in the sense of expressing it completely, the more precisely they are used the better. Progress in understanding would depend on accuracy in the use of words. But if it

[1] *A.I.,* pp. 98-9.

is not always true that words contain the whole of the thought they stand for, the principle will be valid only within a certain area. Within this area, words may be adequate/containers of thought: beyond it they may indicate thought which they do not wholly contain.

If we speak of a physical object, the word wholly contains our thought *when we are in a practical state of mind* and are speaking on the common-sense level. Thought and language are then co-extensive. This applies to the area within which questions are convergent, and the mind then focuses the idea sharply like a lens.

If we take the word "table", for example, as thought of in ordinary life, the conception is as definite and final as the word. But this definiteness has been artificially secured by the concealment of all except the practically useful attributes of the table. Material objects have been made to appear rounded off, definite and self-complete; therefore we are able to use words as containers for them. But if we take a step away from the world so subtly prepared for us in advance, ideas lose this simple definiteness and words cease to contain them. Physical investigation has shown that the word "table" comprises a great deal more than it contains in daily use, and Eddington has been severely criticized by philosophers for saying that there are *two* tables, the familiar table and the scientific table.[1] Perhaps this was not the best way of putting it, but it does bring out the important point that science has converted the table from something which is wholly intelligible to the practical level of the human mind to something which is unintelligible (or becoming so) to the reflective mind. If, when we use the word "table", we mean it to include all that physical science has discovered about it as well as all that it will discover and, in addition, all that it will never be able to discover, then we must admit that the word "table" does not contain all this but acts as a pointer to it.

If we leave the world of physical objects and speak about human attributes, we find, on reflection, that we are again using words as pointers. Love, fear, knowledge, etc., stand for experiences that cannot be contained in exactly defined descriptions. Any psychologist will admit that our emotional life transcends our normally conscious life. One of them has indeed said: "In point of fact, we are never aware of all the experience we are having." How, then, can words contain all our experience? Emotion may be partly expressed by the word, just as a table may be; but much that is inexpressible is attached to that for which the word stands. Only within the realm of practical life do words act as containers.

In modern philosophy, the passage from the full competence to the practical competence of words does not appear to be recognized. If it

[1] See the introduction to *The Nature of the Physical World*.

were, definitions and word-clarification would not be regarded as a sure road to progress but would be seen to have the effect of squeezing out of a word the significance which, as a pointer, it indicates. Creative synthesis makes more progress than analysis: but it makes progress of an individual rather than of a public kind. But the former kind of progress is scornfully dismissed by the kind of philosophy which is animated by science. Precision and clarity, outside the field of practical things, render discussion more and more narrow and academic. The controversialist, immersed in argument, has sunk below the level of clear, synthetic vision and has become the tool of words, after which his thought spreads out into endless ramifications. We can see this kind of thing happening in Logical Positivism.

Intellectually, we inherit much from Greece and from the influence of Aristotle. Some are inclined to associate the clarity of Greek thought with the clarity of Greek surroundings. Small mountains, small islands, small seas abound in Greece and in the Aegean. Nothing suggests questions about the absolute or the infinite. "In the transparent luminous atmosphere even the most distant objects stand out with perfect sharpness; the outline is as hard as the lines of architecture. The eye, and through the eye the mind, grow accustomed to the utmost precision. There is nothing misty or smudged or vague, as in the lands of the North. The poetry of haze and mystery, wraiths fading into the clouds, German romance and Scandinavian symbolism, all that is unknown to the Hellenes. There is no more fog in Greek thought than in Greek landscape."[1] On the other hand, the vast plains of India and the heights of the Himalayas, suggest the immense and the overpowering. "Clarity, precision, moderation—these are excellent qualities as far as they go; but when the mind of man is trying to understand the universe, they do not go far enough. . . . For the Greek, the boundary-line of vision, whether physical or mental, was, as a rule, the boundary-line of existence. What could not be clearly seen was unreal. What did not admit of exact statement was untrue."[2] This has been carried into modern philosophy. From Aristotle, whose influence on the western world was revived during the twelfth and thirteenth centuries, we inherit a word-bound logic and a sense-bound cosmology—the tendency, in fact, to assume that the power of the human intellect and the range of the human senses are adequate for dealing with the entire cosmos. Although this tendency may have been reinforced in the western world by the influence of Aristotle; it has its origin in the innate structure of the

[1] Quoted from A. Jarde, *Formation of the Greek People*, by Edmond Holmes, H.R., p. 7.
[2] H.R., p. 8.

human mind. We are brought again to the tendency of the human mind to arrive at foregone conclusions. "But is it wise of the speculative thinker to fetter his freedom by formulating beforehand the laws which are to regulate his thinking and the canons of correctness to which his reasoning is to conform? Is he not dooming himself to think in a circle, to arrive at last at conclusions which he has proved to his own satisfaction but which were really implicit in the very process of his proof? He who decides at the outset how he is going to think has already gone far towards determining the issue of his thinking." [1] Again the Procrustean problem!

It is probably legitimate to think according to verbal rules so long as the words used really do contain the meanings for which they stand. But when they cease to do so, they cease to be dead symbols or counters suitable for dialectical exercises, they become alive. Edmond Holmes points out that words which are alive in this sense have different shades of meaning for different minds, acquire different shades of meaning from different contexts, and also acquire fresh shades of meaning from age to age. He stresses the danger of introducing logical laws into thinking, which has risen above the level of practical affairs; "for there the words that matter most—*God, man, soul, self, spirit, thought, feeling, will, reality, nature, Universe* and the like—are of all words the most truly alive, the most variable, in respect of meaning, from mind to mind, from context to context, from age to age, and the most fully charged with varying associations, due to centuries of usage, and also with potentialities of further development of meaning. Yet it is in the region of speculative thought, as we shall presently see, that the temptation to use words as symbols, and therefore as counters in the logician's game, is strongest." [2]

There was, after all, some sense in Humpty Dumpty's refusal to allow words to gain the mastery over him. We must never be caught in the machine which public thought creates. Wherever we look, we find that progress beyond a certain point inevitably becomes *individual* progress. There the mind is free to explore and is no longer bound by the rules of public logic. And it is always the individual who is in the van of progress.

Edmond Holmes quotes a pertinent passage from F. C. S. Schiller's *Logic of Use*: "For so far as Formal Logic takes any interest in meaning, it substitutes *verbal* meaning, the 'dictionary meaning' of words for *real* meaning, which is the only meaning that has importance for life and science. The latter always arises in a particular situation, and it is always *personal*; i.e., it is what men mean when they *use* words to express and convey *their* meaning." [3] There is always the danger that philosophical argument may take the form of a game played according to rules and may

[1] *H.R.*, p. 10.   [2] *H.R.*, p. 16.   [3] *H.R.*, p. 23.

degenerate into a competition in scoring dialectical points. Behind it all lies the adapted nature of the human being, which tries to draw all meaning into the scope of words and render it amenable to the convergent thought of the practical world. It is, however, particularly in modern philosophy that this Procrustean habit of science has been taken over. The older philosophies contain more insight and freedom.

CHAPTER XVIII

THE FALLACY BEHIND THE MODERN OUTLOOK

IN the foregoing chapters, we have developed a line of thought which lies outside the procedure of specialists. We turned to the human individual and examined it from a non-analytical point of view instead of turning first to the external world and adopting the analytical method. Our method is not in itself new, for the sages of ancient India and, indeed, all who possessed intuitive insight in the past, realized centuries ago that this was the main avenue to truth. Once we had adopted this mode of approach, we began to see the human being as it really is and the human situation in its true perspective.

We have freely admitted the authority of the specialist in his own field, but we have denied that a valid picture of the whole can be attained by his methods. The outlook of the present day has been founded on the work of specialists and, looking at it comprehensively, we have seen that it owes more to the constitution of the human mind than to the nature of the independent universe. These constitutive factors of the human mind act, we believe, universally. The secret of adaptation in the mental sphere is that the mind and its subject-matter have been previously correlated during the course of evolution. Consequently, outside the area of pre-adaptation, the adapted character of the mind secretly misleads us. When scientists attempt to solve problems within the range of pre-adaptation—problems we have called "convergent"—the adaptation of the mind leads to triumphant solutions. Taking a clock to pieces and examining its parts provides us with a complete explanation of the way in which the clock works. This is because the properties of solids and the laws of mechanics constitute a framework within which analysis leads to definite conclusions. But the attempt to project this method beyond the containing framework leads to results of a very different order.

The cosmic outlook that has sprung up during the last three centuries is the outcome of the assumption that the method which works within the area of pre-adaptation is bound to work universally. So hopelessly out of line is this assumption with reality that humanity, misguided by science, is drifting on to the rocks of illusion.

We may summarize our non-specialist conclusions as follows: (i) So far as applied science is concerned—science in action as we have called it—the knowledge and power it has given created demands that human nature cannot rise to. Therefore this knowledge and power are at one and the same time beneficial and destructive; and the crucial problem is how to adjust this knowledge and power to the almost static character of the human being. (ii) Pure science—which we have called science in discovery —has produced a general concept of the universe which is based entirely on a study of the foreground, and this outlook assumes that only that which appears in the foreground has any existence. It thrusts aside evidence which goes against this assumption.

Nothing could be more vitally important than to gain a true understanding of the situation in which we human beings are placed by mental adaptation or more dangerous than to plan and act on a false conception of it. Having realized that we are mentally as well as physically adapted, but that our mental adaptation is subtly hidden from us, we examined from this point of view the behaviour of mankind in ordinary life. We also examined the sciences from the same standpoint. Always retaining our bird's-eye view: we resorted to synthesis, always turning the faculty of direct awareness upon each situation instead of using a cut and dried logical technique.

We saw at the same time that the entire human mind has not been adapted by the evolutionary process. While its lower strata are in the grip of instinct, its higher strata are informed by direct insight. And these higher strata can be extended so that the human being has the power of becoming increasingly aware. The mind is not a rigidly circumscribed monad but an abstraction with a shifting and ill-defined boundary. Our inquiry pointed to an infinite extension of the real; and it led us to two conclusions: (a) That the world presented by our senses, even when enlarged by scientific exploration, is not the whole; (b) and that the human being, as it appears in ordinary life, is not the whole being. Both these conclusions are fundamentally opposed to the scientific outlook of to-day; and both are of the very highest significance. The scientific perspective (what there is of it) is hopelessly out of focus with reality and the philosophy to which it has given rise is useless as a guide to life. The scientist sees man entirely from his physical aspect. We saw how man's importance seemed to dwindle as this physical investigation was pursued and the earth sank to the dimensions of a speck of dust in the immensity of space; how the life of the human species appears as no more than the twinkling of an eye when compared with the immensity of time; how the universe seems to be no more than a vast complex of unconscious and inanimate forces, devoid of meaning or purpose.

But if we look critically at this specialist examination of the sensory foreground, we begin to see that all this is no more than a *feeling* which overpowers us, tied as we are to our bodily standpoint. What, after all, do these vastnesses of space and time imply? Why should man, as a conscious being, be rendered valueless on account of the smallness of his body or the speck of physical territory he occupies, or the comparative brevity of his duration as a species? Man's body is indeed extremely minute in comparison with the lumps of dead matter with which he is surrounded. His life-history is indeed, by the same standard, inordinately short. But what has all this to do with his *value*? All the matter in the universe occupies no more than a tiny fraction of total space. Is space, then, more important than matter? Has it greater significance? Matter possesses many properties which empty space does not; and we always regard matter as being more important than space. What, then, has the small spatial extent of matter to do with its significance? Again, life is found only in infinitesimally small portions of matter; but we do not regard inanimate matter as being more important than living matter because the former exists in greater quantity. Consciousness is found in only a very small portion of the matter which has life; but we do not regard unconscious organisms as being more important than conscious organisms. Why should man feel himself dwarfed or insignificant because of his physical smallness? Man is just as significant in the universe which modern science has discovered as he would have been if the pre-Copernican picture had been true. The outlook which represents him otherwise has been built up uncritically.

It is disqueting to realize that this uncritical climate of opinion can be so powerful. It grips the most able as well as ordinary minds. What we have described as the scientific outlook is accepted by all kinds of people to-day, not only in the sciences, but in every walk of life. It is possible that some scientific men might deny that they have any general outlook at all. They might claim to be agnostic about everything that has no "positive" scientific proof. But no scientist can, in practice, achieve such a position, if only for the reason that he cannot help being a man as well as a specialist. As a man, he is bound to have a general conception of things; and this is bound to enter into and mingle with his scientific knowledge. And there is also a further difficulty. Laboratory results, though called "positive", are not in reality purely objective. Observations have to be *interpreted*; and the interpretation often depends on the mind of the interpreter. A purely objective observation is what Eddington has called a "pointer-reading". But it is impossible to stop at pointer-readings. The simplest statement, such as: I see that it is twelve o'clock, is full of interpretation. Purely objective knowledge is a myth.

The central feature of the modern outlook is, however, the belief that the universe is without purpose or meaning, without directing factors, without anything which transcends the range of our senses and our powers of intellectual investigation. Man, it is asserted, owes his origin entirely to forces in the physical world which lie within the range of his observation. There is nothing beyond this. There is nothing teleological or supra-teleological. This belief is considered to be justified by the positive discoveries of science, and any view to the contrary is dubbed "mystical" and put down to the result of wishful thinking and illusion—a myth handed down to us from our ignorant and superstitious ancestors. This view, we have seen, rests on a gigantic assumption—in fact, on two gigantic assumptions. One is that the sense-world includes everything. The other is that the human intellect occupies an Olympian position and is immune from unbalancing or deflecting influences and is capable of investigating everything that has any meaning at all. There is nothing that it cannot grasp!

In Chapter IV we quoted S. Radhakrishnan as saying: "We sweep the skies with the telescope and find no trace of God, we search the brain with the microscope and find no sign of mind." This is typical of the first assumption. We also quoted Professor Stace's summing up of the modern outlook, which he himself accepts: "Without the Great Illusion, the illusion of a good, purposeful and kindly universe, we shall *have* to learn to live." The intense preoccupation of science with the sensory world has given rise to the assumption that all that exists lies within it. Also that nothing can exist unless it falls into one of its categories. Purpose, if it exists in the universe at all, must be human purpose or nothing. There cannot be something which bears a certain resemblance to human purpose but yet soars immensely beyond it. The foreground-pattern of causal events in space and time, *must* be the sole and only pattern, because it is the only pattern with which the limited methods of science can deal. But we saw that everything points to a deeper pattern, only that the mind, on account of the way in which it is constituted, turns away from it, and acknowledges only that which lies within its horizon. And this is the *subjective* horizon belonging to the area of pre-adaptation. Awareness that has achieved true balance can see that there is ample evidence for the existence of a "pattern behind the pattern". The possibilities that lie before us in the limitless universe are in reality infinite; but continued reliance on specialist technique has driven us further and further from a truly balanced state of mind. It has augmented our reluctance to look introspectively into ourselves. This is our great mistake to-day. It is the fallacy behind the modern outlook. So long as it is accepted as axiomatically true that the pattern open to sensory exploration is the *whole* pattern, we are not likely to come in sight of anything beyond it: the door to further discovery is closed. And the most important discovery we can make at the present time is not the amassing of further detail about things we already know but the realization that illimitable vistas of reality exist that we cannot prove intellectually but can realize intuitively. We need to realize the subjectivity of the world's boundary and so to obtain a *perspective* which, in our present situation, is more important than positive knowledge.

The result of our inquiry has been to show that the conceptions of the nature of man and of the universe which are prevalent to-day are to a considerable extent due to *caused* thinking. These conceptions fall under the headings of Materialism and Rationalism. Though not clearly defined philosophies, both have taken a firm hold on the mind of modern man and their practical consequences are far reaching and are now becoming disastrous. The key-concepts which terminated Chapters VII and VIII are diametrically opposed to these philosophies or outlooks. The parting of the ways lies between reason under the influence of instinct on the one hand and free awareness in direct touch with the real on the other. It cannot be too strongly emphasized that the choice of paths has an immense *practical* importance for the whole human race. Its bearing on every practical issue is vital. Religion, social organization, national and international politics, the attempt to control the results of scientific achievement, the happiness of individuals and communities all depend on it. It is useless to preach brotherly love in a purposeless universe, where such "love" can be at best no more than a matter of mutual convenience.

The situation in which we find ourselves to-day is one in which Right Thinking must precede Right Action. Both Materialism and Rationalism rest on vague foundations; yet they reflect the mentality of the present time. Materialism is based on the mind's instinctive urge to accept the sense-perceived world as the whole. It is not peculiar to the present epoch: it has merely been accentuated by the climate of thought of the time. It is founded on an instinct which, though illusory, is absolutely essential for practical life. Rationalism is based on the assumption that the human intellect is immaculate, potentially unlimited and unadulterated by instinct. Both Materialism and Rationalism are, at base, products of adaptation, which science has unconsciously taken over and intensified. Because we have these adapted instincts within us, both these ways of looking at things appear plausible.

Unless we pause and consider deeply, it must be admitted that there are facts which appear to give Materialism strong support. One of these is the subordination of our consciousness to the domination of matter. Evidence for this could be found in plenty in academic works on physiology; but it is better to look for it in non-technical places. Dr. V. H.

Mottram, in his book, *The Physical Basis of Personality*[1] cites the case of a soldier who damaged part of his forebrain in a motor-cycle accident and underwent, as a result, a complete change of character. Before the accident, he was ambitious, smart, responsible, respectful to his superiors and an efficient soldier. After the accident, he was familiar and jovial with officers and men alike, fearless, undisciplined, aggressive and useless as a soldier. Mechanical injury to the brain was responsible for these subtle differences; and the case seems to show that our mental and moral life is purely the result of physical and chemical conditions. What are we, then, but a throw-off of organized matter? By physical means, such as electric shocks, it has been found that character can be influenced and in some cases moral defects cured. "*Can* electricity", asks Dr. Mottram, "take the place of a spiritual guide or the traditional much prayer and fasting?" The obvious conclusion tries to take our mind by storm before we pause to reflect. It is, indeed, Nature using her technique for inducing us to take things for granted. But if we *insist* on pausing to reflect, we can manage to remember that body and mind *must* be interlocked with extreme closeness if they are to act in unison. The body, by means of its sense-organs, has to provide the mind with every scrap of information it needs about the external world; and the mind, in turn, has to direct every movement of the body with minute exactness. Correlation must be complete to the point of fusion; and this makes it inevitable that consciousness should be deeply under the influence of the material structure of the brain. The dependence of consciousness on matter is also very widely spread; for the former is at the mercy, not only of the brain and body, but of the material surroundings as a whole. What we know, what we believe, what experiences we have depend on our physical surroundings. Those who live in a totalitarian country, dominated by secret police and lying propaganda, have their minds and characters influenced by these physical circumstances. We cannot escape devestatingly deep effects of matter on mind if we are to live in a material world at all. To a certain extent we must be psycho-physical hybrids: but what conclusion follows from this? The superficial conclusion is that consciousness has no self-existence but is a miasma hovering about the living brain. Or, to put it slightly differently, consciousness is one aspect of functioning, living matter while physiological process is the other. This view appears reasonable—indeed almost compulsive—at first glance. But the moment we begin to reflect, we see that we have been jockeyed into the assumption that visible matter is the *fons et origo* of all things. We have not deliberately decided this; we have taken it for granted unconsciously.

[1] Pelican, Penguin Books, 1946, pp. 48–9.

If we start without this assumption, the problem looks quite different. Taking into account that the incarnate consciousness is not the whole self (which the experience of all highly developed human beings supports and has always supported): taking into account also that the material world does not comprise within itself the whole universe, the evidence for which we have already discussed, we see that matter-dominated consciousness is no more than an abstraction from the total self. The unadapted portion of man (the Intruder) is constantly interacting with the adapted portion, for it is essentially one with it. Although the latter is the slave of the brain, it is yet in touch with the higher states of awareness to which we have so often referred. It is informed and inspired by them, although it can, at the same time, be seized and mishandled by its physical counterpart. This is the verdict of experience; but conditioned thought raises the objection that if the mind is not a mere property of the body— if it has in any sense an independent existence, then it must be an entity which it is possible to produce in isolation within the sensible world. That is obviously Procrustean thinking. The Mind's independence of matter does not fall into any physical category. It is not spatially separate from matter. The mind is not an entity which can be discovered existing alone in the sensible world; nor can it be isolated by any procedure which depends upon the bodily senses. It is independent in a sense we cannot *intellectually* understand—a sense which may be meaningless to the intellect, but which is in some degree perceptible by direct awareness. The matter-dominated mind is an abstraction from selfhood as a whole (even this is to speak in metaphor). From the unabstracted portion come religious experience and the enlightenment of the mystic and, indeed, every thought which has originality and leads to the advance of the intellect itself. Where are the physical correlates of the *sources* from which these things come?

Another passage from Dr. Mottram's book shows how our failure to see things in perspective leads us to absurd conclusions. "We guess and indeed assume that all hereditary characters are carried by the nuclei of the uniting sperm and ovum. And as this assumption fits all the multitudinous experiments of the last forty years upon the mode of inheritance, it is the assumption upon which we shall proceed. Put briefly thus: the nuclei of the uniting sex-cells carry the hereditary characteristics —it sounds a simple and comprehensible statement, but when its implications are considered, it is staggering. . . . It means that all the multiplicity of characteristics which make the difference between, say, Newton and Machiavelli, Marcus Aurelius and Nero, Winston Churchill and Hitler—in so far as they were not distorted by environment and nurture—

were carried in a speck of living matter perhaps not four twenty-five millionths of a cubic inch in size."[1] It certainly is startling; indeed, it might well be called fantastic. J. S. Haldane has already been quoted as saying: "In the exclusive light of existing physical and chemical conceptions, reproduction appears as nothing less than miraculous." But why is it assumed that all these hereditary characteristics, many of which do not possess spatial properties, are carried *in* the nuclei, conceived as pieces of visible matter? Why do we assume so naïvely that matter is revealed in its entirety to our senses? What experiments show, or can show, that nuclei possess no supra-sensible properties? It is not experiment but our own instinctive way of thought which leads us to accept this fantastic view of heredity. For, instinct forces upon us the "island" view of matter; and we obediently accept it without a qualm. Everything points in the same direction. As soon as we leave the world of practical affairs and try to understand what lies beyond it, our conclusions are derived far less from independent facts than from our own mental constitution. We do not see this *because the adaptation of the human mind, and all that goes with it, remains invisible unless seen from without.* For the normal intellect, it is clad in an invisible cloak. The result of this is important beyond measure, for on a true conception of the universe and of man all else in the long run depends. No stable society is possible so long as false views about these all-important things prevail. All that supremely matters depends upon our becoming conscious of just where Nature is leading our minds astray. No lasting structure can be built on a foundation of illusion. To-day Materialism is a widely accepted creed. William McDougall has said: "Mechanistic science, then, is science that excludes, neglects, ignores or abstracts from the processes of mind; and Modern Materialism is the assumption that such mechanistic science can, in principle, achieve a complete and satisfactory account of the world and of man, his nature, origin and destiny."[2]

> *Another voice when I am speaking cries*
> *"The Flower should open with the morning skies."*
> *And a retreating whisper as I wake—*
> *"The Flower that once has blown forever dies."*

The retreating whisper gains the day because it comes from the world to which the human being is adapted.

Rationalism takes the human intellect for granted without criticizing it. "Rationalism may be defined as the mental attitude which unreservedly accepts the supremacy of reason and aims at establishing a

---

[1] *The Physical Basis of Personality*, p. 18.   [2] *M.M.*, pp. 11-12.

system of philosophy and ethics verifiable by experience and independent of all arbitrary assumptions or authority."[1] This definition makes a double appeal, partly to reason and partly to empiricism. The two have often been at loggerheads. A free appeal to experience made by a mind that has succeeded in freeing itself from bias, arrives, as we have seen, at very different conclusions from those at which the intellect arrives when it is under the influence of the instinct, which directs it towards foregone conclusions. The question presented to Rationalism is whether it is going to unearth these instincts and recognize them or whether it is going to fall meekly under their spell. So far it appears to have done the latter: it believes itself to be wholly controlled by unbiased reason. Never for an instant does it suspect that reason may have been tampered with from within. There is a certain irony in the term "free-thinker", when the rationalist applies it to himself. In an article in the *Rationalist Annual* for 1948, Professor A. E. Heath writes: "There is a charming definition of a gentleman as a man who is never *unintentionally* rude. A Rationalist is a man who is never unwittingly irrational." But that is just where the mistake lies. The irrationality of the Rationalist *is* unwitting. Nature converts his reasoning into rationalization. By all means let us put our trust in reason: but let us make sure that we have it pure.

The false conception of the human being, to which adapted thinking leads, results in false conceptions of human aims and human values and a totally wrong view of human society. If mind is only an aspect of matter, physical life embraces everything. What is important on this view is the possession of material goods and benefits. From a social point of view, the individual is no more than a brick in the social structure and this involves a mass-conception of humanity, which is seen as a conglomeration of units to be organized on the basis of statistics. This idea of mankind falls into line with the methods of natural science. We have only to discover uniform laws of man and the human race which can be controlled by the imposition of uniform rules as the scientist controls the activities of atoms. It is extremely unfortunate that this materialist-scientific way of regarding man falls into line with the schemes of dictators. Enforced uniformity is the tool of the power-seeker. "One Church, one Empire was the idea of Charlemagne, of Otto, of Barbarossa, of Hildebrand, of Thomas Aquinas, of Dante. The forces struggling against that ideal were the enemy to be defeated. They won."[2] They won in past history because the uniform view of the human being is radically false, and the desire for freedom and diversity overcame it. But the power of the dictator and the

---

[1] *The Literary Guide and Rationalist Review.*
[2] Lowes Dickinson, *After the War, 1915*, pp. 20-1.

tyrant to-day has been immensely augmented by the gifts of science and the overthrowing of dictators may now involve the overthrowing of the whole world-order. The ideal of the dictator and the mental tendency of the scientist both fly in the face of Nature because they misconceive the constitution of man and try to substitute for the infinite diversity of life a stereotyped uniformity. Arnold Toynbee cites an instance of how the attempt to impose dictatorial uniformity was frustrated by the innate tendency of mankind to rebel against it. "In France, again, Roman Catholic orthodoxy has been disappointed, time and again, of the hope that it had succeeded in re-establishing religious uniformity once and for all by suppressing a heresy. The Albigenses were suppressed, only to break out again as Huguenots. When the Huguenots were suppressed in their turn, they broke out again as Jansenists, who were the nearest thing to Calvinists that Roman Catholics could be. When the Jansenists were quashed they broke out again as Deists; and to-day the division of the French into a clerical and an anti-clerical faction still reproduces the thirteenth century division between Catholics and Adoptionists (or whatever the doctrine may have been that the Albigenses really held), in spite of repeated attempts, during the last seven centuries, to dragoon the French people into religious unity."[1] Science soon becomes bankrupt when it leaves the inanimate world and tries to investigate life; for it is faced with countless individual differences instead of with uniformities which are amenable to general laws and neat statistical patterns. The comfortable rule of Occam's razor goes by the board in the world of life. Nature pours out a profusion of interlocked causes.

Communism is a plan for organizing society based on the erroneous, external view of the human being. It accepts the two illusions whose falsity we have emphasized, the monad-like self-inclusiveness of man and the intelligibility to the human intellect of the entire universe. It is a fellow traveller with Materialism and believes only in the scientific work carried out in the foreground. "We can now see why communism appeals to so many scientific minds; it rests on the scientific, predictable, measurable side of social nature—statistics—while it brushes aside or suppresses the erratic, dissenting, free individual whose behaviour is always original and unpredictable."[2] Communism pictures a visionary Utopia to be attained in this world by imposing a uniform plan of life on all by methods of force and violence. The uniformitarianism sponsored by the adapted mind comes into deadly conflict with Nature's principle of infinite variety. The idea of attaining perfection in this world is based on the misconception

[1] *C.T.*, pp. 165-6.
[2] Salvador de Madariaga, *The Listener*, October 10th, 1946.

o

that this world is the all-in-all. "It is an essential feature of perfectionism that it inevitably must conceive the reform of the whole world in one single plan. There cannot be many paradises but only one. The principles for the realization of the paradise must everywhere be the same. But, whatever the value of the principle, the aberration begins as soon as it is regarded as universal."[1] Without some conception of the true nature of man and of the universe, the mass of mankind cannot realize that the hardships and inequalities of life in a material world are not to be done away with by a piece of political machinery. They are inherent in the situation of man in this world and they appear to have no meaning unless we view them in the light of a larger context.

An examination of human nature shows that the essence of life lies in perpetual struggle and change. Not for a moment would human beings be content with a material paradise even if it were presented to them. In a short time they would become restless in it, would tire of it, would form opposing factions and would destroy it.

Communism lacks the flexibility, the sensitiveness, the sweet reasonableness which belong to the higher levels of man. It shows a mental fixation which strongly suggests the lower instincts. J. M. Keynes, one of the most intelligent and best informed men of our time, said that he could not see that Russian Communism had made any contribution to economic problems of intellectual interest or scientific value. If communism achieves a certain success, he said, it will not be as an economic technique but as a religion. Indeed, it is as a pseudo-religion that communism is spreading over a large portion of the globe to-day. The idealism that filters through from the unadapted levels of the self is here warped and thwarted by the lower instincts.

Some believe that the solution of our present problems is to be sought in science and yet more science. But science obviously creates as many problems as it solves, and the new problems are so difficult to cope with that they baffle mankind and break loose from its control.

The urgent need of our time is not for more and more science but for clarity of vision, which will enable us to raise our eyes from the foreground and to realize something of the importance of those things which lie in the shadow. The true conception of the nature of man and of the universe is the first indispensable foundation of any world-policy which can lead to some degree of security and peace. We *must* see the whole in true perspective and not any longer build on the flat screen which the specialized technique of science has created. Only thus can we hope to see the human situation in its true proportions. Only then will the true

[1] Schwarzschild, *Primer of the Coming World*, p. 68.

character of religion appear and it will be seen, not as something isolated, but as a central core, interfused with all knowledge, and constituting its life and crown. Only then will the first stages of universal purpose and significance come into view. Perspective is necessary before we can see the status of the self, although it will also show us that we cannot comprehend its essence or extent. Yet selfhood is the central hinge on which all depends. The purpose and meaning of life, dimly visible when we glimpse the deeper pattern, lies in what is accomplished *in* us as we pass through this world and not in what we externally do or acquire.

There is purpose and meaning everywhere; but it would be childish to expect it to be spread out before us like a map, plain to see and wholly within our comprehension. We cannot fully grasp it; but that does not prevent us from realizing its presence.

That the scientific era has brought the world to the most critical pass in its history can scarcely be denied. It may be that we shall have to go through the valley of the shadow of death before a new birth and a new civilization arise. But tragedy brings despair only if the cosmos is seen in the light of Materialism. A glimpse of its true nature and of the supra-material reveal in trial and disaster a deeper meaning which converts them into a road to progress, uncomprehended as to its goal, but whose existence is verified again and again in human experience. We may recall the words of Milton: "I cannot praise a fugitive and cloistered virtue unexercised and unbreathed, that never sallies out and seeks her adversary, but slinks out of the race, where that immortal garland is to be run for, not without dust and heat. Assuredly we bring not innocence into the world, we bring impurity much rather; that which purifies us is trial and trial is by what is contrary."[1] It is this wider perspective that brings us in sight of the "immortal garland". Are we prepared to make the effort to grasp it and to rise towards truth? If so, we must criticize and reject the illusions which science has fomented and must turn inwards and seek to know ourselves. At present we try to fit, not only things classed as "paranormal", but also God and immortality into the world of familiar experience, regarding the latter as including in its structure the whole cosmos. We find that they have no place in such a world: therefore we reject them. In order to accept them, we do not so much need specific items of evidence in their favour as a truer outlook in which our familiar world appears as a fragment only of the whole.

Perspective is our first and greatest need; for the central truth is that we are specialized beings in a special world. Around us lies reality—around us and within—but the only gateway to it is intuition or direct awareness

[1] *Areopagitica.*

through the enhancement of consciousness. We must gain our unadapted self by freeing ourselves from the adapted self; and then we shall begin to realize that progress in the future will not lie in *solving* the great questions of philosophy or the great human problems which so darkly overshadow us, but in throwing them into stereoscopic relief. Once we have begun to see the universe and ourselves in true perspective, and to realize the incomprehensible vastness of both, Religion will re-enter the picture, not in the form of a stereotyped institution, but as the core of Reality, integral with science, with philosophy and with the whole of human experience.

INDEX

Printed in Great Britain by
The Camelot Press Ltd., London and Southampton

For Product Safety Concerns and Information please contact our EU
representative GPSR@taylorandfrancis.com
Taylor & Francis Verlag GmbH, Kaufingerstraße 24, 80331 München, Germany

9 7 8 0 3 6 7 2 7 3 5 6 9